IMPROVING LITERACY IN THE PRIMARY SCHOOL

One of the most important challenges teachers face is making sure children can read. It is an absolutely crucial skill, and current educational policy is giving it a very high priority.

Based on one of the largest studies ever undertaken of what primary schools do to improve literacy, this book reports what Professor Ted Wragg and his research team found.

The importance placed on literacy has never been greater. When children learn to read, they are laying the foundations for their entire educational future. Effective teachers can make a huge difference, as a poor start can hinder children throughout their schooling and beyond.

By looking at what actually goes on in classrooms, this volume provides an invaluable insight into what happens to children and how their reading progresses. It shows how particular teachers manage the improvement of their pupils' reading levels, and also follows individual pupils through a school year.

This is a very readable account of a fascinating and crucial area of research that is highly topical. Every class teacher should read it.

Professor Ted Wragg, **Dr Caroline Wragg**, **Gill Haynes** and **Dr Rosemary Chamberlin** are all at the School of Education at the University of Exeter.

D0162101

IMPROVING LITERACY IN THE PRIMARY SCHOOL

E. C. Wragg, C. M. Wragg,
G. S. Haynes and R. P. Chamberlin

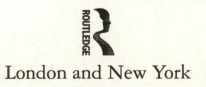

London and New York

First published 1998
by Routledge
11 New Fetter Lane, London EC4P 4EE

Simultaneously published in the USA and Canada
by Routledge
29 West 35th Street, New York, NY 10001

©1998 E. C. Wragg, C. M. Wragg, G. S. Haynes and R. P. Chamberlin

Typeset in Garamond by Routledge
Printed and bound in Great Britain by Clays Ltd, St. Ives PLC

British Library Cataloguing in Publication Data
A catalogue record for this book is available from the British Library

Library of Congress Cataloging in Publication Data
Improving literacy in the primary school / E.C. Wragg . . . [et al.].
p. cm.
Includes bibliographical references (p.) and index.
1. Reading (Elementary)–Great Britain. 2. Educational surveys–Great Britain.
3. Literacy–Great Britain. I. Wragg, E. C. (Edward Conrad)
LB1573.156 1998
372.4'0941–dc21 98–20622
CIP

ISBN 0–415–17287–X (hbk)
ISBN 0–415–17288–8 (pbk)

CONTENTS

TABLES

PREFACE

This book describes the research undertaken during the Leverhulme Primary Improvement Project, a two-year research project funded by the Leverhulme Trust. There were four interlinked studies to the research. Study 1 was a questionnaire survey about practice within primary schools, completed by head teachers or language co-ordinators from a national sample of 1,395 schools. Study 2 involved the investigation of practice in four different local authorities, one of which was Birmingham. Study 3 comprised the case studies of thirty-five class teachers carried out over a full school year and Study 4 involved intensive case studies of 258 pupils.

During the project we used questionnaires, interviews and observation. This variety of research strategies produced rich data both about the contemporary teaching of literacy and how improvement is managed in schools and classrooms.

The chapters in this book describe a comprehensive study of literacy teaching at several levels, from what happens in a large local education authority to the events taking place in a small rural primary classroom.

ACKNOWLEDGEMENTS

We should like to express our gratitude to the Leverhulme Trust for supporting the Primary Improvement Project. We should also like to thank the many local authority officers, heads, teachers, classroom assistants, pupils and parents who co-operated so fully with us.

1

STUDYING IMPROVEMENT

Introduction

How do schools improve the quality of their pupils' achievements in a field
like 'literacy'? Can local education authorities still have an impact? What do
head teachers do to raise standards? What is happening inside the classrooms of those teachers who succeed in increasing their pupils' competence
in reading beyond the average over a school year? Which individual children
in a class improve, and what do they actually do?

These were a few of the questions we addressed in the *Primary Improvement
Project*, a two-year research programme at Exeter University, funded by the
Leverhulme Trust, in which we investigated the efforts being made to
improve the standards of literacy, especially reading, in primary schools and
classrooms. This book describes and analyses what we found.

For two decades or more there has been considerable interest in the
accountability of schools and teachers. Life in the adult world seemed to be
getting tougher as the twenty-first century approached. Employment opportunities, particularly in traditional jobs like those in manufacturing
industry, declined sharply. Millions of unskilled jobs disappeared
completely, as factory automation, alongside developments such as the fork
lift truck, rendered obsolete the need for carrying, lifting and machine
minding (Wragg 1997a). The millennium drew to its close, with parents,
employers, taxpayers and pupils themselves beginning to expect more from
the education service than in previous generations.

It is important, in these rapidly changing and ever more demanding
conditions, to study the effectiveness of what primary schools are achieving,
and this is what we set out to do. Such research can be riddled with pitfalls.
Choose any aspect of the curriculum, let alone one so important as literacy,
our particular focus, and the difficulties soon become apparent. Even
defining what teachers and heads understand is covered by the term
'literacy' is far from being a straightforward matter, though we did attempt
to tackle this, by actually asking them, during the research.

There has been extensive research, especially in the United States, into

1

the 'effectiveness' of individual teachers. Studies of school effectiveness have also become a well-trodden field of enquiry. Research into literacy in general and the teaching of reading in particular is another huge area of research. Some of this is described in more detail in Chapter 2. What we wanted to do was straddle all three aspects by undertaking an intensive scrutiny of particular classrooms in different schools, with a sharp focus on what the pupils and teachers in them actually did to improve literacy.

Studying teacher and school effectiveness today is much harder than it would have been a century ago. In the nineteenth century teacher training institutions were known as 'normal schools', on the grounds that there was a single agreed 'norm' of teaching (Rich 1933). The pluralism of the twentieth century has led to a diversity of teaching styles and there is no clear research evidence that one approach is universally more 'effective' than another, since context, subject matter, pupil ability and prior experience will often influence both process and outcome. Indeed large-scale summaries of the relationship between process and product in classrooms have often stated precisely that.

Barr (1961) summarised several hundred American studies with different definitions of 'effectiveness', some based on test scores, others on observations of teaching by experts, or on the opinions of principals, fellow teachers or pupils. He concluded that teachers who were preferred by administrators or by pupils were not necessarily those whose pupils did well in tests. Doyle (1978) observed that reviewers of research into teacher effectiveness 'have concluded, with remarkable regularity, that few consistent relationships between teacher variables and effectiveness criteria can be established'.

Even reviewers of the same studies have reached different conclusions about them, as Giaconia and Hedges (1985) pointed out in their synthesis of research findings on effectiveness. Some smaller-scale analysis has sometimes found advantages for one style of teaching over another. For example, Gage (1978, 1985) cited studies that tended to show a superiority of 'traditional' over 'progressive' methods so far as basic skills in the early years of schooling were concerned, and Kulik et al. (1979) reported a meta-analysis of American studies of the Keller Plan, a form of teaching involving pupils completing individual assignments, which showed higher learning gains among Keller Plan pupils than in control groups.

Despite the problems, disagreements and uncertainties, however, classroom research can attempt to analyse process and outcome in a way that will give insights into teaching and learning. These may not be universally applicable, but at least they offer some clues about aspects of practice that teachers may wish to consider changing. It is then up to individuals to decide to what extent other people's research findings might apply to them. Unfortunately, as Hargreaves (1997) and others have argued, there is not always the strong relationship between educational research findings and teachers' professional practice that might be found in other professions like

2

medicine. That is not, however, an argument against doing good classroom research, more one for improving its quality, applicability, dissemination and impact.

One example of higher impact occurs in the United States, where Freiberg and his co-workers (Freiberg 1983, Freiberg *et al.* 1990, Freiberg and Driscoll 1992, Freiberg *et al.* 1995) have studied the effects of various classroom processes thought to be associated with pupil learning. In a number of action-oriented programmes they found that when teachers consistently applied certain class management principles, like creating an orderly environment, varying their strategies, supporting a climate of pupil reflection, providing greater opportunities for pupil self-discipline, and establishing closer links with parents and the community, there was more likely to be significantly greater pupil progress in reading, writing and mathematics.

There are no miracle programmes and the advantages reported in these smaller-scale analyses are often relatively slight, not strong enough to support the complete endorsement of one style of teaching or the abandonment of another. They are also frequently related to the particular context in which they occur. Nonetheless each can add a little to our understanding of what may work in certain circumstances. Teachers can then modify their own teaching in the light of what they have learned from others. Successful models are more likely to invade the consciousness of busy teachers than exhortations or vague generalisations. As Gage (1985) has pointed out, medical research into beta blockers and low-cholesterol diets found differences of only 2.5 and 1.7 per cent respectively in the mortality rates of the experimental and control groups, yet the US government implemented the findings immediately. Effectiveness research in education is problematic and difficult but still worthwhile.

In order to locate our research in a context, we decided to study schools in different parts of the country, to select classrooms in which we could observe teachers' and children's practice over the whole of a school year, and to pick out certain pupils for particular attention. We employed a multilateral strategy using a mixture of quantitative and qualitative methods. This involved sending out questionnaires to a national sample of schools; interviewing heads, teachers, advisers, parents, pupils; observing lessons from the beginning of September to the end of July, with up to eight 'target' pupils in each class; testing pupils' reading, and asking teachers to rate their progress, attitudes and behaviour.

We moved successively through these various layers of enquiry via a 'zoom' technique which allowed us to focus on the general and then on the individual. The four linked studies which made up our research are described in more detail below and in later chapters of this book, but briefly, for the time being, they consisted of:

1   questionnaires sent to a national sample of 1,395 schools;
2   studies of local education authorities in general and Birmingham in particular;
3   recording and analysis of the processes, over a full school year, in the classrooms of thirty-five teachers in different parts of the country, from Reception class up to Year 6;
4   intensive observations of six individual children in each of these thirty-five case study classes (plus up to a further two pupils in each class who were thought by the teacher to be 'improving'), to elicit which seemed to make good progress and which did not.

The chapters in this book describe the research we did in more detail. Below there is a description of what we set out to do and how we did it, while Chapter 2 reviews some of the research relevant to our enquiries. The following section reports the first of the various strands of the research. Chapter 3 reports the national questionnaire survey of 1,395 schools. Chapter 4 relates what four local authorities did to improve literacy. There is special attention to the city of Birmingham which invested a great deal of effort in its literacy programmes.

In the middle section of the book we move to individual school level. Chapter 5 analyses the interviews about the organisation of literacy in the school conducted with key players, like head teachers and language co-ordinators; Chapter 6 reports teachers' accounts and observations of their beliefs and practices. Chapter 7 brings together information about the teaching of reading skills from lessons we observed, while Chapter 8 describes the role played by adults other than the teacher, like parents and classroom assistants. Chapter 9 describes case studies of six teachers in more detail.

Chapters 10 and 11 describe the pupils' perspective, an element often ignored in educational research. Chapter 10 presents information on individual children, their performance and views about literacy, while Chapter 11 portrays in more detail a number of 'target pupils' and children who were regarded as 'improvers' by their teacher. Finally Chapter 12 summarises the outcomes and conclusions, and considers the implications of our research for both policy and practice.

'Improvement' and literacy

Even before actually investigating it, the very act of defining a commonly used word like 'improvement' is not as straightforward as it looks. Although we tested several hundred pupils at the beginning and end of the school year in the Leverhulme Primary Improvement Project, we used reading test scores as just one criterion of improvement. In our case studies there were individual children whose actual test scores moved up only a little, but who devoured every Roald Dahl book they could find and whose enthusiasm for, and understanding of, what they were reading deepened considerably.

'Improvement' is a notion which can be studied in general terms or with reference to one particular aspect of learning. In general studies of 'effectiveness' it is easy to diffuse the energy of one's enquiry too widely, and in the end find that 'head teachers make a difference', or reach some other decontextualised conclusion. That is why we decided to focus on one especially vital aspect of the curriculum in the primary school, namely the field of 'literacy', and look in detail at what was happening in schools and classrooms to improve the level of children's competence. As is often the case, close scrutiny of one aspect of education often throws light on other elements, and this project was no exception. One can learn a great deal about how local authorities, schools and classrooms operate generally through focusing on a specific area like literacy.

We thought carefully before deciding to investigate what people did in primary schools to 'improve' literacy in general and reading in particular. Literacy is an especially fruitful field to consider for a number of reasons. First of all it lies right at the heart of primary school work, often occupying a significant period of classroom time. Second, it is an area which is agreed to be important by both professional and lay people. Third, it underpins other areas of the curriculum, for without competence in literacy, children would find it hard to learn effectively.

'Language' and 'literacy' are together important domains in the whole of education, not only in the primary school, but in secondary education and beyond. Their importance has been underlined by, among numerous others, psychologists, sociologists and philosophers. 'Die Grenzen meiner Sprache bedeuten die Grenzen meiner Welt', wrote Wittgenstein (1922) in his *Tractatus*. It is a powerful statement, but unless you speak German its power and elegance will elude you. Translated into English, the sentence reads: 'The limits of my language mean (or 'indicate') the limits of my world'. This assertion, though Wittgenstein modified his beliefs in later life, is a persuasive one, for without the written and spoken word, many functions and transactions we take for granted in adult life would not be possible.

Our society makes great use of audio-visual communication, but the written and spoken language still play a very significant part. In work, recreation and leisure, home and family life, the ability to read well in a variety of contexts, to write clearly and appropriately, and to speak to different individuals and groups, using an appropriate language register, remain vital components of an intelligent society. Being a citizen in the twenty-first century presupposes that members of society will be able to read about and understand their rights, entitlements and indeed their obligations to their fellows. Harrison and Nicoll (1984) analysed the reading competence needed to cope with the literacy of citizenship. They discovered that tabloid newspapers require the reading capability of the average 12 to 14 year old, while the broadsheet national papers need a significantly higher competence such as many adults would not have achieved.

They also found that a number of the more difficult information leaflets that people receive in their morning mail, or come across in public buildings, were about crucial rights, such as the availability of free glasses, or the procedures for complaining about inadequate hospital treatment. Those unable to read well would simply miss out on entitlements available to their more literate fellows. Anyone unable to read a work of literature or peruse the vast amounts of written information in our society, compose a letter, prepare and present a report, or understand and follow written instructions, may find that opportunities for further study, prospects for promotion, or even satisfying personal and social relationships, are diminished. In a fast-moving society poor levels of literacy can have dire consequences.

It is not only in adult life that inadequate competence in literacy can become debilitating. The primary years prepare children for secondary school, where they will have to understand more complex issues and concepts in several specialised fields. Language is learned at any age, but in primary schools words like 'area', 'length', 'volume', 'litre', 'metre', 'square' soon become central taken-for-granted terms in the early stages of the mathematics of measurement. Pupils who do not understand them and cannot use them as part of an everyday active vocabulary would neither grasp the initial stages of measurement, nor be able to progress to higher levels in secondary schools and beyond.

If teachers are to improve the quality of their own practice, then information of this kind about what is happening elsewhere can be a useful starting point. A report into primary education by Alexander *et al*. (1992) stated that teachers should look critically at their own classroom teaching and make judgements about ways of doing it more effectively. A similar assumption has been made in other enquiries into literacy and primary education. In our previous research into teacher appraisal (Wragg *et al*. 1996) we found that only about a half of teachers said they had changed what they did as a result of being appraised. Many primary teachers have taught for fifteen years or more. Indeed, at the time when we did the research some three out of five were over the age of 40. This meant that the teaching profession was rich in experience. The negative aspect, however, is that deeply ingrained patterns of classroom behaviour can be notoriously difficult to change, even when people do read or hear about practice and process in other classrooms. Nonetheless, without fundamental information change can be elusive.

What was studied in the research

As was described above, the Leverhulme Primary Improvement Project carried out research into two important aspects of education in primary schools. The first was *improvement*, what schools sought to do to raise the quality of children's achievement and learning; the second focus was on *literacy* in particular, since this was such an important part of what schools taught. These are both areas of considerable interest to any society, particularly one which is experiencing rapid change.

The timing of a project looking at these issues was also important. The approach of a new millennium, the introduction in 1995 of a revised version of the original 1988 National Curriculum for England and Wales, the increasingly fluid and uncertain job market, were amongst several forces which concentrated the attention, not only of the public, but also of the professionals involved. The pressure was mounting to make the best of the compulsory years of schooling, of which the primary phase was an important element.

In research of this kind investigators have three principal choices in theory, though less often in practice. The first is to study teaching and learning in its natural setting, without any direct intervention, other than being present to observe. The second is to intervene in some way and ask teachers to take certain predetermined actions, so that the effects of these can be monitored. For example, the teacher might be asked to hear certain children read at set times, or to use particular teaching strategies or materials. The third is to conduct an experiment, if necessary away from the school, by setting up an artificial classroom where an attempt can be made to control numbers and age of pupils, subject matter, timing, content of lesson, teaching strategies and other factors. The difficulty with this last approach, valuable though it can be on the right occasion, is that it is often seen as unreal, too unlike what happens in the hurly-burly of daily life in a busy school.

In previous projects we have adopted all of these approaches at some time or another, but on this occasion we decided on the first, that is to observe classroom processes as they occurred naturally, without intervention. We also decided against the second option, an intervention or action project, because our foremost intention was to construct a picture of what teachers and others believed was necessary to improve teaching and learning and then see what actually happened by direct observation, interviewing, testing, as appropriate.

In naturalistic research of this kind investigators are not in a position to prescribe what should happen in schools over a whole year. Classes of children do not start at the same point. They differ, sometimes considerably, in age, size, social background, geographical location, prior experience and a host of other individual and group qualities and characteristics well beyond the control of any research team. Measuring 'improvement' and then ascribing it to some kind of cause, therefore, is no easy assignment. Furthermore, we wanted to ensure a broad definition of the notion of 'improvement', for it would be easy to interpret it too narrowly. For example, if we had only accepted that children had 'improved' if their reading test score had gone up, then this would have ruled out those who developed a more positive attitude towards books, or who read more widely than previously.

Particularly when studying individual children, we wanted to keep an open mind about what 'getting better' at something should mean. Although we tested several hundred children, we did not want our conclusions to be swamped by a single test score, even a carefully compiled one, since this was but one tiny sliver of their life in school over a whole year. We began, therefore, with the intention of looking for instances where a particular aspect of literacy at the end of the school year seemed in some respect arguably 'better' than it had been at the beginning. We could then examine each case in a context.

There are technical as well as conceptual problems when trying to measure improvement. If class A starts the year with an average score on a test of 60 per cent and ends with an average of 70 per cent, then we could say that it had 'improved', since its scores on the test are 10 percentage points higher. This conclusion begs several questions, however. Have the pupils improved because of their own hard work, or that of their teachers, or a combination of both? Or is it simply a case of maturation? After all, children will probably grow 2 or 3 inches (5 or 7.5 cm) taller during a school year, something which would have happened even if they had stayed at home.

Supposing at the same time class B starts the year with an average score of 30 per cent on the same test taken by class A, but ends with an average score of 50 per cent. Have the pupils improved more than class A, since they have gone up by 20 percentage points, compared with 10? If one were so foolish as to reach this simple conclusion without further inspection, then classes which start from a low base would always appear to be doing better, as they have more headroom above them in which to improve, while any class of very able pupils starting in the 90 per cent bracket would appear to remain stationary or even decline. This phenomenon is usually described in statistical texts under the heading of 'regression'. There is no single way of coping with initial differences between classes, so we used a variety of both raw scores and statistically adjusted scores (i.e. scores which have been modified to recognise differences in the first testing) when we analysed beginning and end of year test results to see what differences emerged.

Studying any aspect of classroom life over a whole year is a complex business. Primary schools are teeming places, with thousands of interpersonal transactions between teachers and pupils every single day. It is not easy to select events which are worth further scrutiny, or to identify with any certainty those micro-elements arguably related to improving children's achievement in a particular field. Their learning, or lack of it, may also be influenced by their home and family life, by friends and relatives, by radio and television, and dozens of other forces, for good or ill, in the society in which they live. We interviewed participants to obtain their own views, but people themselves, teachers or pupils, cannot always be sure what has brought about improvements.

Our decision to focus successively on several levels of primary education, therefore, was taken because we wanted a series of related contexts in which to record what was happening. There is nothing wrong with simply conducting a national survey on its own, or carrying out a case study of a single classroom. Given the problematic nature of effectiveness research, however, we decided we wanted to draw on a number of sources and types of information, so as to be able to map out and cross check what we discovered. When there are differences in perception and interpretation, trying to achieve a 'consensus of those able to judge' is one way forward. The danger, of course, remains that people may all share the same misconceptions. Forty thousand football supporters sometimes believe that any referee giving a decision against their favoured team is either blind or of dubious parentage, even if video replay evidence shows he was right.

Denzin (1985) described four means of checking one set of findings against another: (1) *data triangulation*, involving different time, space or people; (2) *investigator triangulation*, where various observers cross check each other; (3) *theory triangulation*, which brings different theories to bear on what is observed; and (4) *methodological triangulation*, whereby more than one methodology of enquiry is employed. These approaches may be used singly, or in combination. All four were employed to a greater or lesser degree in this research. There were qualitative data, as well as quantitative outcomes, from interviews, questionnaires and observations, so various kinds of methodological and data triangulation were employed. These included self-reports of classroom and school practice from head teachers and language co-ordinators, observations of teachers' lessons by four different observers, tests of pupils' reading achievement, interviews with heads, teachers, pupils, parents and local authority officers.

Observer triangulation also took place. The training of observers involved watching videotapes and live lessons, as well as discussing interpretations and conventions, until a high measure of agreement was obtained between members of the team. Throughout the research there was reference back to other members of the research team until agreement was achieved over doubts and uncertainties. Quantitative data were carefully checked and statistical tests run more than once, often using different procedures. Qualitative interview or observation data were usually scrutinised by two, or even three, different people. Theory triangulation was also used, in that no single a priori theory was adopted, as conclusions were grounded in the actual data collected and their interpretation.

The four major studies

Education is a national as well as a local enterprise, so there can be immense variations in custom and practice. Millions of individual children learn how to read and write in thousands of schools and classrooms throughout the land. They are taught by hundreds of thousands of teachers, who in turn work in dozens of different education authorities. We decided to embed our research firmly within several, rather than just one, of the layers in this complex nexus of relationships and so we undertook four major interlinked studies, where each would complement the other. They were as follows:

- **Study 1** questionnaires about practice within the school, completed by head teachers or language co-ordinators from a national sample of 1,395 schools;
- **Study 2** interviews with heads, language co-ordinators and local education authority (LEA) personnel to study policy and practice in four different local authorities, one of which was Birmingham, chosen because it had embarked on a high-profile literacy campaign;
- **Study 3** recording and analysis of the processes, over a full school year, in the classrooms of thirty-five teachers in different parts of the country, ranging from Reception class (4 to 5 year olds) up to Year 6 (10 to 11 year olds), reading tests being given to some of these classes (a total of 355 children) at the beginning and end of the school year, plus interviews with forty-seven head teachers and twenty-five language co-ordinators;
- **Study 4** intensive observations of 258 pupils to study which individual children seemed to make good progress and which did not. In the first instance, six children from each of the thirty-five case study classes were selected (wherever possible three boys and three girls, one of each sex representing 'high', 'medium' and 'low' ability, as perceived by the class teacher). In January, after one term of the school year, each teacher was asked to select two pupils who were thought by the teacher to be 'improving'. In some cases the selection was made from the existing pupil sample and occasionally the teacher felt unable to identify any children as 'improving'.

These studies have certain commonalities as well as differences, so in this book the reporting of them is bound to overlap, as comparisons and contrasts emerge. We tried to be thorough in our analysis of the perceptions of different groups, so we might include a number of the same questions in a questionnaire to one sample of head teachers that were posed in an interview with another group of them, or ask the same questions of both teachers and pupils to see what similarities and differences emerge.

Some samples were quite distinct from each other. For example, we did case studies in thirty-five classrooms, but these were selected separately, not drawn from within the 1,395 schools that responded to the national questionnaire. Heads and teachers often complain at how busy they are. We did not want to overstretch their goodwill by imposing ourselves too often on the same people. Our case studies ran from September through to the following July, with ten visits being commonplace, sometimes even more.

Classroom observation

Classroom observation is not always undertaken when teaching is studied and there are strong arguments for and against using it, just as there are numerous different approaches. Some investigators take a quantitative approach, using schedules or checklists, whereby events are tallied and counted as they occur. Others employ qualitative methodology, studying events, looking for meanings and patterns, making notes and then interviewing participants, a more social anthropological approach. The many issues and procedures have been described more fully elsewhere by one of the present authors elsewhere (Wragg 1994).

Classroom observation is useful not only in its own right, in providing valuable data about events, but also in helping to focus and verify interviews. There is a danger that observers may influence events by their very presence, and Samph (1976) recorded classroom interaction with and without observers present, finding that teachers became slightly more child centred when observed. Such problems are lessened, however, when the observer makes several visits and becomes a more accepted part of classroom life. In the present research each teacher was observed on at least six occasions through the year and several were seen at work more frequently. The observation period was most frequently between 45 minutes and 2 hours, though sometimes we observed for about half of a school day. A balance has to be struck between being present often enough to see something worthwhile in fairly natural circumstances, and becoming an irritation or source of stress. We felt the advantages of observing lessons outweighed the disadvantages, and also that interviews were enhanced by the observer's first-hand knowledge of classroom events.

One of the problems classroom researchers must face is *when* to observe. A great deal of time can be wasted visiting lessons in which the aspect under scrutiny does not occur. For example, we could have watched art and physical education lessons, but there was little likelihood that children would spend as much time on learning to read in these sessions as in lessons where literacy had a sharper focus. We asked teachers, therefore, to give us the times of lessons when improving children's literacy was likely to be the major concern, and we fitted in our visits accordingly. This does *not* mean that literacy cannot be nurtured in science, technology or music lessons. It is simply the case that most lessons we visited were called

11

'English', 'language', 'literacy', 'reading', 'writing', or something similar. Other areas of the curriculum offer important subject matter on which children can hang their literacy. They often learn to read, write and speak the language of mathematics ('rectangle', 'probability') and science ('variable', 'force') in lessons specifically allocated to those subjects on the timetable, but these were not usually the lessons nominated by teachers as the ones when the *principal* focus would be on literacy, so we saw relatively few of them.

Observers made notes under several headings. The general ecology of the classroom was noted during visits: layout of room, resources available, displays, seating arrangements. Changes in this picture of the environment were also recorded, so in later chapters of this book there will sometimes be reference, for example, to displays of books by a particular author being changed or remaining the same during the school year. Records were also made of the eight individual target pupils in each class (six pupils of different abilities plus the two 'improvers'), what they did, how they behaved, what reading and writing they produced, how they interacted with their fellows and the teacher. Two observation tasks were regularly undertaken. These were:

1   *On-task and misbehaviour* A study of every individual child in the class, including each of the eight target pupils, to see whether they were applying themselves to their work and if they were behaving well or badly. Each child was studied in turn for 20 seconds and then recorded as being 'high' (14–20 seconds), 'medium' (7–13 seconds) or 'low' (0–6 seconds) on-task, as well as 'not deviant', 'mildly deviant' or 'very deviant'. Observers were trained on videotapes of classroom scenes until there was a high (over 80 per cent, often over 90 per cent agreement between them and there was discussion about what kinds of act would be coded as mildly deviant (e.g. noisy or irrelevant chatter, illicit movement) or very deviant (e.g. physical aggression towards another pupil, gross insolence to teacher). Two scores are then computed by converting the figures obtained to an 'on-task' and 'deviancy' index which can range from 0, if no one is on-task or deviant, to 100, if every child were to be on-task or deviant (Wragg 1994).

2   *Critical events* Observers looked for events, however fleeting, that appeared to be related positively or negatively to children's learning of literacy. The approach is a modification of the 'critical incidents' technique developed by Flanagan (1949). Any such event is recorded as it happens under the headings 'What led up to the event?', 'What happened?' and 'What was the outcome?' The teacher is then interviewed after the lesson to explore the reasoning behind the event. Where classroom interactions are described later in this book, these are often transcriptions from such critical events, where the observer judged

they were illuminative of some particular principle and therefore worth preserving.

Samples

Like any research design, however well intended, this one is not perfect. 'Sample mortality' is the somewhat forbidding phrase used to describe the difficulty of maintaining a sample, when there are population movements or changes within a school. Try as one might to keep samples of pupils together, there are forces at work that conspire to defeat the best-laid plans. This is especially difficult in classes of younger pupils, or in areas like Birmingham, where many children may move house in a year. One of the Reception classes we studied changed its membership three times during the school year, as new children arrived in January and April, while others left to make space for them. By July there were only eight pupils left who had started in the previous September. Fortunately these were our six 'target' pupils and two 'improvers', as the school had agreed to keep them together for the whole year.

Another difficulty, with so intensive a programme of observation, interview and testing as we undertook, is obtaining full sets of data, especially on all the pupils. We could not give reading tests to all the children we should have liked to test for several reasons. Sometimes the school was giving a different test of its own, so our particular testing programme, using a reading test from the National Foundation for Educational Research, would have got in their way, or overloaded the class. On other occasions the school was in any case planning to administer the same test as we were using, but at a different time of the year.

Inevitably some children will be away from school during a particular visit, so an observation, a test score, an interview, an example of the child's written work that day, will not be available. A research team has to collect more data than can possibly be used, as forces beyond its control will conspire to reduce the validity of some of it. Researchers cannot impose their will on schools. We had excellent co-operation from large numbers of heads, teachers and others in the education service, but since this research is not a controlled experiment, rather a series of snapshots of classrooms as they are, we could not tell people how to run their school for our benefit. In Study 4 it was remarkable, in the end, that we managed to obtain an almost complete record on over fifty measures taken at several points in the year from the sample of 258 pupils. Table 1.1 summarises the numbers involved in each of the studies.

We endeavoured to conduct as large and thorough a study of the field as we could within the time and resources available. It would be easy to claim either too much or too little for what we have found. No project solves the riddles of the universe, so we shall certainly not claim to have answered the

Table 1.1 Numbers in samples for each of Studies 1, 2, 3 and 4

Study 1 – the national questionnaire	
Number of schools from Birmingham	151
Number of schools from other LEAs	1,244
Total number of responses	1,395
(All 109 English local authorities were represented)	
Percentage from combined junior and infant schools	59
Percentage from infant and first schools	26
Percentage from junior and middle schools	15
Study 2 – case studies of LEAs	
Number of LEAs	4
Study 3 – case studies of schools and classrooms	
Number of heads interviewed	47
Number of language co-ordinators interviewed	25
Number of teachers studied over a year (30 female, 5 male)	35
Study 4 – case studies of individual children	
Number of high-ability pupils studied	70
Number of medium-ability pupils studied	70
Number of low-ability pupils studied	70
Number of 'improvers' studied	65
Total number of pupils in case studies (referred to in the text as sample A)	258[a]
Boys studied	130
Girls studied	128
Number of pupils tested	416
Number of pupils for whom complete test data are available (referred to in the text as sample B)	355

Note

a: Total does not add up to 275 as some 'improvers' were also in the original sample of six target pupils, and three pupils (two medium, one low ability) left during the year.

14

questions conclusively. Nor should we, at the other extreme, seek to disarm entirely what we have found, despite our own reservations about the limitations of research into such potentially diffuse notions as 'effectiveness' and 'improvement'. To study any aspect of literacy and reading in primary schools and classrooms, however, is to touch on many of the vast issues to do with teaching and learning generally, so we had to limit ourselves strictly to a relatively narrow scrutiny.

Towards the end of the Primary Improvement Project there was a change of government, and in 1997 a Labour administration replaced a long-serving Conservative government. 'Literacy' was stated to be one of its highest priorities and a number of working parties were established and various initiatives were proposed, such as the establishment of a regular 'literacy hour'. In 1998 a detailed framework was introduced for the literacy hour, with two 15-minute periods of interactive whole class teaching, followed by 20 minutes of individual or group work and 10 minutes of whole class review. Strong pressure was applied by the government for all primary teachers to adopt it for all classes, irrespective of age. It was not a pattern that we had observed being applied in any classroom on a regular basis. However, teaching children to be literate in general, and to read in particular, is a timeless activity, so we did not reorientate our analysis towards any particular political agenda.

There are numerous findings in this research, some of which confirm what a number of investigators have discovered, others which offer fresh evidence, and it will take several chapters to describe them. We have tried to keep the language of this book straightforward and readable. Some of our inferences and conclusions, however, are based on the statistical treatment of data. The findings from these analyses are written up as clearly as possible, and we have described the techniques used in terms that most readers should be able to follow. Since we guaranteed anonymity to all the schools, teachers and children taking part in the research, any such names in this book are pseudonyms.

2

RESEARCH INTO EFFECTIVENESS, IMPROVEMENT AND LITERACY

The long-standing international concern about the need to improve standards of education in general and literacy in particular, described in the previous chapter, has prompted many investigations of different kinds. In a multi-level project such as the Primary Improvement Project, it was necessary to consider previous research in several different fields. Since we were looking at how LEAs, schools and teachers help pupils to *improve* their literacy, their reading in particular, we had to take account of studies not only into school effectiveness and improvement, but also of the vast body of research into literacy itself, and how it was taught. In a single book chapter it is not possible to give a full account of these vast fields, so we can describe only a few reports of research to be found in them.

The effect of schooling and 'effective' schools

Parents often believe that schools differ and that sending their children to one rather than another will make a difference to the way they are taught, but findings in educational research have not always been consistently clear. During the 1960s and 1970s there was considerable emphasis on the importance of social class and family background on children's achievement, thus minimising the role played by schools. At that time some studies did conclude that school effects existed and might even be quite large (Gath 1977, Reynolds 1976, Edmonds 1979, Weber 1971, Brookover *et al.* 1979), but there was a predominant belief in the overwhelming importance of family background, so these findings were often treated with excessive caution.

It was in 1979 that Michael Rutter *et al.*'s study, *Fifteen Thousand Hours: Secondary Schools and their Effects on Children*, began to change the climate. Rutter *et al.*'s conclusions met with some scepticism, and there was concern as to whether sufficient background information had been collected to show whether it was *schools* that really did exert an effect, or unacknowledged family differences. However, other studies with a wide range of information on intake continued to find differences in outcomes. Although Reynolds *et*

16

al. (1989) chart how opinion moved from believing first that school effects were large, then that they were small, and later that they were large once more, there was general agreement that some school effects must exist. It was not that the influences of family were suddenly thought to be unimportant, but rather that the focus changed from parents – whose beliefs and behaviour were perceived to be outside the control of teachers, LEAs or government – to schools, which were thought to be more amenable to influence. If some schools were more successful than others in promoting the learning of pupils from a similar background, then questions had to be asked. These often concerned how they did it, what they were like and what others schools could learn from them.

In contrast with the United States, Scandinavia and parts of continental Europe, research into school effectiveness and the related field of school improvement in Britain is relatively recent. The purpose of the studies varies, from seeking to establish that differences exist, to explaining why this might be, and finally to determining how the successes of some schools could be copied by others. Most British research is of schools as they are, but elsewhere intervention studies have been used, with experiments to test theories of what is thought should improve teaching and learning (Fitzpatrick 1981, Nitsaisook and Anderson 1989, Van der Sijde 1989, Phillips and Norris 1996).

Sparse in Britain, but more popular in the Unites States, are studies of schools already judged to be excellent (Weber 1971, Wilson and Concoran 1988, Wynne 1993). Research methods vary along the quantitative–qualitative continuum, from studies which analyse data without ever studying pupils directly, to participant observations of a single school or class. Bondi (1991) and Hutchinson (1993) used a variety of techniques to allow for differences of intake, when they compared the results of standardised tests from different schools, taken from the local authority records. Both found that schools differed in the amount of reading progress their pupils made. The Office for Standards in Education (Ofsted) study (Institute of Education 1994) adopted a similar approach in its analysis of schools' results in the General Certificate of Education, making use of census data to provide information on the pupils' backgrounds.

Other data studies, such as that by Aitken *et al.* (1981), have reassessed previous research. More common, however, are primary research studies focusing on one or more schools. These may be longitudinal studies over a period of years (ILEA 1986, Galton *et al.* 1980), or snapshots at a particular point in time. They are often mainly quantitative, and reliant on 'before and after' test scores, sometimes with the addition of teachers' accounts of what they do, like the study by Bennett (1976), in which he clustered teachers into groups sharing similar practice, and then compared the test scores obtained in the classrooms of each group. Equally they may be predominantly observational and concentrate on the learning and social processes in the classroom, as did the ORACLE project (Galton and Simon 1980, Galton *et al*. 1980).

The introduction of national tests and league tables of school performance in the early 1990s made comparisons between primary schools seem easier, if more controversial. Before then it was only secondary schools that had available public examination results which could be compared, so it was not surprising that most British research was carried out in the secondary sector. There was, however, one major study in the 1980s – the Inner London Education Authority (ILEA) Junior School Project (ILEA 1986), which found differences between the fifty London primary schools it studied. A smaller study of infant schools by the Thomas Coram Institute (Tizard *et al*. 1988) found that while *attainment* was related to background factors, school *progress* was not. Tizard *et al*. studied the differential progress of black and white, male and female infant pupils, and so were not specifically looking for differences between schools' overall level of effectiveness. Nevertheless they did in fact find some, but realised that while correlations could be established, causes were harder to discover, concluding:

> The fact that children made more progress in some schools than others does not mean that those schools were more effective (in the sense of 'causing' their children to make more progress than children in other schools) ... more research is needed before we can make statements about what makes an effective infant school.
>
> (Tizard *et al*. 1988: 106)

Discovering that differences exist between schools is only the first step down a lengthy and tortuous path if teachers are to be helped to improve the education they provide for their pupils.

Once the existence of different degrees of effectiveness was widely established, the direction of much research changed to an investigation of the reasons behind such differences. In the year in which Rutter *et al*.'s *Fifteen Thousand Hours* was published, Edmonds (1979) put forward a 'Five Factor Theory of School Effectiveness'. This set out five characteristics of effective schools which have since been widely used and adapted. The factors were high expectations; involved and committed staff; frequent monitoring of students; orderly and secure environment; and emphasis on basic skills. Some of these characteristics have been disputed. For example, it is suggested (Clauset and Gaynor 1982, Scheerens 1992) that the relationship between teachers' high expectations and their pupils' success need not be one of cause and effect, for the teachers' high expectations could be the result of their pupils' achievements or the two might be bound in a reciprocal relationship. The benefits of frequent testing of pupils have been questioned, also (Levine and Lezotte 1990), on the grounds that some schools waste time testing instead of teaching. In their review for Ofsted of the characteristics

18

of effective schools, Sammons *et al.* (1995) reiterate Levine and Lezotte's emphasis on appropriate monitoring as opposed to the excessive use of tests. Scheerens identifies the circularity involved in judging a school's effectiveness by tests of basic skills and then citing emphasis on basic skills as a characteristic of effective schools.

Despite marginal differences, many lists of the characteristics of effective schools were drawn up similar to Edmonds' original five, sometimes with the addition of 'good links with parents' and 'good leadership'. In the Junior School Project (ILEA 1986), Mortimore *et al.*'s list of attributes which correlate with effective education contained several which relate to the work done by individual teachers within the school, while others were to do with school policy and 'school climate'. Subsequent research placed greater emphasis on the importance of having an effective head teacher. In their booklet for governors on what makes an effective school, Barber *et al.* (1995) put 'professional leadership' at the top of their eleven-point list, while the National Commission on Education (1993) put 'Strong, positive leadership by the head and senior staff' as the first of ten characteristics of effective schools.

There are fewer studies of 'good reading schools' than of 'good schools' *per se*, but the Junior School Project mentioned above found that schools which were effective in one area, and for one group of pupils, were usually effective in other areas and for other pupils. Her Majesty's Inspectorate (DES 1991) concluded that, in schools successful in teaching reading, firm leadership was given by the head and often by the language co-ordinator. It also noted that reading was given a high priority and taught by a balanced mix of methods, with practice in the classroom consistent with a clear well-documented school policy, attention to the needs of individual pupils and a wide variety of appropriate books, organised and matched to individual needs. Mortimore *et al.* (ILEA 1986) say that while lists of attributes of successful schools

> do not constitute a 'recipe' for effective junior schooling, they can provide a framework within which the various partners in the life of the school – head teacher and staff, parents and pupils, and governors – can operate.
>
> (p. 138 of part C)

As Mortimore *et al.* are aware, recognising key factors shared by many effective schools is easier than transplanting them to other less successful schools. It is at this point that the research on school effectiveness becomes linked to the separate but related subject of school improvement.

Improving schools

In the United States, the relationship between school effectiveness research and school improvement has been closer and of longer standing than it has in Britain. Early American effectiveness studies concentrated largely on the relationship between the input of resources and the outcomes of examination passes. School improvement studies similarly stressed material resources rather than anything as nebulous-sounding as 'ethos' or 'climate', and identified the main question as how to disseminate new ideas and successful teaching techniques. One belief was that the best way to improve schools was to develop products and get them adopted (Miller and Lieberman 1988). This approach of producing a 'package' for all teachers to deliver re-emerged in Britain as part of the National Literacy Project. Introduced in selected LEAs in 1996 and throughout England and Wales in 1998, *The National Literacy Strategy Framework for Teachers* (DfEE 1998) set out precisely what should be taught to each age group in each term. The alternative approach of looking at the process, rather than the product, though discernible as early as the late 1940s and 1950s, did not become established until the 1970s, when Seymour Sarason's *The Culture of the School and the Problem of Change* (1971) emphasised the cultural perspective and the need to look at participants' understanding.

The school effectiveness and school improvement traditions clearly have a great deal in common and sometimes people who have taken part in one scheme move on to another. One of the members of the Junior School Project team went to Canada to work on the Effective Schools Project, run by the Halton (Ontario) School Board of Education (Stoll and Fink 1992). The Halton Project, based on both school effectiveness and school management research, was of particular interest as an example of an education authority's effort to improve the education given by all its schools. Attempts at more widespread school improvement are often less effective than initiatives in one school, as innovations brought in from the top may become diluted or distorted during the translation down to classroom level, while the effects of the traditional way to improve teachers' practice – individual professional and in-service education – have often been short lived, and restricted to one teacher and one class.

In one of the largest analyses of what was thought to be effective in terms of influencing pupils' learning, Wang *et al.* (1993) conducted a wide-ranging survey of several hundred studies and expert appraisals in the United States. Their perusal of relevant research produced a list of 228 variables which were thought to have some effect on pupil learning. They grouped these into six sets covering (1) the State and District factors; (2) Home and Community; (3) School Demographics; (4) Design and Delivery of the Curriculum; (5) Classroom Practices; and (6) Pupil Characteristics.

The first important finding was that what the authors called 'proximal' factors, that is to say what happens within the school, are far more influential than what they named 'distal' factors, that is aspects such as State or District policies. Regional policies only made an impact on pupil learning if classroom processes changed. Second, the two elements 'classroom practices' and 'pupil characteristics' consistently featured amongst the most influential factors. Third, within the heading 'classroom practices' it was classroom management that seemed to bear most strongly on effective learning. It confirmed that, although there may be some disagreement about exactly which teacher practices and procedures affect pupil learning, they do seem more influential than distal policies:

> Distal variables such as district and state policies may set the stage for classroom practices that affect student learning, but findings from the present review provide little supporting evidence. Distal policies are likely to make a major difference in learning only when they affect proximal practices.
>
> (Wang *et al.* 1993: 279)

The Canadian Halton Project was, of course, intended to affect what Wang *et al.* called the 'proximal' practices of schools and classrooms, and after considering ways of implementing change, they rejected both the top-down method and that of training one person from each school to disseminate to the rest, deciding that it was better for the whole school to be the unit of change, and for the whole staff to have responsibility for school improvement. Teachers and schools had to identify their own areas of need and make their own development plans. Stoll and Fink (1992) both advised on and studied the process, and concluded that leadership, teacher involvement and a shared vision are critical to successful school development. Halton's 'top-down, bottom-up' approach was considered to have worked well, as it combined the benefits of greater commitment from teachers with the outside help they considered essential.

The relationship between effectiveness research and school improvement continued to grow closer. The notion of school improvement came to wider public notice in Britain in the 1990s with the controversy about the introduction of school league tables based on test scores. This prompted a search for a fairer way of comparing schools, and coincided with a general demand for improved standards and more accountability. In this climate, emphasis was sometimes put on comparing rather than on improving. The assumption seemed to be that, once a school had been identified as 'ineffective', change would be simple.

In some cases links were made between the research community, LEAs and schools to develop and study programmes designed to improve pupil performance. Essex LEA, for example, worked with the University of Cambridge Institute of Education and local schools. The Two Towns Project linked secondary schools in Stoke-on-Trent, the LEA, FE colleges and Keele University's Centre for Successful Schools, while the Improving Schools' Effectiveness Project was funded by the Scottish Office and carried out by Strathclyde University and London University's Institute of Education. Describing the plans for the latter project Mortimore and MacBeath (1994) said that twenty years' research had left us knowing that good leadership, firm, fair discipline, high expectations, strong links with parents and an atmosphere conducive to learning are characteristics of the effective school, but that the research:

> has told us more about the what of good schools than the how of making schools better. It has been descriptive rather than prescriptive and has had more to say about correlations than causes and effects.
>
> (p. 14)

Following this variety of localised projects to raise standards, efforts are now being promoted, by the government, to extend this to all schools throughout the country. While many local initiatives included a 'bottom-up' element, attempting to involve teachers more directly in the improvement project, the frequent criticism of teachers and schooling by press and politicians was often interpreted by teachers as being mistrustful of them and dismissive of their skills.

Effective teachers

While studies were being conducted into the atmosphere and ethos of schools, and the ways in which they could change and develop to become more effective institutions, the individual teacher continued to be the focus of other strands of effectiveness research. A very large study in the United States (the Co-operative Research Program in First-Grade Reading Instruction, commonly referred to as the 'First-Grade Studies' (Bond and Dykstra 1967)) had looked at the early stages of reading, comparing the teaching methods of twenty-seven projects. This study, like other methods of comparison research, was based on the assumptions that it should be possible to identify the 'best' method of teaching reading and that teachers using similar methods would work in similar ways and be equally effective.

Teachers vary in more respects than solely the methods they use, and when the First-Grade Studies and other enquiries failed to find clear evidence of one 'best' method of teaching reading, researchers began to consider the teachers themselves. Teachers' 'style', the amount of time and opportunity to learn they gave their pupils, the importance they put on literacy and the expectations they had, the quality of the questions they asked and the example they set, have all been the focus of research, as have other factors which might arguably be related to achievement, such as the effects of whole-class or group teaching, and parental involvement.

In accounts in the mass media, research into teachers or teaching methods has sometimes been presented in terms of a battle between two different camps, usually called 'progressives' and 'traditionalists'. The research by Bennett (1976) into the effects of different styles of teaching on primary school pupils' progress was one such study. His cluster analysis of questionnaire responses from teachers about their own classroom practices produced twelve teaching styles. These differed from each other in classroom management, curriculum, methods of control, instructional strategies, motivational techniques and assessment procedures. These twelve groups of teachers were eventually reduced to three teaching styles, named 'formal', 'informal' and 'mixed'. This research attracted much attention from the media because of its apparent endorsement of 'traditional' teaching methods, although Bennett had concluded:

> It ... seems to be curriculum emphasis and organisation rather than classroom organisation factors such as seating, grouping, and degree of movement and talk, which are crucial to pupil performance.
> (Bennett 1976: 160)

At the time of Bennett's earlier study of teaching styles, educational research was predominantly quantitative and relied to a large extent, as Bennett had done, on teacher's own assessments of the way they taught. Classroom observation had been criticised for being too subjective and unscientific, but Galton and Simon (1980) believed it could be shown to be a valid method of investigating the relationship between teachers' styles and the behaviour and attainment of their pupils. The ORACLE (Observational Research and Classroom Learning Evaluation) project was a longitudinal study spread over several years. The authors found the junior classrooms they studied to be orderly, work orientated if rather uninspired, with a traditional curriculum, an emphasis on literacy and numeracy, and the teacher in close control.

So far as teaching style was concerned, both Bennett's 'formal' teachers and Galton and Simon's 'class enquirers' appeared to get better results in basic subjects than teachers using other styles. However, one of Bennett's most 'successful' teachers was 'informal'. It appeared that success could come from either 'traditional' or 'progressive' methods, in so far as these were useful or meaningful concepts, and indeed, there can be a great deal in common between them. Orderly and disorderly classrooms, for example, are not exclusive to one particular style of teaching.

In the search for the elements of effective teaching which more often, but not always, were found in more 'formal' classrooms (Gage 1978, 1985), several possibilities were investigated, and explanations suggested. Sulzby and Teale (1991) cite findings by Weinstein (1985), Marshall and Weinstein

(1986) and Brophy (1986) that teachers' expectations exerted a powerful influence on achievement, and Tizard *et al.* (1988) also found that teacher expectations were related to children's progress, though, as we stated earlier, these may be the response to pupil learning, not necessarily the cause of it. The amount of curriculum content covered and whether a child was considered a pleasure to teach have also been cited as possible influences, while co-operative learning has been said to aid motivation and reduce anxiety (Slavin 1987).

Time spent on the task in hand has been scrutinised in a number of projects. In itself time is an empty concept. How it is spent is more important. Bennett (1976) had noted that children in successful classes spent more time on their task, but Galton *et al.* (1980) concluded that success was due not so much to the amount of time spent on tasks or interacting with the teacher, but to the nature and quality of such elements. They concluded that successful teachers made more use of task statements and questions, and provided regular feedback.

The level and nature of teachers' questions and other speech acts became a popular area of research, with a general assumption being made that asking probing open questions must be an effective strategy. There was no hard evidence, however, that persuading teachers to do this improves their pupils' attainment. Other 'teacher-talk' believed by some investigators to be useful is clear instructions, and explanations which help students to become aware of what they have learned and why it is useful (Pressley *et al.* 1987). Modelling appropriate problem-solving behaviour, with children talking and thinking aloud about their strategies, is believed by some to help children to understand the thinking behind tackling a problem. Shayer (1996) worked specifically in the field of science. He found that, when teachers trained children systematically to understand scientific thinking, they did better in national tests of science and mathematics.

Organisational and planning factors which may influence successful learning have also been investigated. It may come as no surprise that effective teachers take care to ensure that routines proceed smoothly and are generally well organised (Galton *et al.* 1980), or that they match the children's work to their ability (Bennett *et al.* 1984). Subsequently Bennett has criticised the excessive emphasis given to the 'opportunity to learn' and the corresponding neglect of what is learned. In 'The search for the effective primary teacher' (1987) he says:

Exhortations to increase curriculum allocation or to improve levels of pupil involvement or industry are of no avail if the quality of the tasks set is poor or not related to pupils' intellectual abilities.

(p. 56)

Clearly the importance of matching the task to the child's ability and to what needs to be learned should not be overlooked.

In all discussion of effective schools it should be remembered that it is an international issue and that notions of effectiveness will to some extent be dependent on a nation's aspirations and ideologies. For example, Scandinavian schools, as described by Ekholm (1988), are expected to foster democracy, co-operation, independence and high self-esteem, and have to do this if they are to be judged successful. American schools, especially if they cater for large numbers of immigrant children, are expected to foster the values of patriotism and 'Americanness'. Korea is an interesting example of publicly stated aspirations for the twenty-first century. It is a country that moved rapidly from a principally agrarian society to having a 166 billion dollar volume of trade by 1993. The aims of Korean education for a prosperous future are stated in official documents to be 'humanisation, refinement, informativeness, human welfare and open-mindedness', and the intention is to raise 'a self-reliant individual equipped with a distinct sense of independence, a creative individual with a sense of originality, and an ethical individual with sound morality and democratic citizenship'.

In Britain there has been no single state version of this kind about national aspirations. The 1990s saw a mixture of beliefs, some based on the preparation of children for life in a twenty-first century dominated by high technology, others on nostalgia for a real or imagined golden past. There have been debates about whether schools should foster competition or co-operation, pursue a curriculum of basic competence in numeracy and literacy, or try to cover everything from economic awareness and the enterprise culture to contraception, drug abuse and traffic safety. With very few exceptions, however, schools usually claim that they put a high priority on the teaching of literacy, the principal focus of this piece of research.

Concepts of 'literacy'

In 1970 Oxenham commented with surprise that almost 5,000 years passed between the invention of literacy and serious world-wide attempts to determine what level people needed to reach. Since then, however, there has been a large volume of enquiries into the nature of literacy, as well as investigations of literacy standards and literacy teaching in schools. Two basic models of literacy have emerged. In the first, the *autonomous model*, learning to read is seen as important in that it develops such cognitive skills as precision, memory, logical thought and detachment, and because of its use in a society's social and economic development. The second, the *cultural model*, looks at the meanings and uses of literacy in different cultures.

Different groups are found to emphasise different literacy skills, and research, often from an ethnographic perspective, is done to find out what are the valued skills and which develop from literacy itself and which as a

25

result of schooling. The differences between the autonomous and cultural models of literacy use, found in anthropological and sociological studies of adults, might seem to have little practical relevance to the teaching of reading in school. After all, everyone acknowledges that one major aim of reading is to acquire understanding. There are, however, differences between the view that this is 'simply' a case of getting at the author's meaning, and the idea that readers bring their own experience to the text and create something that has meaning for them. Thus, making sense of a text can be seen as an act of reconstruction, or of construction, and the emphasis can be on the text, or on the reader. These differing views of what people are actually doing when they are reading involve a variety of ideas on how children learn to read, which, in turn, affect theories of how reading should be taught in schools.

There are also several interpretations of what counts as 'being literate', which may partially explain the discrepancy which exists between the public perception that standards of literacy are declining, and research findings (Brooks *et al*. 1995) which show no overall decline. As Gardner (1986) points out, the requirements of industry and commerce are different from those traditionally promoted or tested in schools, for while employers require workers who can understand instructions, extract information and formulate plans, school English lessons have been mainly fiction based. *Chambers Concise Dictionary* gives two definitions of 'literate': first, 'able to read and write' and, second, 'learned, scholarly'. In 1942 the United Nations used 'the ability to read and write a simple message' as a working definition of literacy. In 1962 UNESCO defined a literate person in the following relativist terms:

> A person is literate when he has acquired the essential knowledge and skills which enable him to engage in all those activities in which literacy is required for effective functioning in his group and community, and whose attainments in reading, writing and arithmetic make it possible for him to continue to use these skills towards his own and the community's development.

People can be 'functionally' literate with only rudimentary competence, if simple basic skills are all that is needed in their community. What might have counted as literate for a village farm worker a hundred years ago is illiterate for a secondary school pupil today. The reference to personal development shows that UNESCO's definition is not purely utilitarian, but the emphasis is on an adequate level of capability, and literacy programmes coming from this perspective tended to be rather narrow and work related. By contrast, Paulo Freire's political definition of literacy (1985) is that it is about 'reading the world', liberation and helping the powerless to challenge dominant assumptions.

Although there are always one or two voices claiming that in an age dominated by audio-visual technology books may be outmoded and literacy overrated, the vast majority of parents and teachers are anxious for children to learn to read and write. There may be disputes about whether standards have fallen but there is general agreement that, as the literacy needs of the twenty-first century are likely to be increasingly exacting, they need to rise.

Barber (1996) drew attention to the complexity of the problem when he pointed out that although standards at GCSE and A level had risen steadily, as had the numbers of pupils staying on at school and of those entering higher education, for a significant minority of pupils standards might be static or falling. He cited evidence from the Office for Standards in Education (Ofsted) and the National Foundation for Educational Research (NFER) that reading standards in primary schools may have fallen in the early 1990s, and mentioned the concern sometimes expressed by secondary school head teachers about the number of pupils entering secondary education with reading ages of 9 or less. He also drew on research from Keele University on pupils' attitudes, which showed that 5–10 per cent of secondary school pupils were regularly truant, another 10–15 per cent were disaffected and disruptive, while another 20–30 per cent were unmotivated and disappointed in their experience of school. Barber concluded:

> While half or slightly over half are doing reasonably well, concern over the rest remains justifiable. ... If this is the overall national picture, then it should be borne in mind that the gloomy parts of it are likely to be accentuated in Britain's urban areas.
>
> (Barber 1996: 8–9)

He found cause for optimism, however, in the work done in cities such as Birmingham and Nottingham, where standards in urban areas were thought to have risen.

In 1997, the incoming Labour government set the target that, by the year 2002, 80 per cent of 11 year olds should reach Level 4 (the putative 'average' level for 11 year olds) in English national tests. This renewed the debate about how such mass increases in competence could be achieved. Earlier Barth (1990) had drawn attention to the importance of encouraging discussion amongst staff about successful teaching methods. Barber (1996) wrote of the need to encourage 'a learning staff', as well as the value of schools having a clear sense of direction with specific targets. Some advice was derived from research evidence, but much was based on supposition.

Teaching reading

There are two theoretical perspectives from which we may view the act of reading, and each is associated with different methods of teaching children to read. One view is that reading (or writing) is essentially the same process, whether done by an expert or a beginner: always a search for meaning (or attempt to communicate), and always an interaction between the writer and the reader. This meaning-based perspective is influenced by psycholinguistics with its emphasis on how we make sense of our world through the use of language. Reading is seen as the active *construction* of meaning, rather than the simple *reconstruction* or comprehension of the author's own meaning. The process is seen as starting with readers who have expectations of what a text will reveal, who then test these theories and confirm or reject them as they proceed. This perspective underpins those teaching methods which stress the importance of the reader's response to a text and emphasise 'top-down' skills – the use of semantic and syntactic cues. The alternative view is that reading is the uncovering of the writer's meaning and that in learning to do this children go through different stages: they begin by learning the alphabetic principle, then apply this to enable them to decode words so that, after practice, they can comprehend the text. This perspective, at its behaviourist extreme, sees reading as lots of little behaviours to be mastered one by one, and subscribing to it completely would entail reliance on teaching methods which emphasise phonics and word recognition – the 'bottom-up' skills of decoding.

Few teachers subscribe to one or other view exclusively, and so, in the classroom, they have commonly used a mixture of different teaching methods. Research into the teaching of reading, however, was dogged by problems similar to the polarisation and tendentiousness encountered in studies of effectiveness, although some writers in the field now believe we may be moving away from the disputes between the opposing stereotypes of 'progressive' and 'traditional', 'phonics' and 'look and say', 'reading schemes' and 'real books', and think that there is now a measure of agreement about the necessary conditions for developing literacy (Beard 1993, Riley 1996). This consensus is not simply a compromise until the one best method is discovered, but is due to a growth in understanding of the complexity of the reading process and has been built on the accumulated findings from several different lines of research.

Fluent readers and successful beginners

One area of study involved looking at successful beginners to discover what other skills and knowledge they had which may have contributed to their success, and findings about the relationship between early success and other variables show a large measure of agreement. Children's knowledge of nursery rhymes was found to be related to their reading ability (Bryant *et al*. 1989), and Juel (1991) suggests this is because experience of rhyme directs children's attention to the *sound* of words and so enhances their phonological sensitivity. Tizard *et al*. (1988) found that children used to hearing stories are better able to benefit from reading instruction, as readers need to know a lot about print, books and stories before they are able to learn to read, and the children who come to school fully aware that print carries meaning and with a rich experience of what books are about and the conventions of story are ready to make a flying start. Pre-school children's knowledge of letter names was found to be a very accurate predictor of their later success (Chall 1967, Bond and Dykstra 1967), and a good vocabulary at the end of nursery education (Tizard *et al*. 1988) is also related to later reading success.

Finding a correlation, however, is not the same as proving a causal relationship, and teaching children some of the skills associated with early reading success did not always produce the hoped-for improvement in children who had made a slow start. For example, teaching letter names to school children who found reading difficult did not appear to advance their reading a great deal. Attempting to explain this, Adams (1990) suggested that the reason learning letter names before starting school helps is because, through this teaching, children's attention is drawn to different letter shapes and focused on the alphabetic principle. Thus it is not knowledge of the names themselves which helps, but a confident early understanding of the alphabetic principle which is a necessary foundation for acquiring the bottom-up skills of decoding.

Adams (1991) claimed that the appearance good readers give of not attending to individual letters and letter patterns is misleading. Although they appear to read too quickly to process words 'letterwise', they do look at the letters and syllables, and are able to process them quickly because of their memories of previously recognised sequences of letters. Using letter–sound relations, they break words down into syllables and graphemes and recognise quickly which are the common letter strings. They also scrutinise orthographic patterns and make analogies with words they already know, and because of these abilities, they can read pseudo-words and nonsense words – something poor readers find very difficult.

It is now widely agreed that a thorough knowledge of phoneme–grapheme relations is of crucial importance, and that children need phonemic awareness (the realisation that oral words are sequences of meaningless sounds) and an understanding of the alphabetic principle (Chall 1967, Clay 1987, Juel 1991). Juel (1988) also found that primary school children who were good at decoding were exposed to about twice as many words as those who were not, so the effect of early success appears to be cumulative.

Phonological awareness

Learning about phonemes and phoneme–grapheme correspondence is a difficult as well as important task. The evidence that it is difficult comes from experiments in which children were asked to make judgements about phonemes of a kind that literate adults or older children could easily make (Bryant and Bradley 1985, Goswami and Bryant 1990, Liberman *et al*. 1974). That children can distinguish between 'cat' and 'hat' is obvious from their conversation, but they find it difficult, if not impossible, either to say how many phonemes there are in words, or to say what a word would sound like if a particular phoneme were removed.

Illiterate adults and those who have learned to read a non-alphabetic script such as traditional Chinese orthography have similar difficulties. As Beard (1993) points out, if alphabetic knowledge has little part to play in reading, then the difficulty children have will not matter, but other research evidence suggests that there is a connection between children's ability to understand grapheme–phoneme correspondence and their success at reading. The understanding that words are made up from meaningless sounds and that these sounds can be represented by letters is fundamental and there is a strong correlation between reading levels and tests of awareness of phonemes. Poor readers have difficulty in coping with pseudo-words as these cannot be guessed, but can be read only by applying knowledge of grapheme–phoneme correspondence (Frith and Snowling 1983, Baddeley *et al*. 1982). When Morais *et al*. (1987) compared illiterate and recently literate Portuguese adults, they found the literate ones did much better distinguishing phonemes than the illiterate ones, suggesting that it was not through maturation that the ability to distinguish phonemes came about, but through being taught the alphabet.

Beard (1993) argues that these three research findings – (1) that phonological distinctions are difficult; (2) that they are connected with learning to read well; and (3) that they do not come about unaided – together add up to a strong case for teaching phonics, a case which now seems to have been widely accepted. This consensus is comparatively recent. HMI's 1990 review of language and literacy (DES 1991) did not mention phonics specifically, although it stressed the importance of a wide, structured language curriculum, a variety of language activities, discussion about meaning, interesting books, and home/school initiatives. The 1991 review (DES 1992), however, did recommend the teaching of letters and sounds, and a balanced mixture of methods is generally recommended now for both pragmatic and theoretical reasons.

Teaching methods

Partly because skilful readers appear to recognise words without concentrating on individual letters, and partly because English has many exceptions to its phonic rules, the assumption had been made that children would learn more quickly if they were not taught to rely on phonics. The belief that children recognise whole words by their shape was behind the look and say method of teaching reading, but it failed to explain how they could recognise words written entirely in capital letters that they might not have seen printed in that case before. Practical problems were that children had, in effect, to learn every word from scratch, as if learning a logographic script like Chinese, and that, when faced with an unknown word, they had no strategies with which to decode it.

In the late 1960s, Kenneth Goodman (1967) had put forward his famous and influential theory that reading was a 'psycholinguistic guessing-game' in which readers selected the word they expected to find. The theory that readers recognise a word because it is the word they expect in the context, however, has been investigated, and Just and Carpenter (1987) and Adams (1991) argue that while we do use context, it is only *after* a word has been identified. Fluent readers have at their disposal a variety of strategies and appear to use whichever method of getting at the meaning of the text is the easiest. They do use their knowledge of grammar and they make predictions of meaning, but because of their ability to decode, they rely less on syntactic and semantic clues and make fewer guesses than those children who find reading more difficult (Stanovitch 1980).

Thus the combined weight of evidence suggests that although some words are recognised by their shape, and others are guessed at from the context, knowledge and use of letter–sound correspondence are vitally important. While the earlier debate about phonics, however, focused on *whether* letter sounds should be taught or not, the later question was *how* they might be taught. What is sometimes called the 'new phonics' represents an attempt to overcome the main problem of the partially irregular letter–sound system of the English language and is seen as something that should not only be taught to beginners. Attention is focused first on learning how to represent the forty-four phonemes which make up English speech, rather than learning that the twenty-six letters of the alphabet are pronounced /a/ /buh/ /cuh/ – something which is often not the case. Children may be taught to separate words into the initial sounds before the vowel (the *onset*) and the vowel and the rest of the syllable (the *rime*), to attend to alliteration and to segment the syllables or individual sounds in words (Adams 1990).

Enthusiastic readers

There is more to reading, however, than the ability to decode, or even to decode and comprehend. Fisher (1992) describes the skilled reader as

> one who can decode efficiently, but who can use that knowledge appropriately and effectively, continually refining his/her information processing skills. To this should be added the dimension of reading for pleasure and the acquisition of a habit for life.
>
> (p. 13)

Neither gaining pleasure nor using knowledge is as easy to measure as word recognition, yet they are an important part of being literate, and much of the disaffection with reading schemes or traditional phonic teaching methods came from teachers concerned about the children in their classes who were able to read but did not do so.

Waterland (1985), an infant teacher, was disillusioned with what she called her 'feeding the cuckoo' methods, by which she stuffed her 'chicks' with a diet of Books 1, 2 and 3 until they were ready to fly off and feed themselves, but often chose not to. Starting from the belief that reading may be learned by an apprentice working alongside skilled practitioners, she made the Apprenticeship Approach popular. It was often linked with the 'real books' approach and combines emphasis on meaning and enjoyment with awareness of the part parents play. This has been developed or refined as Paired Reading, with a skilled reader, perhaps a parent or older child, reading the text with the beginner until he or she indicates the desire to take over (Topping 1995).

Waterland believed that using her Apprenticeship Approach and selecting good children's books produced great improvements in her children's attitude to reading. Finding the best method of teaching reading, however, is complicated by three problems: (1) every method of teaching will appear to work for some children; (2) new methods, introduced in the hope of bringing about an improvement, are often believed by their instigators to work better than previous approaches, especially as the experimenter, whether teacher or action researcher, often has a significant personal stake in their success; (3) the *Hawthorne effect*, named after the Hawthorne factory of the Western Electrical Company, where each experimental condition tried out by investigators led to improved productivity, largely because of the attention and interest being shown in the workforce.

Chall (1967) found that enthusiasm or apathy, and excitement or boredom, existed independently of the method of reading instruction, but were affected by the atmosphere of the classroom, the pace of activities and the active involvement of the teacher. Newly introduced methods and materials were found to be more successful, and Chall thought this was partially due to the intelligent and optimistic nature of those who innovate. However, another reason for the success of the new was thought to be that teachers who brought in, or were instructed to use, new methods did not dispense with their old ones, and so, for a time, children received the best of both approaches. In this way they received the broad-based instruction which is now believed to be important, for reading is a complex, multi-faceted activity during which we use many skills in order to decode, understand the author's meaning and assimilate it into our own experience. Children need to learn processing skills, using context and knowledge of syntax to focus on the general meaning of the whole, and also decoding skills focusing on individual letters and words. They need specific teaching of both 'top-down' and 'bottom-up' skills; a certain amount of phonic instruction; careful monitoring in order to give early help to those who make a slow start; interesting meaningful texts; teachers who are enthusiastic about literacy throughout the whole primary range; encouragement from home; and lots of practice.

The contribution of parents

The deterministic view that home background was the only important factor affecting children's attainment had been replaced in the 1970s by a belief that schools could make a difference. The Plowden Report (1967) on primary education devoted a whole chapter to the role that could be played by parents. Young and McGeeney (1968) experimented in London schools by involving parents in attending school functions, hearing their children read, and various other forms of participation. They found some improvements in reading performance compared with control schools where there was no such participation. Many studies of parents simply record the implementation of specific projects, while others report the teachers' and parents' attitudes to such studies. A few studies have been conducted on parents coming into school to help, but the majority are on parents helping at home.

McNaughton and Glynn (1980) and Kemp (1986) investigated the 'Pause, Prompt, Praise' technique taught, with apparent success, to parents of children having problems with their reading. In contrast, the Haringey Project (Tizard *et al*. 1982) was one of several attempts to ameliorate the results of social deprivation throughout the school by involving the parents of all the children. Parents were encouraged to help but not taught specific techniques. Hewison and Tizard (1980) had found, in Dagenham, that informal participation by parents hearing their children read was the most important variable in determining children's success in reading.

The study by Hannon (1987) of working-class children who took books home for three years, however, showed only marginal gains in reading attainment, while Share *et al*. (1987) found a negative correlation between parental listening and children's reading ability. There are plausible explanations for Share *et al*.'s findings. Although Hannon's sample of children was encouraged to take books home, the study included many parents who were already hearing their children read, and so it did not chart the progress of a new practice. This was even more marked in the case of Share *et al*., who studied what parents already did, rather than a school's attempts to get them more involved, and it is possible that parents who felt their children had reading problems were more likely to hear them read than the parents of fluent readers.

Despite the findings of these two studies there is still a widespread belief that involving parents in their children's reading must be beneficial.

Parental help is encouraged by most primary schools, with growing aware-ness of the need for schools and parents to work together. Phillips and Norris (1996) compared three groups they had issued with the same set of books. One group used the books only at school, one used them only at home, and the third, which used them at home *and* school, made the most progress. The realisation that parents often need help in knowing how to help, plus understanding about the importance of the pre-school years, has prompted many Family Literacy projects.

It is interesting to note that, as Hancock (1991) points out, the involve-ment of parents in their children's learning sits more easily with meaning-based approaches to teaching reading than with those emphasising the acquisition of skills. It remains to be seen, therefore, whether the renewed stress on the importance of phonics and decoding skills will halt or alter the direction of the move to involve parents in the teaching of reading. When reading is seen as an enjoyable shared activity, the aim of which is understanding, then parents, relatives and siblings can all join in. If reading is seen as a series of skills to be mastered, however, then teaching it is more likely to be claimed as the prerogative of the professionals, although when we interviewed parents in the present project, some of them quite clearly emphasised decoding, and monitoring their children's progress, not solely enjoyment, as will be reported in Chapter 9. We may have reached the stage at which the complex nature of learning to read is recognised and the differing contributions of parents and teachers may be considered equally important.

The role of parents in their children's education is an interesting point at which to conclude this chapter, as it brings us almost back to where we began, with the research finding that parents were not the only factor influ-encing children's academic success, and that effective schools might make a difference. It finishes with the conclusion that what parents do both before and during their children's school days is nonetheless of some importance. There may be limits to what schools can do to compensate for the social circumstances of some children, but there are many steps they can and do take. It was to try and identify a number of these that we undertook the Leverhulme Primary Improvement Project, and it is to the findings of our four major studies that we now turn.

3

THE NATIONAL SURVEY

The first part of our analysis of what schools do to improve literacy, Study 1, was based on a national survey of a large sample of primary schools. The 'zoom' strategy we had adopted, whereby we planned to move from the large-scale national and regional perspective to the individual classroom teacher and pupil level, required a broader picture of practice to be assembled. We decided to send out a wide-ranging questionnaire to head teachers of primary schools to help construct this overall description of what schools said they were doing.

Drawing up a 'national' picture is not easy. With millions of children in thousands of different primary schools, there is bound to be considerable diversity. An 'average' or percentage, therefore, will conceal numerous individual differences. The use of questionnaires is common in these circumstances, as it allows researchers to gain a great deal of information from a large audience of respondents, many of whom are at a distance from the investigators and might not be easy to reach. It also permits respondents to reflect on their responses in private, without feeling the face-to-face pressure that an interview might engender. The disadvantages of mailed questionnaires are also well known. Amongst these are: that there may be a low response rate, 10 per cent being often the case, that the respondents might not be 'typical', that the investigator cannot verify easily what is written, and that the information is often in a form that is easily quantified and may, therefore, oversimplify the issues. Oppenheim (1992) has written a full account of the use and construction of questionnaires.

Nonetheless, we decided that it was worth trying to collect some national data, as these would form a useful background to the more fine-grained and longer-term scrutiny of local authorities in Study 2, and of individual teachers and pupils in Study 3 and Study 4. In order not to influence these three further sets of data, therefore, we did not analyse the national questionnaires in Study 1 until we had completed all the other case research. This allowed us to conduct our other studies independently and then refer back to the national picture.

The national questionnaire

A questionnaire for Study 1 was constructed which elicited reports from head teachers, or their designated respondent. Most replied themselves, though about 20 per cent delegated the task to their deputy head or language co-ordinator. The questionnaire was constructed from the interviews we had conducted with head teachers, in which elements thought to be important in the teaching of reading had been identified. It contained sections on 'organisation and language policy', 'the teaching of reading', 'assessment', 'LEA involvement' and 'constraints'. Many of the questions involved responding to a set of predetermined categories, but some invited freehand responses. Analysis and statistical calculations were carried out using SPSS (Statistical Product and Service Solutions) for the quantitative data, and a consensus 'rate until agreement' principle for the qualitative data. This latter involved discussion between members of the research team on what meaning was being inferred from written freehand statements until a particular interpretation was agreed.

Copies were sent to a random sample of one in eight primary schools, producing 1,395 returns, a 53 per cent response rate, with some replies from every local authority in England. This is a good response for a mailed questionnaire. Nearly 59 per cent of the replies were from combined infant and junior schools, 26 per cent from infant and first schools, and 15 per cent from junior or middle schools. About half the schools were urban, while a quarter each said they were rural or 'mixed'.

We wrote to all Birmingham schools (excluding those previously included in head teacher interviews), since the city was a particular focus in the Leverhulme Project, and 151 responses were obtained. There were 1,244 responses from schools in the other English LEAs; hence the grand total of 1,395 schools. In order not to distort the 'national' picture by overweighting it with Birmingham schools, we assembled a special 'national sample' consisting of the 1,244 responses from English LEAs and twenty Birmingham schools chosen at random from the 151 respondents, so as to include roughly the same number of Birmingham schools pro rata as the rest of the sample. Thus the 'national sample' in this chapter of the book consists of 1,264 schools.

One of the sections of the questionnaire asked schools about what their local authorities were doing in the field of literacy. The whole of the next chapter will be devoted to reporting what LEAs do, so at this stage we shall only report that, in their answers to the national questionnaire, 46 per cent of head teachers replied that they were aware of a local authority initiative concerned with the teaching of reading. In Birmingham the figure was a much larger 94 per cent.

Organisation and the role of the language co-ordinator

Most primary schools said they gave a high priority to literacy, as one would expect, and that the language co-ordinator, a feature in virtually all schools, was a key person responsible for organising and supporting the efforts of others. Some fascinating detail emerged from the survey about the role of language co-ordinator, including the following:

- Over 90 per cent of schools said that they had a language co-ordinator who took special responsibility for literacy.
- In 10 per cent of the schools it was the head or deputy who held the post.
- Only 3 per cent of schools said that nobody had special responsibility for language.
- About 40 per cent of post-holders are not paid any special allowance for their responsibilities.
- About 30 per cent of post-holders do not have any non-contact time to do the job.
- Amongst those that do give non-contact time to their language co-ordinator there is considerable variation – nearly 20 per cent of respondents have one period of time per week or better, and a quarter are given time for specific tasks, rather than on a regular basis.

These overall averages and totals conceal a wide variety of practice, as Chapter 4 will show, and the position is noticeably different in Birmingham, where 94 per cent of language co-ordinators are paid a special allowance and 86 per cent are given non-contact time. Other comparisons between Birmingham and schools in the other 108 local authorities obtained from Study 1 will be further reported in Chapter 4.

The role of the language co-ordinator is generally regarded as crucial. Almost all schools said that a major responsibility was to ensure teachers knew the school's language policy, though not all the individual teachers we interviewed seemed fully knowledgeable about it. Beyond this assignment, the ten most common functions of the language co-ordinator, in descending order of importance, can be seen in Table 3.1. The need to monitor language teaching and give regular advice to other members of staff, mentioned by 84 per cent and 81 per cent of all schools, were regarded as being right at the top of schools' priorities.

Almost all schools said that they already had a written language policy (87 per cent) or were currently preparing one (12 per cent). Most of these policies were said to have involved a wide range of people. About 90 per cent of schools stated it was compiled mainly by the language co-ordinator and the class teachers, working with the head. Some three-quarters mentioned the special needs co-ordinator. The predominant influence on

Table 3.1 Ten major responsibilities of language co-ordinators (1,264 schools)

Responsibility	Percentage of schools mentioning
1 Monitoring and evaluating teaching	84
2 Providing advice to staff on a regular basis	81
3 Advising on reading materials	68
4 Leading in-service training	66
5 Ordering resources	60
6 Organising the school library	42
7 Running meetings for parents	35
8 Devising language resources	35
9 Working with teachers in their classroom	35
10 Assessing children's reading problems	19

this policy was from the head and teaching staff, but about half cited the governors, and a quarter said they had involved the LEA and classroom assistants, though how profound or perfunctory this involvement was we are not able to say from the questionnaire responses.

Many of the written comments of heads were about the heavy workload of what were called variously 'English', 'literacy' and 'language' co-ordinators. They also mentioned the constraints under which they laboured. The head who suggested that English co-ordinators are unnecessary because all teachers are supposed to know about teaching English was overwhelmingly outnumbered by those who felt the job was too big for one person, especially for someone with a full-time teaching commitment. This theme was often accompanied by references to funding, as these two comments reveal:

> Our deputy head is the language co-ordinator. She has several other areas of responsibility too. I am concerned about her work load and the pressure she is under. The severe financial constraints do not allow her non-contact time to fulfil her role as she would wish.

> Fulfilment of her role and of my post-holder's potential is hampered by our constant, perpetual, never-ending lack of money to support initiatives by freeing staff during the teaching day.

Heads of small schools frequently pointed out their particular problems:

> In a small school we all take on subject co-ordinator roles in two or three subjects.

> Often in a small school like ours the co-ordinator is not the specialist.

> In a small rural school, three full-time staff means that the head teacher is responsible for, or leads, all curriculum co-ordination.

Heads took the responsibility for literacy for other reasons also: because they did not have teaching commitments, because of its importance, and sometimes because of the difficulty of finding someone else to do the job to the head's satisfaction.

One way some schools attempt to overcome the problems of excessive workload is by sharing the responsibility, though for others this was not always feasible:

> The work of the language co-ordinator is of major importance since it impinges on the whole curriculum and is central to it. The role ... is really too great for one person to carry out and in an ideal world with a greater level of staffing available, a language team should be created to include the special needs co-ordinator and the school library organiser – each with language responsibility points.

Although most evaluative comments on the role of language co-ordinator were positive, some were negative. Problems mentioned were related to staff ability, knowledge and attitude:

> As a newly appointed head teacher I found that the subject co-ordinators had not got any job descriptions nor any real concept of the role of a co-ordinator.

> The language co-ordinator has reluctantly taken responsibility.

The teaching of reading

When it comes to books and teaching methods, most schools believe in the 'pick and mix' approach. Despite frequent press reports that teachers have abandoned the use of reading schemes, or indeed systematic and structured approaches in general, our survey showed a different picture. We asked for information about several aspects of teaching and learning that were of interest for different reasons, either because they figured in debate and speculation, or because they were commonly believed to be important elements of practice. The answers in the questionnaire provided both quantitative and qualitative data.

The areas addressed included the following:

1. the use of reading schemes;
2. the colour coding of books according to difficulty;
3. the use of approaches like 'phonics', 'real books' and 'look and say';

4   current initiatives in the school;
5   the teaching of children with reading difficulties;
6   the involvement of parents and others;
7   what respondents thought teachers could do to raise standards of reading.

Summaries of lesson observations by HMI (DES 1991, 1992) concluded that very few teachers used one exclusive approach to the teaching of reading, only 5 per cent of teachers being said to use exclusively the 'real books' approach, and only 3 per cent to employ a solely phonics-based strategy. Since the National Curriculum in English requires children to acquire 'phonic knowledge', to develop a sight vocabulary of words they can recognise instantly, as well as to read a range of fiction and non-fiction, it would be very difficult to justify using one sole strategy to the exclusion of others. A wide variety of findings emerged from this part of Study 1, including the ones described below.

Reading schemes, books and teaching methods

- Some 99 per cent of schools say they make use of reading schemes.
- About 53 per cent of schools (infant stage, 54 per cent; junior stage, 52 per cent) say they use several schemes.
- About a third of schools confine themselves to either one or two reading schemes for their classes (infant stage, 38 per cent; junior stage, 20 per cent).
- One principal use of reading schemes for a minority of schools is as a 'safety net' for certain children (infant stage, 12 per cent; junior stage, 23 per cent).
- Differences in practice within the school appear to be discouraged, as only 2 per cent of schools replied 'yes' to the item 'some teachers use reading schemes, others do not' (infant stage, 1 per cent; junior stage, 3 per cent).
- Approximately half the schools (infant stage, 48 per cent; junior stage, 47 per cent) employ colour coding to identify the difficulty of books.
- Some 97 per cent of schools say that they prefer 'a mixture of teaching methods'.
- More schools mention the importance of 'phonics' (31 per cent) than 'look and say' (10 per cent) or 'real books' (8 per cent) when describing their 'main' or 'most favoured' approach.

This last finding may be either a true reflection of practice, or an 'expected' response, given the criticisms in the press about the supposed lack of structured methods in the teaching of reading. Phonics was used mainly in the infant school and where necessary for less able children in the junior phase. Many schools talked about 'structure' and 'progression' and timetabled phonics sessions seemed common:

> Written phonics policy with clear progression used throughout school – some commercial, some home-made resources. Part of, but not whole, approach to teaching reading.

> Children are assessed on arrival at school (junior school) on their phonic knowledge. From this assessment children follow a programme until they have *learned* sounds, blends etc. Children are withdrawn in groups of 4–6 for this.

> [Phonics] plays an integral part in our school. Each day at 10.20 the whole school work in sound workshops for 20 minutes. Each teacher runs a different workshop (progressive) and the children work at their own pace throughout the workshops.

In the popular press 'look and say' is often reported as a 1960s' progressive approach to reading which displaced phonics. The meaning that most lay people would naturally attach to the phrase is that children would look at a word and pronounce it, much as adults do. Developing a sight vocabulary of instantly recognisable words is not exactly a recent phenomenon. In an attempt to clarify possible confusions, Goodacre (1975) distinguished between 'look and say', where the teacher would often give children a word, speak it, and then ask them to repeat it, and the 'whole-word' approach, where flashcards might be put onto pictures, or taken home to be learned. 'Look and say' responses to our questionnaire revealed diversity in interpretation and practice. Many respondents tended to use the approach for building up early sight vocabulary. Some linked it to their reading schemes, while others were rethinking, feeling that words on their own might mean little:

> Children start with this [look and say] via the Ginn 360 scheme, taking flashcards home.

> We have just stopped the practice of sending home reading scheme words (decontextualised) in boxes. Now they still go home, but can make sentences.

'Real books' is also a confusing term for both lay and professional people. On the one hand it describes a methodology or, more precisely, a set of approaches to the teaching of reading, some of which involve using a range of fiction and non-fiction, graded according to their difficulty, instead of working through a reading scheme. The common meaning of the term in everyday speech, however, would embrace the actual books that one might find in any library or bookshop. Responses to this section of the questionnaire revealed a range of interpretations of the term. Some indicated that real books were used mainly by more 'competent' readers, while other schools talked of their use at the very earliest stage of reading. Others indicated that they had colour coded the real books and had integrated them into their core reading scheme:

> Whilst we recognise the need for good quality books and the need for a range of reading materials we do use the structure of a scheme. 'Real Books' are graded and colour coded to fit in alongside the scheme to give the child the breadth and balance they need.

Several respondents were vociferously opposed to the use of real books as the sole approach to the teaching of reading. Indeed, some said they had tried the approach earlier but discontinued it:

> [We are] totally opposed to this approach. Yet we believe in real books being used to support children whose reading is taking off.

> The children are surrounded by books throughout the school and are encouraged to 'use' them ... but osmosis is out!

> We originally just used real books but found that some children learned very little from this and required some structure. We still have a lot of real books and prefer them for our more fluent readers, although we don't prevent the others taking them.

> [Real books] had been in place prior to my arrival. Not working – very poor results.

The phrase 'mixture of methods' has become a common feature of reports by HMI, such as those in 1991 and 1992 (DES 1991, DES 1992). It represents not just an eclectic but a pragmatic view of teaching. Few schools in our sample seemed to be committed to an exclusive approach, the overwhelming majority (97 per cent) preferring flexibility. The main reasons for this seemed to be (1) the belief that children need as many tools as possible when learning to read, and (2) that there is a need to match strategies to a child's individual need. Some expressed their regret at extreme polarisation in discussions on the teaching of reading:

> Reading has to be a joint approach. No one method or scheme would enable a child to learn to read adequately.

Word recognition and phonics run side by side. A fluent reader needs to have both in order to succeed and be able to tackle unknown texts.

Our emphasis is on reading for *meaning*. Children are encouraged to use any clues available from context, pictures, sensible prediction etc. I emphasise diagnosis of individual need and provision of an approach to meet that need.

It is unhelpful for different approaches to be presented as if it is an either/or issue. This has not served the reading debate well. Planned teaching of skills plus quality literature and skilful assessment are needed.

Current initiatives – involving parents

When it came to the question of whether schools are taking any special measures to improve reading, some 58 per cent of schools reported that they currently had a particular initiative. These are included in Table 3.2 in descending order of frequency.

Perhaps we should have included a definition of the term 'initiative', but we did not. As a result schools described a varied set of practices, many of which may have been new to the school concerned, but would have been regarded as commonplace in other schools. It is difficult to state, in reply to a questionnaire, that no initiatives are being taken, of course, as this might imply that the school is complacent or inert, so perhaps some heads felt the need to report something under this heading. The result is a substantial collection of comments on what respondents report as a novelty in their own

Table 3.2 Current reading initiatives reported (1,264 schools)

	Percentage of schools
Involving parents	20
Evaluating current policies	9
'Reading recovery' (or similar)	8
Paired reading	8
Getting additional adult support	7
Reviewing/updating reading schemes	7
Changing/reviewing assessment procedures	7
Group reading	7
Working on 'higher-order' reading skills	5
'Enrichment' activities	5
Improving library	5
Staff development	5

school, and the majority of these are about either specific new projects, or changes in policy or practice.

Initiatives involving parents were top of many schools' priority list and they fell into four major groups, with considerable overlap. These were:

1 Parents helping in school.
2 Parents helping at home.
3 Informing/educating parents about policy/child development/how best to help.
4 Improving parents' own literacy and language skills.

In the first group, the fact that parents were parents was almost incidental. They were in school as helpers:

> Early Years Reading Workshop. Teachers, ancillaries and parents work with small groups to develop a true understanding of the world of reading: discussion, comprehension, information gathering etc.

> Each day begins with a 30 minute reading session to which parents are invited.

Similarly in the second group, parents were convenient and important helpers whose ability to help at home was often taken for granted. Reading diaries were mentioned, but in some cases the taking of books home became more structured, with a period of intensive activity and/or systematic instruction:

> Shared reading project – 8 weeks annually. Intensive programme of home reading, checked daily in school.

> Reading project with Year 3 children. Parents are asked to hear their children read every day for 8 weeks. Many now think their children no longer need to be heard and are amazed at their improvement over the 8 weeks.

> Six weeks' training for parents of new children in the term before main school entrance (*after* training for all staff – teaching and non-teaching) covering the relationship between learning to speak and learning to read, approaches, choices, parents' views, making literacy games, sharing a book.

Some initiatives were targeted on particular groups of parents. Occasionally the focus was on fathers, but by far the most common targets were parents of nursery, Reception or pre-school children. There were also programmes aimed at those families where English was not the first language, or where levels of literacy might be low:

> We are currently talking to fathers about ways in which they can encourage and motivate their sons in literacy skills.

> We are spending much time with parents of nursery pupils encouraging them to become involved with 'early learning' activities. To help this we have produced a booklet and a pupil pack for children to work with at home. As this is a 'family stress' area, children don't have pencils, crayons etc at home.

> (We run courses in) English for Bengali speaking mothers.

> A family literacy project running, whereby a group of parents work with their own child with support of a teacher and adult tutor. The parents then work with the Adult Education Tutor to improve their own literacy skills and the children get time with the teacher in a small group situation.

Schools were asked whether various groups of adults, not just parents, were involved in the teaching of reading 'frequently', 'occasionally', or 'not at all'. Classroom assistants were the biggest category of adults who were not the class's regular teacher, followed by parents and grandparents. The results shown in Table 3.3 do not signify that every class in a school had a classroom assistant, parental help, or whatever. Schools were simply asked if people other than class teachers helped at all.

Sending books home for children to read with parents is virtually universal, only two schools in the whole sample saying that they did not do it. Most schools say they send home spellings and key words, but the frequency varies considerably. About half the schools say they use a booklet

Table 3.3 Percentages of adults other than class teacher involved in teaching reading (1,264 schools)

Adults involved	Frequently	Occasionally	Not at all
Classroom assistants	80	15	5
Parents/grandparents	69	23	8
Special needs teachers	61	25	14
Other volunteer adults	49	32	19
Head teacher	22	53	25
Student teachers	18	52	30

or video for parents on how to teach reading, while two-thirds have a school bookshop. Half run meetings for parents. Table 3.4 shows some of the relevant figures.

Table 3.4 Home/school links reported (1,264 schools)

Home/school link	Percentage of schools
Reading record sent home	92
Spellings sent home to learn	90
Key words sent home to learn	82
Meeting on reading for new parents (pre-school)	79
School bookshop	65
Booklet or video on reading for parents	50
Meetings on reading for current parents	50

Current initiatives – evaluating policy and changing organisation

Evaluation of policy and changes in organisation were the main or partial focus of a number of the initiatives that heads described. Some schools worked alone, developing staff expertise on projects such as:

Reviewing phonic progression.

Research into gender differences in reading achievement.

Looking at book provision ... how we plan and assess reading.

Totally revising the English policy and scheme looking for ways to make it more efficient.

A two year School Effectiveness Project with the local university to focus on extending the more able readers by extending our current classroom practice and provision and knowledge of children's books.

Banding in ability groups.

Emphasis on literacy in Reception by 'sidelining' other areas of the national curriculum.

Reading Roundabout – where children are taught reading in a systematic way ... organised in groups and there are 5 reading related activities every day. Each group visits one activity each day throughout the week on a rota basis.

Giving certificates for reading effort and achievement.

Rewards (given) for building a list of books read at home.

The introduction of new teaching methods was mentioned frequently by respondents. Many schools were trying some version of group reading, sometimes in mixed, sometimes in similar, ability groups. The substance of this activity varied from groups of children hearing each other read to groups with additional classroom support being taught 'strategies for reading, meaningful guesswork, phonic and picture cues ... punctuation, writer's style and much more'. Paired reading, and its transatlantic relation 'Buddy reading', were also being introduced, sometimes between children and parents, but more frequently between children of different ages. Specific remediation programmes like 'Reading Recovery' and its offspring OWL (Our Way of Learning), Kickstart and Freshstart, also received favourable comment:

We now have individual support monitored by our ('Reading Recovery' trained) special needs co-ordinator, delivered by classroom assistants trained by her. We are thrilled by the results and received £2,500 from the LEA's initiative for raising reading standards. We are now finding that having dealt with the worst difficulties, those children have overtaken the group above. Most significantly, the trained classroom assistants are taking the skills learned with individuals into group and class situations.

We currently have a Reading Recovery teacher based in the school – the most valuable resource any school should have.

We are in our second year of using Reading Recovery. ... This has influenced many teachers' understanding of the teaching and learning of reading.

This programme (Project Read) started as a response to failing readers in American inner cities. It is highly structured and involves reading and writing skills. It is fun. It is small group oriented and can be used with 6–8 children at a time. It is therefore economical compared to Reading Recovery.

The events and procedures covered by the 5 per cent of schools that reported 'enrichment activities' included poetry workshops, authors in residence or attendance, dramatic performances, book weeks, a library club, competitions, bookshops, the 'production of school-published reading books based on our environment, using a grant from Birmingham's Year of Reading', and 'A story telling event with local schools. We aim to publish one story from each school in book form.'

Children with reading difficulties

The two shortest replies to our question about what schools were doing for children who had difficulties with their reading were 'Very little' and 'Not enough'. One respondent said this 'should be covered in daily individual reading work', and another 'We try not to think of it as a problem ... but as a child needing a different approach over learning – slower pace etc.'

The most commonly mentioned provision was extra help or extra time, and this could be provided by a wide range of people: the class teacher, part-time teacher, special needs teacher or co-ordinator, Reading Recovery teacher, LEA support teacher, head teacher, nursery or classroom assistant, parents, reading volunteers, Dyslexia Centre. A number of schools complained that financial problems prevented them from giving all the additional help they would wish, and some were cutting back:

> Sadly, for the first time in many years, due to budgetary constraints, there is no member of staff free from a class commitment. Children with special needs (particularly reading) are not given the individual support they need to help with their problems.

> Programmes drawn up with help of special needs consultant employed from supply budget four afternoons a term. Teacher assistants – some deployment. Totally inadequate but we can't afford learning support. As teaching head I am also special needs co-ordinator (not to mention half a dozen other things). Very, very difficult.

Respondents frequently described the use to which the extra time was put, sometimes by withdrawing children in groups, or sometimes by giving individual help in or out of school time. Use was also made of 'named' approaches and commercial programmes – Reading Recovery, OWL, Skillteach, DISTAR – and other methods such as paired reading, extra phonics. Individual learning plans, sometimes developed in consultation with parents and/or other teachers, were often drawn up. Advice was also obtained from various LEA agencies, including educational psychologists.

The importance of screening, monitoring and dealing with problems early in a child's school life were emphasised, though the chosen time differed:

> Through daily monitoring, children with problems are identified very early in Reception, resulting in increased pre-reading activities using classroom assistant and parent helpers. After one term parents are alerted and a home–school partnership begins in which parents agree to work with their children at home on activities which will reinforce school work. Levels of progress are monitored and a wider range of language activities is introduced to build up vocabulary and confidence. Monitoring and review will show child no longer requires extra input, or that help from outside agencies is needed.

How can reading standards be improved?

Very few schools, only 3 per cent of respondents, believed that standards of reading could not be improved. Three choices of response were offered, as shown in Table 3.5, and the majority answered 'yes' to the question 'Can reading standards be improved?', though 29 per cent thought it would be difficult. Some of the respondents followed their apparently unequivocal 'Yes' answer with an equivocal comment explaining how difficult this would be, so the 68 per cent 'Yes' value in Table 3.5 is probably inflated.

Table 3.5 'Can reading standards be improved?' (1,264 schools)

Yes	68%
Yes, but it will be difficult	29%
No	3%

A number mentioned areas of concern where there was room for improvement, without necessarily saying how these would be addressed. Many referred to the problems of an overloaded curriculum:

> The curriculum at Key Stage 1 is still overloaded. We wish wholeheartedly that we had the time and flexibility we had a few years ago to devote to teaching 'basics'.

> We need to give greater emphasis to extending at Key Stage 2. Lack of time and resources are holding this back.

> Finding the time to teach reading is very difficult, the national curriculum is so demanding.

Some respondents felt that the best way ahead was to target certain individuals and groups, often picking out specific aspects of reading such as 'higher-order skills' or 'information gathering' which could be developed. Almost every aspect of reading, every level of ability and every age group were identified by one head teacher or another as being a ripe target for improvement. A number mentioned the relatively poor performance of boys in their school:

> Our standards are high. However, it is worrying that a number of boys, [aged] 8+, no longer see the value of functional reading and reading for pleasure, in spite of having: a) daily opportunities for personal reading, b) access to appropriate books, c) a wide variety of books.

One interesting group of heads was those who had taken up their post recently. Most felt charged to inject improvement in some form, in order to justify their appointment, especially where they felt the previous head had not been sufficiently proactive:

> Standards were poor when I took up the headship two years ago. One reading scheme in place to the exclusion of virtually all other reading material. Literacy had a low profile, parents were not involved in any positive way. We are making headway – governors approved expenditure on books, parents are more involved and we have a home/school reading project.

> Took over the school 12 months ago, standards poor. Few real books, reading schemes in poor condition, lack of choice, not graded or coded, no library, few non-fiction. There was not a good range, limited genre. There was little recording of progress and no formative assessment or diagnostic work. We are gradually putting the resources in and working hard to get schemes of work in place. We know we have a long way to go and many of my staff are on a vertical learning curve (but willing!).

> Historically: 1. Low expectations of children. 2. Higher order reading skills and other basic skills have not been a part of the planned reading programme. 3. Poor provision of books. 4. Lack of confidence/knowledge at Key Stage 2 (teachers). 5. Poor/non-existent reading records. 6. Lack of consistency. 7. No monitoring of progress.

Some heads said that, although the school seemed to achieve high standards on the whole, there was a particular aspect of reading (higher-order skills, reading for pleasure) or group of readers (boys, able readers, children with special needs, older pupils, etc.) where improvements were planned.

> We have high reading scores (68% level 3 SATs) but I am always looking to improve the standard of reading provision. Consequently, I am training as a Reading Recovery teacher. This is proving very successful. Parents are really pleased with the results so far. We also constantly look for ways to challenge our excellent readers. This is an issue as well.

Most respondents did not pin their hopes on a single strategy for improvement, but mentioned several. Some stressed they had moved towards more active direct teaching, both for teachers and parents, rather than simply hearing children read:

> Current work on sharing texts is already generating a marked rise in achievement, particularly for Key Stage 2 children.

> One clear factor emerging as a link between fluent and literate readers is the input parents have in reading to and talking about the literature, rather than just correcting errors. This really puts meat on 'modelling' and it is this approach we are trying to develop. Teachers model reading methods for their pupils.

Most of the small group of respondents (3 per cent) who said standards could not be improved did so because they believed that they were 'good' already. Some acknowledged the help given by parents. Some cited as evidence their SATs results (all Year 2 children at Level 3), reading ages (vast majority above chronological age) or their Ofsted report.

When it came to the means by which improvement might be achieved, there were numerous categories of answer. The two most important approaches advocated both related to setting a climate in which reading was important, either within the school and classroom, or in the home by involving parents in partnership. This would be aided, it was thought, by the presence of a good selection of books and resources and by monitoring children's progress on a regular basis. Table 3.6 shows the analysis of respondents' written comments. These figures do not add up to 100 per cent because many replies covered more than one category. Nor should it be assumed that respondents did not value or advocate other approaches. In freehand replies many people simply record their most pressing response, rather than write an extended essay.

Table 3.6 Means of improving reading standards (1,264 schools)

Getting a positive atmosphere and ethos	35%
Involving parents	33%
Having good-quality resources	24%
Regular monitoring and assessment	22%
Having enough class time to devote to reading	17%
Teacher's own professional knowledge	13%
Hearing individual children read regularly	13%
Differentiation for different abilities	13%
Using praise and encouragement	12%
Having a whole-school reading policy	11%
Effective planning and organisation	9%
Using a variety of approaches	9%
Staff development	9%

Most respondents were not short of ideas on how to improve children's reading. Their replies may be divided into those relating to issues beyond schools' and teachers' control; those focusing on the school as a whole; and, by far the largest group, those which concentrate on what the class teachers should do (or be).

Factors that were beyond the schools' control were often under the jurisdiction of LEAs or government. These included extending nursery provision, cutting class sizes, especially for the 5 to 7 year old age group, reducing the demands of the National Curriculum, and improving resources:

A period of stability in education. An improvement in teacher status, morale and an appreciation of their hard work. A realistic national curriculum with more flexibility to address literacy in a creative interesting way. Abandoning League Tables and pretending to measure the immeasurable.

Get up and fight (preferably with their Union) over class sizes. Let's tell and keep telling parents and media that in a 'normal' day a child in a class of 35 mathematically has the right to a teacher's time of 6 minutes. Until we stop pretending everything is all right, nothing will happen.

The school's ethos was seen to be the most important factor, and this could be broken down into smaller notions that related to such matters as the attitudes of teachers towards improvement, professional dialogue and the sharing of ideas, as exemplified by aspirations like:

Corporate aim of striving to improve.

More collegiality when problems arise.

Agree on the reading policy and ensure that it is implemented consistently through good planning.

Spend time, as we did, to create a structured format to ensure success by addressing assessment, evaluation, planning, reporting and recording as a whole which runs alongside the practice.

There must be a whole school approach to the teaching of reading with agreed policies for monitoring and assessment. The policy should promote an interest in and love of books and literature (more difficult now in the computer age!). Ways of disseminating research work and methods. Greater sharing with colleagues who have demonstrated good practice in the teaching of reading and language. In the early years, teachers should not be 'swamped' by national curriculum demands, and devote more time to encouraging, reinforcing and building up positive relationships with parents.

The need for teachers to be 'constantly developing professional expertise' was seen as an issue both for school management and for individual teachers. Schools should provide good in-service training and teachers should 'ensure they have a top quality professional knowledge re the teaching of reading, well supported with clear, detailed guidelines'. Exhortations to improve teachers' knowledge were sometimes accompanied by strictures on initial training:

[Teachers must] become more skilled themselves and more aware of research and analysis of the skills children use when learning to read. We none of us feel that we were *ever* trained to teach reading and sadly that still seems to be the case in universities and colleges today.

Discussion of what was read was also recommended, and there was appreciation of the fact that giving children 'quality time' might mean that they were not heard as often as they used to be:

Give children time to discuss their reading material, always developing language in all its aspects. It isn't just about listening to children read, it is also about creating the right kind of unhurried approach and calm atmosphere.

Alongside the emphasis on direct teaching mentioned earlier in this chapter, the importance of making reading enjoyable and attractive was also stressed, and there was much that teachers were urged to do to achieve this:

> Making books important; clear and concise reading displays in classroom; interest in reading themselves and showing this to children; positive approach to children; variety, but consistent approach to methodology; wide range of reinforcement materials; beautiful books; reading corners in all rooms (comfortable); regular reading sessions.

The need for teachers to 'read to children regularly, choosing good quality texts and reading aloud with skill, intonation and enthusiasm' was frequently mentioned, partly to introduce children to good literature and partly to model enthusiastic reading. High expectations were cited as important, but so were praise and the celebration of small successes. Good planning and structure were considered, by some respondents, to be indispensable for the improvement of literacy standards, along with monitoring and assessment, which were necessary so that teachers could provide differentiated instruction and materials and also pick up problems early. One respondent said:

> Teachers need to be more analytical in their view of each child. Comments like 'super reading' or 'well done' don't give anyone clues as to where any particular child needs to focus in order to improve.

Involving parents was also seen as a significant task for the classroom teacher – sometimes to urge them to play a more active role in their children's learning and sometimes to slow them down a bit. 'Ideal' parents – fathers as well as mothers – understand the school's approach to teaching reading, are aware that reading encompasses a range of experiences, and they discuss and enjoy what is read with their children rather than pushing them through the scheme. They also value books above the television. Some parents may need to be educated to fulfil this role.

There was, of course, some divergence of opinions among respondents, and a difference of emphasis. Overall, however, a common view of the ideal school emerged. It was a stimulating place where staff worked together to ensure reading was given the highest priority. In an attractive, well-resourced and literacy-rich classroom, enthusiastic, knowledgeable teachers used a variety of high-quality texts and provided well-planned, structured, interesting instruction in the multi-faceted skills of reading. Parents were involved in their children's learning, and other appropriate help was directed to those children who were shown, through diagnostic assessment, to need it.

Assessment of progress

Assessment procedures also vary from school to school, and between Key Stages. Standardised tests are much more in evidence with 7 to 11 year olds at Key Stage 2, while phonic checklists are more common in the earlier years at Key Stage 1. Assessment is a topic which occurs many times in this research, especially in the studies of individual schools and classrooms. The summary of main results from the national questionnaire is shown in Table 3.7.

Table 3.7 Principal methods of assessing reading in 1,264 schools (864 schools had both Key Stage 1 and Key Stage 2 pupils; 213 schools had Key Stage 1 pupils only; 187 schools had Key Stage 2 pupils only)

Form of assessment used	% at Key Stage 1	% at Key Stage 2
Record of books read	80	76
Phonic checklist	71	43
Sight vocabulary test	55	43
Teacher record of strategies and behaviour	51	83
Miscue analysis	45	40
Standardised reading test	43	67
Pupil self-evaluation	20	41
Statement banks	12	9

Baseline assessment

Three-quarters of schools said that they carried out baseline assessment when children entered the school. Almost exactly half of these schools said that they had designed their own form of entry assessment, while about 4 per cent had used or modified a procedure devised by their LEA. The figure for Birmingham schools using baseline testing was notably higher, at 95 per cent, as will be reported on further in Chapter 4.

There were some different interpretations of what a baseline test actually was, even though we had defined it in the questionnaire as 'The assessment carried out at the end of nursery school or during the child's first term at school in order to establish a baseline against which a child's progress may be measured'. Most respondents did use this definition, but there was also mention of monitoring throughout the first year in the school and testing at the end of it. Some schools stipulated a time limit – within the child's first four or six weeks, the first half term, or the first term of school. There was a range of complexity, with some schools opting for a 'simple check on motor control skills and mental abilities' and others going into much more detail. A few respondents listed a hierarchy of skills, starting with interest or awareness of books, and extending to knowledge of letters, words and ability to read certain books. Most were less specific.

Depending partly on whether a school was responding as an infant or junior, some schools' baseline tests are related to the National Curriculum so that progress can be assessed. A number of schools mentioned parents (e.g. 'Baseline begins with parent interviews'; 'Linked in with individual sessions with parents and children'). There were examples of parent–teacher interviews, the teacher listening to the child reading with a parent, and booklets with sections for parents to complete on what their children could do at home, such as dressing themselves. Responses sometimes seemed to reflect notable differences in the expected achievement of children on their arrival at school.

Positive and negative comments were made about baseline testing. Favourable observations included three possible benefits in use: (1) an aid to monitoring progress and the 'value added' that had accrued during a child's school career; (2) the assessment of a child's starting point for purposes of planning and also for the identification of special educational needs; (3) a basis for discussion with parents. Some respondents neatly encapsulated all three:

> Useful starting point and gauge of a child's progress for teachers and parents.

> It provides staff with a guide for trying to give appropriate input to the individual child. It informs the parent of the child's achievement. It gives an indication to child, parent and teacher of the effort and improvement made over time.

In some cases the 'value-added' argument was broadened to include the direct involvement of children in their own learning, in others it was seen as a tool for teachers, even as a boost to their morale when progress could be seen:

> Essential in relation to: taking children on from where they are; building on strengths; diagnosing weaknesses/gaps; involving children in seeing/planning progress; value added.

> Very important as a method of showing progress, particularly if that progress is small (to encourage despondent teachers).

> It is vital to us. We do need to know what attributes our children bring. If education is a journey by train, some of our pupils may not reach the intended destination. Some run like hell to even catch the train. Baseline helps us to measure the journey our pupils have travelled.

Some heads saw the potential of baseline testing to act as a defence against external criticism, including that emanating from parents or Ofsted:

> [It] might shame some parents into giving children more time before they come to school. It's also time the public recognised that results depend at first on raw material.

> It also shows awkward parents why they should be pleased with their child, rather than criticising the school for not getting the child to a particular standard.

> ... the hidden agenda is that it shows how difficult our particular situation is with children from a disadvantaged area – and is ammunition to use against criticism from OFSTED *et al*!

Other benefits of baseline testing mentioned were: to gain extra resources; to identify high fliers; to enable teachers to group children earlier; and to raise teachers' expectations:

> It has made staff realise that, despite the fact that we serve a catchment area where children often don't have a great deal of literacy/numeracy input at home, nevertheless they start school with a wide range of abilities and understanding, and that teaching needs to be differentiated from the beginning. It has raised teacher expectations.

On the question of national or local versions of baseline testing opinion was divided. Some heads wanted a standardised, national or county-wide test, perhaps related to national tests, while others thought it would only be useful if it was geared to the specific children, school or area, detached from national assessments, as these contrasting responses show:

> [I] wish it was formalised throughout England.

> If it's to be used as a performance indicator it needs relating to SAT areas which aren't necessarily appropriate in Reception.

> Needs to be tailored not only to school's particular intake but also to school's particular interests and expectations. Not in favour of national checklists!

> I have real concerns about the kind of baseline assessment which simply provides number-crunching information for value added comparisons with SATs results.

Some thought baseline testing was only useful if it was conducted in the first two, four or six weeks of term, while others warned that children vary in the length of time they take to settle into school and so should not be tested immediately. Many were concerned about the time it took and the disruption it caused when children were settling in, with some stressing that the test should be basic and simple, and others wanting more detail:

> *Very* simple form of sharing information. Would rather spend time supporting progress than collating data. Too much analysis leads to paralysis.

> Very useful if efficient and not too time-consuming. Unfortunately they [baseline tests] are seen as a protection against critics rather than a tool for planning for the individual child's needs in the present political climate. They must be carried out for the right reasons, have a clear purpose, be manageable and be completed as part of the day to day observations rather than through contrived tasks.

Almost all the negative comments were about the quality of the tests themselves or their effectiveness, or else queried whether testing was even necessary. Specific criticisms included that: testing is 'often too time-consuming and quickly becomes outdated'; 'standardised checklists can be very prescriptive and not reflective of the whole child'; many pupils are transient, or do not speak English; the tests are hard to standardise, varying from year to year and being carried out by different people; comparisons with more detailed tests by educational psychologists show them to be not very accurate; they are 'too crude to be really useful'; they are not graded and so 'provide very little information about the children's capabilities other than the minimum'.

Some heads dismissed them completely:

> Some of the tick box variety don't do a lot for me. If they focus on what the child can do, it's a deluge of wasted information, if they focus on what they can't do it's a deluge of negative information, often out of context with maturity and background.

> We are quite apprehensive about this issue. We are concerned about the parental pressure on young children. It is a very sensitive issue and needs more clarification and discussion.

> What purpose does it serve? Get on and teach them to read.

Target setting

Assessment is often closely related to the setting of specific targets, as it is the means by which judgements are made about the extent to which such targets may or may not have been met. We asked schools two separate but related questions: first, whether any use was made, in the context of reading, of target setting for the whole school, and second, whether targets were set for individual pupils. The answers were an almost exact mirror image of each other. The result was that 70 per cent answered 'no' to the 'whole-school' question (in Birmingham two-thirds answered 'yes', see Table 4.3, p. 84). By contrast, about 70 per cent answered 'yes' to the 'individual pupils' question, though targets were set mostly for children with special educational needs. Table 3.8 shows some of the national questionnaire answers to these two questions.

Table 3.8 Target setting in reading for the whole school and for individual pupils (1,264 schools)

Whole school reading targets set?	
Yes	24%
No	70%
No response	6%
Individual reading targets set?	
Yes, set for all children	26%
Yes, but set only for children with special needs	44%
No individual targets	21%
No response	9%

Perhaps our questions were slightly ambiguous, as respondents answered 'yes' in two different ways. One respondent pointed out: 'Learning objectives may be for class, group, pairs and individuals.' While some respondents were clearly referring to 'all' children as individuals, each with their own distinct targets, others were thinking of children as members of groups, classes or school, all of whom were expected to reach certain standards or fulfil certain requirements.

This is certainly an area where greater conceptual clarity is needed. The notion of 'targets' was being interpreted in different ways, in some cases quantitatively, such as a specified number of books, authors or genres to be read by a certain time, actual pupil scores on specific tasks which had to be carried out. Sometimes there were particular skills to be mastered, or standards to be reached. Specified quantitative targets were almost always 'group' targets. Not all 'group' targets, however, were quantitative.

In the case of individual pupil targets there was a wide variety of responses. Many were quite specific and systematic, with frequent references to pupil profiles, reading records, planning, assessment and informing parents. A connection between these elements often occurred, and in a number of responses heads described the involvement of pupils themselves in the process:

> A reading interview is completed each term with the child which includes comments from the teacher, the parents and also from the child on how they think they have progressed. From this interview a target is set which has to be met before the next interview.

> Targets are set on pupil profiles which parents read on open evenings.

> [A Book Week during which] children are encouraged to read at home for 20 minutes each evening – this is the expectation throughout the year too in the context of reading homework. It is formalised during Book Week – parents fill in a form to state that this target has been achieved and children receive a merit award for reading.

> Reading Assessment Record has targets for each individual child.

> At the beginning of each term children negotiate curriculum and social targets with their teachers. These are written down and signed by both.

> Some children, especially in Years 5 and 6, set their own targets in consultation with the teacher in the form of a reading contract.

There were many schools which stated their individual targets in terms of pupil scores on either standardised tests or national tests at the ages of 7 and 11. Some referred to specific criteria to be mastered, but most involved comparisons with national norms and standardised tests. Criterion-referenced targets included: spelling various word lists by certain stages; knowing key words; phonic knowledge; 'Reading aloud to be clear and expressive, with awareness of audience'; time-scales for progressing through colour-coded books, finishing the 'look and say' stage, and completing the reading scheme. Some norm-referenced targets were highly specific and applied to all pupils, like the junior school which stated: 'All pupils to achieve a reading age of 9.6 and above' and the infant school aiming at '80% of pupils reading at national curriculum level 2 or above'. Others in the same vein included 'That every child has a reading age within 12 months of its chronological age', and the more ambitious 'All children aim to have a reading age above their chronological age'.

Standardised tests were used to give the basis for setting targets, for example:

> We are now starting to assess pupils annually using a standardised reading test. We will then use this information to set targets for year groups and individuals.

> Each year group has specific benchmarks which each child is expected to achieve. We record percentages for 'above target', 'on target', 'below target' on a regular basis. We evaluate results and aim for at least 80% achieving our targets. The 20% below will have individual targets set by the special needs co-ordinator and language co-ordinator. The results of our benchmarks are presented to the Governing body at the end of the academic year.

Amongst those who set the kind of targets that required an improvement in scores on a year-by-year basis, some expressed caution about such comparisons:

> [We express our targets] in terms of improvement against previous best relative to SAT results (but how do we know we compare like with like?).

> We set targets for the first time this year directly related to SATs in order to raise the percentage of children gaining level 2 or above, with the caution that this must be directly related to progress for individuals.

In some cases the notion of 'target' was much more diffuse, seeming to be little more than a synonym for 'trying to make headway', with no reference to time-scale, plans for how the aim was to be achieved, or ways of identifying when the target was reached:

> Generally to progress through the reading scheme at a rate appropriate to individual ability.

> An overall approach in order that pupils can read and also enjoy books of all types.

> For all pupils to enjoy reading, to make use of all resources and be able to read for meaning in all their work.

Aim to have everyone enjoying and willing to read as soon as possible.

Answers to the two questions about target setting for the whole school and individuals reveal that, although there is, on the surface, a great deal of positive response, there is also a considerable amount of caution. Moreover, there is no real consensus about what is entailed and some interpretations seem to stretch the concept beyond its limits.

Constraints

Teachers were asked to describe the major and minor difficulties that they faced in the teaching of reading. Table 3.9 shows the ten most commonly stated major constraints. The most frequently mentioned were the time taken to cover the National Curriculum, class size, funding, and lack of classroom or parental support. Measures to cope with the issues of class size, curriculum overcrowding and insufficient time for teaching literacy were subsequently taken by the Labour government in 1998.

Table 3.9 Ten most common major constraints in teaching reading (1,264 schools)

Type of constraint	Frequency of mention (%)
Covering other National Curriculum subjects	68
Too large a class	57
Inadequate funding	50
Lack of auxiliary staff	36
Lack of parental support at home	29
Media attitudes	28
Lack of space	21
School starting age	9
Teacher ability and knowledge	7
Pupil misbehaviour	6

Respondents who believed standards could be raised, but only with difficulty, described some of the constraints, especially about time (the overloaded curriculum) and money:

Class sizes are creeping up, especially at Key Stage 1, which means a smaller amount of individual time for each child. The budget for the next financial year looks very bleak and we will probably have to lose our 0.5 part time teacher.

Large classes and too broad a curriculum limits the time for this.

It is difficult to know what more can be done. Resource and staffing considerations become more of a problem as the budget becomes more difficult.

We know what we would like to do. We know how to do it. We just want the human and physical resources to bring it about!

The Reading Recovery type resource would be beneficial and, I feel, cost effective, but without resources it is a vain hope.

Our budget has been drastically reduced, making huge reductions in books/equipment/staffing unavoidable. Our school is situated in an area of high socio-economic disadvantage (88% free school meals). Many parents are not functionally literate and find it diffi-cult to support their child's learning. Many pupils have little access to books/reading materials at home. We have approximately one third of pupils on the SEN register, but we have very little addi-tional staffing/support. The pressures of SATs (and published results) is having an adverse effect on staff morale – comparisons with more advantaged schools cause even more damage.

Large classes; Year 3 pupils arrive unable to read; bilingual pupils; some parents not literate in their own language; family pressures for survival, education not given a high priority; Muslim children, 1–2 hours' attendance at Mosque each evening; transitory element in school population; society does not value reading; adults do not read; national curriculum pressures – coverage is still a problem.

A number of respondents recognised that some of the difficulty in improving standards lay with themselves and their colleagues. Some were critical of experienced teachers' knowledge of how to teach reading, or that of newly trained teachers:

Poor planning. Staff feel they have had training, that their teaching is effective ... so they need cushioning: classroom organisation is poor; behaviour of children is poor; reliance on photocopied sheets; no diagnostic records; poor levels of understanding of staff; low expectations of staff about the children as most children are ESL; poor speaking and listening opportunities; large class sizes; parents cannot speak/read English.

Many (most) of my infant teachers do not have a clue about how to 'teach' reading – they seem to think hearing children read occasion-ally is teaching them.

Initial teacher training appears to be woefully inadequate. For example, every teacher in New Zealand (I understand) uses running records and diagnostic assessment in a highly skilled and routine way, whereas almost all British teachers are very wary of them and have difficulty in using the insights gained to effect.

Other problems mentioned included disruptive pupils, as well as references to the wider community, such as the perceived evils of television and computer games, motivating children to read, the decline of reading in society, lack of support from parents, and even overdemanding parents:

> Before teachers can do anything the Government needs to take steps to support discipline in school. Teachers should not be denied the right to teach by disruptive pupils.

> Television is killing reading.

> The TV video of the book often replaces the actual reading at home and parents think to know the story is actually the same as reading the book.

> Reading is not perceived as being so important – influence of TV and multimedia information technology. ... Reading for enjoyment by outside community much less valued and practised.

> Parents are becoming neurotic about reading. They are frantic if their child doesn't get another 'reading scheme' book almost every day. We have high reading standards, but I believe the media are feeding parents' anxieties.

Some heads were dismissive of the effects of constant change and whim, making a plea for consistency. Certain practices, they felt, should be explored, improved and then persisted with, rather than discarded for the next fashion:

> For too long there have been too many 'in-things' for teaching reading: ITA, Look and Say only, Real Books, free choice. ... It's time to use all skills and take the best from the past and present to keep consistent.

> When I taught in New Zealand, their Education Department policy was to take one initiative and give training to every teacher in a quality fashion. Over here we just start on one approach, e.g.

Reading Recovery, and when it gets going we abandon it and start Reading Centres or such.

The national questionnaire used in Study 1 has yielded a great deal of valuable information about what was said by senior practitioners to be happening in local authorities and schools. It filled out a useful and comprehensive background for our research into the detail of the practices we went on to observe in local authorities and individual schools and classrooms in Study 2 and Study 3. It is the role of local authorities in general and the city of Birmingham in particular, that we shall now address.

4

THE IMPACT OF THE LOCAL
EDUCATION AUTHORITY

Despite changes since the 1988 Education Act, when more money and
responsibilities were devolved from LEAs to schools, there was still a
requirement that LEAs should be concerned about the quality of education
in their schools. The relationship was no longer meant to be the proprietorial one that had existed before the 1988 Act, with the LEA clearly 'in
charge', but there was still a role for LEAs. We wanted to know what part
local authorities, in their modified form, might be playing in the improvement of literacy, so Study 2 of the research was devoted to a detailed scrutiny
of four LEAs in particular. This was intended to yield some understanding of
their ethos and their plans, and to investigate whether and to what extent
they appeared to be making an impact on what happened in schools.

Local authorities after 1988

In the years that followed the 1988 Education Act, LEAs went through a
period of change, as many of their traditional functions were taken away,
modified, or threatened. Local Management of Schools (LMS) meant that
funds previously allocated by the LEA were now in the hands of head
teachers and school governors, and functions previously carried out by the
LEA, regardless of whether schools had appreciated them or not, had to be
attractively packaged and sold. Relatively few primary schools had chosen to
become grant maintained, but the possibility remained that they might do
so, thereby diminishing further the LEA's funds and influence. Fewer advisory staff were employed, and advisory *teachers* were becoming an endangered
or extinct species in many areas. Alongside the reduction in the number of
advisers employed, there had been changes in their responsibilities, as the
emphasis shifted from 'advising' to 'inspecting', and many advisers had
trained as Ofsted inspectors. The original reason for this had been to enable
them to advise schools on how to prepare for inspection, but some advisers
also carried out Ofsted inspections in other parts of the country, so time
spent inspecting schools elsewhere could not be spent advising teachers in
their own authority.

Other more fundamental changes to the organisation of the LEA had come from the greater separation of advisory and support services, with the latter becoming semi-autonomous bodies, which had to survive on the income they could generate from selling their services to schools. LEAs were in the position of having some of their powers delegated to schools and governing bodies, while central government had tightened its hold on local government budgets. Our period of research coincided, however, with what Barber (1996) has identified as a 'positive revival of morale and activity' for LEAs. In 1994, as it became clear that in many local authorities there would be relatively few schools opting for grant-maintained status, LEAs began to find a new role which Barber described as:

> in many ways ... more creative and constructive than the old management and administration functions ... [they had] ... been forced to surrender.
>
> (Barber 1996: 19)

Study of previous research suggested limitations on what external bodies like education authorities might achieve. Wang *et al*. (1993), in their large-scale review of effectiveness research mentioned in Chapter 2, claimed that 'distal' variables, such as school policy and organisation, school demographics, and state and district policies, exerted less influence on children's learning than did 'proximal' variables – classroom management, student characteristics, home environment and student and teacher interaction.

Despite this, on the surface, gloomy prognosis, LEAs have to believe that policy can help change classroom practice for the better, and studies of successful initiatives from education authorities do exist. After studying the Halton Project in Ontario, Stoll and Fink (1993) had concluded that providing high-quality staff development and support was important, while the use of a 'top-down, bottom-up' approach by the Halton education authority secured the commitment from teachers which was essential to its success.

The study of four LEAs

In Study 2 of the Leverhulme Primary Improvement Project we wanted to discover what LEAs planned in the way of literacy and school improvement policies, and whether LEA policy was perceived, by heads and teachers, to involve and support them in their efforts to address their concerns. We conducted intensive case studies of four different local authorities, drawing data from the following sources:

1   interviews with LEA personnel from our four target LEAs from the Midlands, South East and South West England;

2　documentation provided by those LEAs;

3　interviews with forty-seven head teachers, twenty-five language co-ordinators and thirty-five class teachers from fifty-one schools in those LEAs;

4　replies to our national questionnaire survey in Study 1 from 1,395 schools in all 109 LEAs in England.

We had guaranteed anonymity to schools, teachers and pupils participating in our project and therefore refer to them using pseudonyms. It seemed only fair to extend this to LEAs as well and call them A, B, C and D. Authority A serves a large urban population with significant rural parts in its area. It would be disingenuous to pretend that Authority B, a large city in the Midlands, involved in a well-publicised 'Year of Reading', carrying out various school improvement policies under a nationally known Chief Education Officer (CEO), is anywhere other than Birmingham. Birmingham LEA was involved from the beginning of the project and this chapter contains, therefore, a much fuller account of Birmingham's attempts to improve literacy standards than of those made by our other LEAs. Authority C serves a number of towns, some quite large, and numerous rural village schools in between them. Authority D is predominantly in a rural area, though it does have several market towns and one or two larger centres of population.

The greater amount of space devoted to Birmingham in this chapter is not intended to suggest that the other LEAs were stinting in the assistance they gave us. It is simply that we began with Birmingham, as its efforts to improve literacy were well developed. Our knowledge of other LEA plans is, therefore, less detailed. The four LEAs in our sample, though situated in central and southern parts of England, were selected to cover rural areas, commuter villages, medium and large towns, with areas of deprivation in inner city and peripheral estates. They served a diverse population and included Afro-Caribbean and Asian ethnic groups.

It was not our aim to undertake a detailed *comparative* study of LEAs' different ways of working, as the services provided for schools by the four different LEAs were not strictly comparable. For a start, they were organised in different ways, with different terms and titles for their departments and personnel. Because of this diversity, although concentrating on the policies, practice and perceived impact of local authorities, we conducted individually focused interviews, tailoring our questions to advisory and support services' personnel to their particular circumstances. The responses we received from LEA officers, therefore, are not suitable for quantitative presentation, but provide, instead, a background picture against which to set our study of literacy in schools.

We interviewed staff from advisory and support services, including some of those responsible for curriculum development, schools' library services, pre-school education, pupil support, and special needs advice. Access was also obtained to internal reports, statistical data, materials provided for schools, in-service training sessions and, in Birmingham, meetings for head teachers on raising literacy standards. In this way we assembled a picture of what LEAs provided for and demanded of their schools, of what they hoped and planned to do, and of the constraints they encountered.

The four LEAs had been affected differently by the changes of the previous decade and had responded in different ways to the pressures that were created by their changing role. In the largest authority, Birmingham, the political decision had been made to increase overall spending on education, especially in primary schools, but much of this money had gone directly into schools' rather than central LEA budgets. A and D had suffered from severe financial pressures and there had been a drastic reduction in the number of staff employed, which had brought about a frustrating contraction of services and increased workload. An adviser from A with responsibility for English said in interview:

> When I joined this Authority I was one of three advisers who had responsibility for English. ... We had a six person advisory teacher team and two language co-ordinators, so we had a very broad based group of people that we could use to support work in schools. At the end of this term the sole advisory teacher is leaving. As LEAs are shrinking ... it obviously makes the service to schools difficult.

Some of the LEA staff who remained expressed satisfaction at having survived these changes and felt they had successfully risen to a daunting challenge.

In Birmingham there were reservations about the assignment of responsibilities and about liaison between the new agencies, which seemed to be competing against each other for 'customers' for their courses. For example, Birmingham's Curriculum Support Service, which dealt with the whole curriculum and therefore included English, arranged conferences, courses and in-school in-service training, provided materials and publications to help schools improve their practice and gave pre- and post-Ofsted advice. There was a cross-departmental group on literacy, but when we asked its officers 'How would you like to develop the service?' the reply included improving contact between themselves and the LEA advisers. The English adviser described how they managed in a free market:

> We try to make sure that things are done jointly or that we are not treading on their toes, because obviously they've got to make their own living because they're delegated.

In D, however, the need to generate an income in a free market seemed less of a problem, possibly because fewer staff were employed. The sole member of the Learning Support Service kept in frequent contact with educational psychologists and English advisers.

The power of schools to determine what happened in classrooms and to select the services they required from the LEA was considered by advisers to be, at best, a mixed blessing in their drive to raise educational standards. Setting out the baseline of what she felt able to achieve in the circumstances, the adviser responsible for literacy in primary schools in A said:

> My main concern is that where schools feel there is something they
> need to look at more closely, the support and guidance are available,
> and that we are able to provide it.

An adviser from D told us that while the benefit of the LEA's reactive role was that schools actually got what they thought was relevant to them, the disadvantages were that advisers had no access to schools which did not invite them, and, if schools did not recognise their needs or failings, there was little D's Advisory Service could do. Consequently, long-term, county-wide planning was difficult, as everything had to be self-financing, and the managers of advisory and support services had to be very sure that their products would sell before committing resources to their development.

Advisers from all four LEAs ran courses, gave advice and made pre-Ofsted inspections if asked. All were aware that their services now had to be 'bought in', but their perception of how proactive this enabled them to be varied a great deal. At one end of the spectrum was the attitude that little or nothing could be done except react to demand and provide the services that schools asked for. At the other, great efforts were made to involve all schools in large-scale schemes to improve literacy across the authority. LEAs in between promoted smaller-scale initiatives working with those schools willing to get involved.

Illustrative of the *non-interventionist* stance were the comments made by a member of D's advisory staff that their LEA:

1   could not distribute a literacy policy, as schools buy the services they require, and there had been no demand for LEA policies;
2   did not ask schools to provide their national test results as there was nothing the LEA could actually do with them;
3   had no mechanisms for monitoring standards county-wide;
4   had no power to force literacy initiatives on to schools.

As a mainly rural authority, D had its own particular problems to overcome, including the demands made on its budget by high transport costs and the upkeep of many small and ageing schools, as well as the difficulty of providing accessible in-service training for their scattered and sometimes isolated teachers. A project to set up a network of schools to share practice through e-mail had not developed past the initial stages. Much to their disappointment, a package of in-service training and materials on literacy which the advisory staff had developed had been bought by only five schools.

By the beginning of 1996, however, new procedures for collaborating with schools on the subject of school effectiveness were being considered, and a report to the Education Committee signalled a change of direction, saying:

> The LEA has a strategic role which can assist schools.... In relation to its work with schools the LEA needs to:
>
> – clarify and resource its monitoring role
> – make clear statements about its expectations of schools.

Until that point the philosophy of D's policy was, as described by its CEO, that:

> We have for some years delegated the maximum amount of funding to schools and think less in terms of taking initiatives in specific areas.... Advisory Service staff spend much more time these days effectively operating to an agenda set by individual schools.

Policy and practice in Birmingham

Whereas local authority D adopted a reactive and sometimes resigned stance, Birmingham, in sharp contrast, sought to be much more proactive and interventionist, attempting to set the agenda in the raising of standards of literacy. In 1993 there had been significant changes in the leadership of Birmingham LEA. The ruling Labour group selected a new leader of the city council and a new chairman of the education committee. Tim Brighouse, who had achieved a formidable reputation as CEO of Oxfordshire and as Professor of Education at Keele University, was appointed CEO. In the same year an education commission, set up by the city council to look at the provision of education in the city, had criticised the authority for giving schools a low priority and made twenty-five recommendations for improvement.

In 1993, a full audit of reading amongst 7 to 11 year olds, carried out by the city's English advisers, had identified areas where improvement was needed. Questions had been asked about resources, progression, approaches to assessment and policy making, and, significantly, about each school's perception of the achievement of its pupils. Answers indicated that many head teachers were not happy with the level of achievement, and the recommendation was made by LEA officers to give schools more support and to help them set achievable targets for improvements in literacy.

It was decided that, as a way of focusing attention on the importance of raising standards of literacy, a 'Year of Reading' would be held throughout Birmingham, running from September 1994 to December 1995. This was planned to be more than simply a matter for schools and the Education Department. Public libraries were to be involved as well as the Schools Library Service, and pre-school, post-16 and adult education services would also have an important part to play. As the officers' report to a joint meeting of the Education and Leisure and Community Services Committees in June 1994 said, it would:

> stimulate, focus and develop work by all those involved in the learning and promotion of reading in both statutory and voluntary capacities.

It would build on the work already done with schools, which included: (1) the setting up of a quality development programme and resource base, (2) the introduction of baseline testing of children on their entry to school, (3) the provision of assessment materials, and (4) the introduction of primary and Early Years 'Guarantees'. We followed these initiatives, studying them at two levels – the plans of the LEA officers, and the impact they actually made in the schools.

Birmingham's 'Guarantees' to parents and the community were a novelty. They contained specific commitments, on behalf of the LEA and its schools, of the input, outcomes and experiences which Birmingham children were to be entitled to receive. For example, commitments were made to provide children with specific experiences, such as that 'Every 6 year old and 9 year old will take part in a public performance', or that 'Each class of 10 year olds in groups of 5 or 6 will write a story, illustrate it, turn it into a book and present it to 5 year olds.'

These were activities which many children in schools throughout the land might have been doing anyway. The purpose of putting them into the form of a 'Guarantee', and specifying *when* they would happen, was to help parents become more aware of what they could expect from their children's schools, and to try to ensure that no Birmingham child missed out.

Other parts of the Guarantee were potentially more controversial. The publishing of children's test results was viewed by many teachers as a threat. The proposal was put forward that Birmingham schools should use the criteria arising from the national tests given to 7 year olds, audit the number of children at each level, and then set targets for year-on-year percentage improvements in each school's scores. It was certainly much more interventionist than what was being done in the other LEAs we studied.

The leadership style of the CEO, Tim Brighouse, played a significant part in the largely positive reaction to these events. He had personally visited every primary school in Birmingham after his appointment in 1993, addressed numerous meetings of head teachers and teachers, and made special efforts to identify and disseminate what appeared to be successful practice in Birmingham schools. This meant that he was seen more as an advocate and supporter than a critical outsider.

The relationship between Birmingham LEA and its schools was constantly portrayed by both parties as a partnership, and this concept permeated communications from the LEA to schools. The implicit and explicit message was that schools and teachers were already doing a good job, wanted to do even better and would be helped to achieve their aim. The phrases 'sharing good practice' and 'improving on previous best' were used frequently. Heads and teachers were asked to contribute their own accounts of action they had taken which they believed had made a difference. These were gathered together and published by the Schools Advisory Service in a book called *School Improvement Butterflies*.

The philosophy appeared to be that incentives and support would be more effective than criticism and conflict, and that, as well as making demands, the LEA provided help. For example, statements of reading attainment which could be reproduced for each child and highlighted when appropriate were circulated for teachers to use, and a file on 'Sharing Good Practice in Reading', containing ideas provided by schools, was distributed to all primary schools. We saw it being used during the classroom observation phases of the research project. While teachers in some LEAs had to work individually to translate the demands of the National Curriculum into their own schemes of work, Birmingham's English advisers circulated a 'framework' document, with grids that could be filled in, to support teachers in their planning for English and save time and duplication of effort.

The Guarantees were not exclusively promises from schools to parents. There were specific responsibilities on the LEA as well as on the schools, and even the setting of targets for year-on-year improvements to national test scores for 7 year old pupils was, like most of Birmingham's initiatives, voluntary. Head teachers may have felt under moral pressure to join in, but, at a time of low morale amongst teachers nationally, many were prepared to take on the assignment, and that seemed significant.

One example of the diplomatic way in which initiatives were launched occurred in a series of meetings for primary head teachers. After Birmingham's 1993 audit of reading, the heads had indicated that literacy achievement was lower than they felt it should be, and at a series of meetings with the CEO held throughout the spring term of 1995, they were again invited to say that they believed standards could be raised. A series of meetings, some of which we attended, was arranged, so that the CEO and various officers could meet all the primary head teachers from the LEA in groups of around twenty. This size prevented LEA officers from being heavily outnumbered and made it easier for them to get their message across.

At a skilfully structured meeting held for the longest serving head teachers, potentially some of the most resistant, since they had a long-standing stake in the city's education service, a short questionnaire was issued. In it the heads were asked if they thought that standards in their schools (1) had risen in the previous few years, and (2) could rise still further. Nineteen out of twenty said 'Yes' to both questions, whereupon the replies were then used to convey the message back to heads that they had already taken successful steps to raise standards, and clearly believed that they could do even better.

The LEA, they were told, would draw on their own successful experience to help them and others make further improvements. The focus was thus neatly shifted away from the question of *whether* standards could be raised, and targets set, and on to *how* this should be done. Concerns about pupil mobility, changes in catchment areas and coping with a 'bad' year were dealt with by the reassuring message that head teachers knew their own schools best and would be setting their own targets. The introduction of baseline testing, they were told, would help also, because the individual circum-stances of their schools would then be taken into account. Most heads realised that they were being led inexorably down a pre-planned path to baseline testing and setting targets for year-on-year percentage increases in their national test scores, but still they went along with the idea.

Once the vast majority of head teachers had agreed to the idea of setting targets for improving their reading standards, the LEA had to deliver its promises of support. On offer to schools were a variety of in-service training courses, resources and advice to help planning and assessment, and funding for specific literacy projects. Birmingham was taking part in the national project for Reading Recovery, and also ran a scheme for training reading volunteers to help in schools.

As part of the Year of Reading, in-service training on an Open University reading course was offered for two teachers from each school wishing to participate, with the costs being shared between the LEA and the school. It was decided to require the participation of *two* teachers, because of the belief that one teacher often returns from a course fired with enthusiasm which may subsequently dissipate under pressure of daily classroom life, or possible cynicism or lack of interest from the rest of the staff. It was originally hoped, by LEA officers, that teachers from all Birmingham schools would undertake the training, but in the event, take-up was lower than anticipated, owing, officers believed, to the cost.

Schools could also bid for grants of £250 for specific literacy projects, and two of our case study schools had received these – one making a video for parents about reading with their children, and the other focusing on the subject of bilingual stories. Twenty-eight schools which received grants in 1994–5 gathered for a conference in November 1995 to present their results, and the city's cross-departmental group on literacy concluded that though the sum of money was small:

> The schools benefit as much (if not more) from being part of a developmental network and having access to some support.

It was decided to continue to fund such projects from central funding, even after the end of the Year of Reading, and sixteen more schemes were chosen for the year 1995–6.

Many of the Year of Reading initiatives were voluntary, but there appeared to be no shortage of takers for most services. This readiness to avail themselves of help from the LEA can be seen in schools' responses to a range of LEA services on offer, as well as the specific Year of Reading initiatives. The great majority of Birmingham's schools continued to subscribe to the various services annually, while others bought on an *ad hoc* basis. Attempts were made to recoup some of the cost by selling services and materials to other authorities, and there were moves in some parts of the service towards marketing themselves as a resource for the whole region.

The various initiatives rippled through the community as well as the schools. The Year of Reading received wide publicity in the local media and achieved a high profile in the city. As mentioned previously, it was not confined to statutory education services, and an important place was accorded to Early Years education. A 'Centre for the Child' was set up in the Central Library which contained areas for under-5s and early readers, as well as providing information for their parents. The LEA promised an increase in the budget for five years to expand quality nursery provision, working towards a minimum entitlement of part-time nursery education for all rising 4 year olds whose parent(s) wanted it, and as the pre-school worker co-ordinator told us:

> Reading had been a focus, right down to babies.... Since Tim Brighouse came, Early Years has been a focus. It's wonderful having someone at his level who recognises that babies are important and that little children are important.

The work planned for the Year of Reading built on work already done in the field of pre-school education and attempts to involve parents. There had been an earlier Home Learning Project with workshops linking what parents do at home with children's first experiences at school, and just before the Year of Reading there was a Community Education Project which included multicultural weeks and baby weeks. Among the targets of process or experience in the Early Years Guarantee was the promise that all children under 5 should have an opportunity to join in a variety of 'Leading to Reading' projects, and the one which developed as part of the Year of Reading was a project called Shopping to Read. This was started in one supermarket, later spreading more widely, with pre-school workers handing out cards of activities for parents and children to do before, during and after shopping. Other, similar schemes were organised at children's clinics in an attempt to make contact with parents of pre-school children and educate them in the value of the contribution they could make to their children's educational success.

Local authority initiatives and schools' responses to them

Given that schools, since the 1988 Education Act, were meant to be more autonomous, it was not always clear what an LEA could and should do to improve literacy. In practice there was a great deal of case law. Policy, to some extent, became what local authorities were actually able to do. 'Baseline testing' or 'entry assessment', the systematic attempt to make some measurement of competence when 5 year olds first enter primary school or leave nursery education, is an interesting example of this. Both Birmingham and Authority A had introduced such tests on a voluntary basis, and their different approaches demonstrate the dilemma faced by LEAs and teachers over the matter.

Birmingham's test was designed to be simple and quick to administer. By contrast, A's test was more comprehensive and, containing sections on social interaction and physical skills, did justice to more than basic mathematical and language ability. Teachers completing it would take children through a series of intellectual and physical tasks at different levels. They had to note down not only who knew the names of letters or could count, but whether they could hop (and how many times, and on one or both legs), walk up and down stairs using alternate legs, bounce balls in hoops, run weaving in and out of a row of skittles and so on. It contained questions on a child's ability to converse with adults and play with other children, and their understanding of mathematical language. It provided a detailed diagnostic assessment of each child so that teachers could plan appropriately – and it was extremely time consuming. Following the pilot, A's baseline testing procedures were later simplified.

Birmingham was not the only LEA to consider having a Year of Reading in order to highlight efforts to improve the standard of literacy in its schools. Authority C published a discussion document which, rather like Birmingham's Guarantees, set out targets of input, process and outcome for schools and the LEA. This document was the product of a working group made up of head teachers, LEA officers and advisers set up in the summer of 1994 to consider how schools, groups of schools and the LEA could 'further enhance the quality of education'. The LEA's targets included publishing booklets of good practice, revising induction programmes for head teachers and finding ways of improving support to schools before their Ofsted inspections. Suggested 'targets of outcome' were also put forward including progressing towards 85 per cent of pupils reaching Level 2 at the age of 7, and 95 per cent reaching Level 3 at the age of 11 in English, maths and science. Schools were also invited to suggest feasible targets for their own year-on-year improvements. The discussion paper suggested having a special focus each year, starting with literacy, which would be

> supported by a range of activities, including for example confer-ences, training courses, support for working parties and the publication of good practice.

Most heads interviewed in C were not aware of the Year of Reading or the activities involved with it, though one head in our sample commented:

> They have produced a document which says children should have experience of making a book and so on. The targets are not remark-able. My problem is that a product doesn't necessarily imply quality.

This comment might equally have applied to any of Birmingham's outcomes of experience, but heads showed markedly more negative attitudes towards the LEA in C than in Birmingham.

Authority A had only one adviser responsible for literacy in the primary school, and she had some responsibility for English in secondary schools as well and was involved in Oftsed inspections. There was also, however, a Reading Task Group, made up mainly of advisers, but also involving primary and secondary heads and teachers. This issued to schools advice on good practice, key research findings and suggestions of aims, objectives and children's literacy entitlement. While not issuing literacy or language poli-cies, A had a curriculum statement setting out the recommended philosophy. It had just been revised and was due to be discussed with heads and chairs of governors.

Schools in A were advised to identify literacy as the main target of their School Development Plan. They were given self-evaluation materials to help them review their literacy teaching and plan its development. This was voluntary, but about two-thirds of schools did focus on literacy as suggested. Despite cut-backs in funding and staff, A also pioneered a particular form of group reading which encourages children to work together and develop planning and higher-order reading skills. This was started in one secondary school and its feeder primaries, and later taken up by other schools. A large day conference was held which was attended by teachers from many other LEAs. A video was made and a book written, partly to spread the message and partly to defray the costs.

Differences between LEAs' philosophies and levels of provision were reflected in the responses given by head teachers both to our interview question 'What is the role of the LEA?' and to the question in our national questionnaire survey in Study 1 about awareness of LEA initiatives and involvement of the LEA. Tables 4.1 and 4.2 show the considerably greater extent to which Birmingham heads were aware of literacy initiatives, as well as the stronger involvement of the LEA in helping develop language policy, not only when compared with the other three authorities studied (Table 4.1), but also with all the other 108 English LEAs (Table 4.2). This seems to be the result not only of the efforts of Birmingham's officers and advisers, but of the much more effective communication that existed between them and schools, through regular meetings with primary head teachers, skilful use of local press and broadcasting media, and newsletters disseminating ideas.

Table 4.1 Responses of heads from four target LEAs to two questions: 'Are you aware of any initiatives organised by the LEA to do with literacy?' and 'Was the LEA involved in the development of your school's language policy?'

LEA	Aware of LEA initiative	LEA involved	Number of schools
A	54%	23%	26
Birmingham	94%	36%	151
C	87%	22%	9
D	13%	24%	25

Table 4.2 Comparisons of the responses of heads from Birmingham schools and those of heads from all other LEAs to two questions about the LEA (151 Birmingham schools and 1,244 other schools in 108 local authorities)

	Birmingham	Others
Head aware of current initiatives by LEA	94%	46%
LEA involved in developing language policy	36%	28%

All LEAs had their supporters and their critics, but the proportions were varied. Birmingham heads from our interview sample were, on the whole, much more impressed by the level of support they received and they were better able to specify what the LEA did. While four heads from Birmingham said that the LEA provided them with money (in addition to capitation), no heads from other LEAs mentioned this. There was some criticism of Birmingham for being 'too frightened of upsetting people' and 'not specifying more directly what constitutes good practice' but much more praise, for the courses, advisers, the CEO, and the general level of support and encouragement provided. Comments made in answer to our question on the role of the Birmingham LEA included: 'very supportive' (from several heads); 'It's about trying to improve on previous best and we've adopted the principles'; 'We've had some very useful hand-outs from the English adviser.'

> Our adviser is very keen and he's in frequently, and of course Tim Brighouse has placed standards generally at the top of his agenda and reading is the most important one.

> Our adviser is focusing on writing and we find his comments very helpful.

and:

> We've got this wonderful new CEO who's given us a really high profile.

In other local authorities there was not always as much enthusiastic support. The general feeling in Authority A was much more negative. Heads reported that, in their view, the LEA's role was 'diminishing', 'decreasing' and consisted of 'not a lot actually'. One stated:

> There's a feeling that it's the lucky few that get involved. It's not seen as an entitlement for all schools.

Yet those involved in the group reading project – the 'lucky few' perhaps – were very enthusiastic, both about the initiative and about the support they received. Others spoke of not knowing what they could afford, of advisers leaving and not being replaced and 'a growing sense of isolation … it seems very fragmented and little of it'. This feeling was echoed in Authority C. One head there described the LEA's input as 'Very little now, I would have to say.' Another thought that C was now 'actually taking a lead on approaches to literacy … but until now it's all been decidedly *ad hoc*'.

Most heads in the sample we interviewed had attended LEA courses and received visits from the advisory team. One head teacher from Authority D thought things were improving, but the majority in that LEA disagreed, describing the LEA's role as 'diminishing', and 'not much'. Comments made included: 'We haven't been too impressed', 'I can't think of anything specifically', 'They seem to be driven by the latest whim', while one head said curriculum advice was available 'for what it's worth'. However, there was praise, in D, for the pre-Ofsted inspection service and for help from the adviser on evaluating and developing the school library. There was particular praise from D's head teachers for the Schools Library Service which made up topic packs, gave advice and arranged a buying scheme as well as the more common lending service. It was described as 'wonderful' and 'brilliant' with one head saying: 'It is one of the few services to schools I wouldn't do without', while another was very complimentary about the choice of books available.

The written replies from our national questionnaire survey in Study 1 showed that our interview sample was not atypical in its mixed views of the service it received from its own LEA. Some heads clearly appreciate what is on offer:

> Reading Recovery – brilliant! Funding stopping. Reading Enrichment – possibly even more brilliant. Staff have been inspired and it's having a real effect on philosophy, understanding of practice.
>
> (Birmingham head)

We had marginally more comments, however, from the unimpressed, who ranged from the ironically uninformed:

> I did *hear* that a common test was being *considered*. We are in the country and don't always get involved with town initiatives.

through the cynical:

> You must be joking! This LEA is involved in radical reorganisation.

and:

> They make no firm recommendations or decisions – they seldom do!

to the more aggressive:

> I haven't got time to bother with them or any superficial temporary high profile projects to get our picture in the paper or keep some LEA office employee in a job. WE GET ON WITH TEACHING THE CHILDREN TO READ, YEAR IN AND YEAR OUT.

It would be easy, but mistaken, to assume that the response from heads was a simple reflection of the quality of their respective LEAs. The picture is more complicated than that. Even within our sample of interviewees, some head teachers believed they received a better service and more help than they had done previously, while others, from the same LEA, thought it was getting worse. These varying perceptions were clearly affected by the nature and level of their involvement with the advisory and support services, by the quality of the services they were currently receiving, and by their personal disposition. Organisational changes within the LEAs appear to have affected the provision of services in different ways, spreading help more thinly, but more widely, or concentrating help on those schools which sign up to what is on offer, or specifically ask for help. A manager from Authority C's Schools Library Service explained the way the new arrangements had affected it and the schools which subscribed to its services:

> I think the way we deliver the service has changed. ... Whereas previously we served schools very much on demand, now we have written down what they can have. And for some schools, that's less than they had in the past. ... We'd go into schools and work for a week sometimes, reorganising their library. ... The demand wasn't out of control so we could do that. But if you are saying: 'The money is delegated and these are the services we offer', then you have to offer it equitably to everybody.

Thus one effect of radical reorganisation within LEAs, and other changes, was that with some services, like the library service, schools did have a clearer idea of their entitlement. What was different, however, was that the limits of that entitlement were tightly drawn. If they subscribed to a particular service they would get exactly what they paid for, no more and no less. This might consist of an agreed number of days when they would receive advice, or training. Since they were now dealing with a business unit, if they wanted more they had to pay for it. In the past head teachers who were particularly enthusiastic, determined, knowledgeable, or were new to their post had been able to secure as much help as they wanted, but those days were now over.

Conversely, in other areas, like those the LEA had taken a policy decision to stimulate, the provision of services to schools seemed to be moving in the other direction, with what the head from Authority A called 'the lucky few' getting involved in local initiatives, and the level of service to the rest of schools declining. Advisers were not always aware of this as they were often busy raising income, while many schools that made few demands or chose not to become involved with LEA initiatives got little attention.

For the schools that are involved in an LEA-favoured initiative, 'help' from the LEA can be a two-way process, with the head and teachers contributing to the initiatives, sitting on committees, doing action research in their schools, reporting back and often helping to disseminate good practice, rather than just becoming recipients of wisdom. Teachers at those schools may thus benefit in terms of career and professional development, but such participation depends on the head and staff of the school already possessing confidence in their ability to contribute.

A case of 'self-help' in a new town

Another development in the relationship between the LEA and its schools is the sort of self-help project we saw in a new town in Authority A. Built in the 1960s, it houses some 33,000 people, mainly families with school-age children, in a mix of low-cost private and local authority housing. It is an homogeneous area, both in the age and income of its residents, and, although hit by unemployment, the majority of residents still had incomes just above benefit level. As the level of deprivation influences the funding schools receive, several heads and teachers in the town felt the schools were losing out, with parents neither poor enough to attract additional funding nor rich enough not to need it.

Concerned about the levels of literacy in their schools, the schools decided to co-operate in a project to raise standards. They planned to liaise with each other to develop and improve literacy teaching in school, and to work with parents and the community. As a group they then approached A's advisers for help in starting off their project. The advisers began by carrying out a survey of all aspects of the schools' language teaching. They interviewed staff, parents and children and did some classroom observation. They assessed the provision and use of resources and provided money for an NFER reading test, which showed, as did the national tests, that the attainment of most children was average or below. After this initial input, however, the schools developed their literacy project together. They joined together for their in-service training and heads and language co-ordinators continued to meet to discuss how to address problems exposed by the survey. They compared and discussed language policies and came up with policies which were similar to, though not the same as, the LEA's.

Joint projects were undertaken to benefit all the parents rather than just those in any one catchment area. Courses were set up for parents in several schools targeting those parents most in need of help and using an external grant for adults who had problems with literacy. The course varied slightly from school to school, but sixty-five families were involved initially, with a number of parents progressing to other further education courses. A joint booklet on helping children to become readers was written for parents, explaining the development from pre-school children through to GCSE.

Another joint project was the distribution of a list of 'good' books. However, there was no bookshop in the town at the time, and although the supermarket sold some books, many of these were not considered to be of particularly good quality. Therefore the schools approached the supermarket, discussed children's books, and listed some quality modern children's literature. The result was that the supermarket gave some money, the schools provided £100 each, the library gave advice and the leaflet 'Psssst! Want a good book?' was published and handed out at the check-outs. The local management of the supermarket planned to show the leaflet to the head office of their chain, with a view to distributing it, or something similar, more widely.

The heads found the liaison extremely useful, not only because they were able to share expertise, but also because it helped to present a common front to parents. The involvement of the secondary school was felt to be of great value, and in interview the heads expressed only one reservation about the project. They had undertaken it because they did not feel they were getting the level of support from the LEA that they needed to tackle their problems. Having completed it, in their view successfully, they feared that they might have proved that they did not really need any help in the first place! Although the project schools were able, by working together, to compensate for the lack of concentrated, sustained LEA help, it would be wrong to conclude from this that LEAs have no role to play. Authority A had provided a considerable amount of support early on to schools. This had enabled them to identify their needs and begin to address them by co-operating with others in a similar position. Not all schools would have the cash and the expertise to be able to do this on their own.

Schools' perceptions of 'good' LEA practice

The overwhelming message received from heads and teachers in our interview and national questionnaire samples was that what they appreciate from the LEA (or would if they could get it) are specialist advice on what is perceived to be 'good' practice, stimulating courses, funding, and experts to turn to for practical help with specific problems. Some would like a more definite lead from the LEA, either to save time, or because they believe that LEA advisers have valuable knowledge and experience and should pass it on. They are disparaging about followers of fashion, and dislike inconsistency, lack of continuity or direction, or anything they see as 'harassment'.

Our research in Birmingham suggests that, although there will always be some grumbling, many teachers respond well to the challenge to make their practice more effective, if it is done in a spirit of partnership with the necessary support provided. We found that Birmingham's efforts to give school improvement and raising literacy standards a high profile and to make its teachers aware of the services it provides, appear to have made a considerable impact on policy and practice in schools. Many more Birmingham schools were aware of what the LEA was trying to do than was the case generally. They were far more likely to give non-teaching time and cash rewards to teachers who take on the post of language co-ordinator. Even before these became national policy, Birmingham schools were more likely to have undertaken baseline testing and set targets for improvement.

Table 4.3 shows some of the most notable differences which emerged from the national questionnaire in Study 1 between Birmingham and 108 other LEAs in certain policies and practices relating to attempts to raise literacy standards. All the differences were significant at beyond the 0.001 level of probability when chi-square tests were carried out. In other words, there was less than a one in a thousand probability that the differences could have occurred purely by chance. Head teachers in Birmingham were not only more likely to know about LEA literacy policies, as shown earlier, but also more likely to do something about implementing them.

Table 4.3 Comparison of responses of heads from Birmingham schools and those of heads from all other LEAs to various questions relating to the LEA, showing most notable differences (151 Birmingham schools and 1,244 other schools)

	Birmingham	Others (108 LEAs)
Baseline assessment carried out	95%	75%
Head aware of current initiatives by LEA	94%	46%
Language co-ordinator has an allowance	94%	46%
Language co-ordinator has non-contact time	86%	49%
Current reading initiatives in school	83%	62%
Use of target setting for whole school	66%	24%

What we are *not* able to say, of course, is whether or not this greater awareness, or whether the higher degree of implementation of policies like target setting and baseline testing, has actually led to higher achievement in reading. It is simply not possible to do the kind of controlled experiment that might give some credence to that sort of conclusion. Birmingham's national test scores for English and reading in primary schools did indeed improve at a rate beyond the national norm, not only in the year we were studying its schools, but in the following year, though the city began from a low base, and it is easier to improve faster from a low than from a high starting position. In 1998, however, there was a very favourable inspection report from Oftsed, albeit with a number of reservations, which concluded that Birmingham was, in general, the best of the local authorities inspected up to that time, and that its test scores had been improving. Nonetheless, it is still not possible to say whether differences in practice like those highlighted in Table 4.3 brought this about directly.

The personal contribution of a CEO, like Tim Brighouse, who visited schools, thought up ideas, celebrated success, and publicised what the LEA was trying to do, can clearly be significant in terms of inspiring the trust and co-operation of heads and teachers. So too can a well-staffed, reasonably financed, committed LEA with advisers who are able to be both reactive and proactive. One of Birmingham's English advisers, when asked if the LEA distributed a written literacy policy to its schools, had much more faith in action than written words:

The curriculum statement is being rewritten. I'd be very surprised if many schools even knew it existed or opened it. I would say that the written policies probably have minimal effect on schools. I would doubt very much whether the written policies are much referred to when schools write their own policies or renew them. But I think, like any LEA, Birmingham has an unwritten policy in terms of the sort of courses that are put on, the messages that are given to schools, the things they are asked to do. For instance, the targets in the Primary Guarantee, the kind of discussions that go on, the reading statement banks. So I think the LEA does have a policy which influences schools, but I don't think it's the written one, I think it's the discussion and the messages that go through other routes.

On the other hand the direct involvement of parents in the classroom was somewhat lower in Birmingham schools – around 60 per cent of schools compared with the national figure of nearly 70 per cent. One or two heads said that there was little point in involving parents, as many were not even literate in their mother tongue. Yet there were other schools in the city with similar intakes which did make efforts to engage parents directly in the classroom helping with reading, so this explanation is not entirely convincing. This issue will be discussed again in Chapter 7.

Nonetheless, Birmingham is an interesting model of an LEA which appears to have more influence on its schools than do many others. The six major elements of Birmingham's greater success appear to be:

1 A reciprocal model, which embraced the ideas and enthusiasm of senior officers, especially of the CEO, as well as systematic dissemination of the ideas and enthusiasm of teachers and heads.
2 Winning schools' support, rather than appearing to impose measures from above.
3 Effective communication though meetings with heads and skilful use of local media.
4 Increasing the level of resources and support available.
5 Monitoring and feeding back results to schools, including them in the collection of data.
6 Involving all schools, rather than a lucky few.

Initiatives that were applauded in Birmingham were sometimes dismissed out of hand, or not even known about elsewhere. This is partly because of poor communication, or of a belief that ideas were being imposed from above. In Birmingham, because there was both 'top-down' and 'bottom-up' innovation, there seemed to be more a co-equal, circular or reciprocal kind of relationship in operation, so the customary hierarchy of 'top' and 'bottom' was minimised. Much of what happened in Birmingham could be replicated in other local authorities, though the inevitable uniqueness of charismatic individuals like the CEO is not so susceptible to cloning. There are, however, many other successful ways of offering leadership, support and inspiration.

5

THE ORGANISATION OF LITERACY IN SCHOOLS AND CLASSROOMS

In the preceding chapters we have concentrated on the national and regional perspective as elicited in Study 1 and Study 2 of the Leverhulme Primary Improvement Project, the national questionnaires and the scrutiny of local authorities. In order to investigate in more detail the processes for improving literacy inside individual schools and classrooms, we undertook Study 3, which consisted of a set of thirty-five case studies of individual teachers. These classrooms were selected from fifty-one schools we had visited during the pilot phase of the research.

Study 3 began with interviews with heads and language co-ordinators in the original fifty-one schools. These schools had been selected partly at random, by contacting schools of different sizes and locations from a list of schools in the four local authorities we were studying, and partly on the recommendation of local authority advisers, nominating schools they thought might be of particular interest in the teaching of literacy. It was also, as is usually the case with intensive case studies, a sample of schools willing to participate.

There were infant, first, junior, middle and primary schools from rural, suburban, and affluent and deprived urban environments in the sample, with sizes ranging from forty to 798 pupils. We began by interviewing forty-seven head teachers and twenty-five language co-ordinators in these schools, a total of seventy-two people in all. Three of the head teachers interviewed also acted as language co-ordinator in their school. This initial phase was then followed by studies of thirty-five class teachers, selected by the head teachers of eighteen of the schools. These were schools that seemed, from interviews and visits, to represent a mixture of types and locations, and be likely to offer interesting insights into the development of children's literacy. Some of the schools were regarded as 'good' schools by their local authority, though not all were in that category.

The thirty-five teachers, two from each of seventeen schools and one from the eighteenth, were mainly volunteers, though some had been selected by their head teacher, usually because they were esteemed as skilful practitioners in the field of literacy. We tried to obtain a spread of classes across the primary age range, from Reception up to Year 6. In the event we succeeded in observing the full range, though there was no Year 4 class in the sample. Almost all the teachers were well regarded by their head teacher, though one head 'volunteered' a teacher hoping to motivate her to improve her teaching of reading. We observed their teaching on several occasions throughout a whole school year, from early September to late July. Full interviews were conducted with them before, during and at the end of the school year.

The principal focus of the first set of seventy-two interviews with heads and language co-ordinators was on their role in developing the literacy curriculum and ensuring it was taught satisfactorily throughout the school. We wanted to gain an overview of philosophy and practice in these primary schools, and to chart the range and variety to be found. The beliefs, approaches and teaching methods employed were to be studied, so questions were asked in the interviews about how literacy teaching was funded, resourced, organised and assessed, and who was responsible for developing staff expertise and ensuring policies were in place. The content and nature of these policies, how they were developed and implemented, the involvement of parents in their children's learning, were also analysed.

Eighteen schools were subsequently used for intensive classroom observation and in these case study schools we had opportunities for further discussions with the head teachers and post-holders, and sometimes with special needs teachers or co-ordinators as well. Ten of the language co-ordinators originally interviewed were also amongst our sample of class teachers, so this offered further opportunities for discussion of their stated policy and observed practice. During interviews with class teachers we asked their views of the literacy policy and the opportunities they had to discuss literacy teaching with their colleagues. We also had access to documentation provided by the schools and, in a number of cases, the school's report from Ofsted.

Heads and language co-ordinators presented, on the whole, a united front. In some instances both were interviewed together, so real or apparent unity might be expected. In most cases, however, where they were interviewed separately, there appeared little disagreement about matters of policy and practice. On only one occasion were adverse comments made about the ability of the other person.

This chapter focuses principally on the seventy-two head teachers' and language co-ordinators' own accounts of what they did to raise and maintain high standards of literacy. The role of head teachers in school effectiveness research has been widely recognised and was described in Chapter 2. Less well documented, perhaps, is the role played by primary 'language', 'literacy' or 'English' co-ordinators (from now on the term 'post-holder' will sometimes be used as a generic term to cover all of these roles), although their influence and the responsibilities placed on them are increasing. In our investigation of how the teaching of literacy was organised in schools, we studied both tiers of management. We gathered information on their experience and responsibilities, how they were trained, rewarded and resourced, as well as on their views about improving literacy and how they perceived their roles. In addition to this, the views of the thirty-five classroom teachers in our case studies have been included where these provide additional insight into the issues discussed.

Experience and training in the teaching of literacy

The experience of headship amongst our sample varied from four months to twenty-three years, with two acting heads in the sample. A majority had been in charge of only one school. We asked heads if they had had specific training in teaching literacy, and most replied, 'No', 'Not recently' or 'Nothing useful'. Courses they had attended varied from one-day heads' conferences or in-service days shared with neighbouring schools in their 'cluster group', to Open University Reading courses, Reading Recovery training and Masters' degrees. One head said she had been to 'about 5,000', another to 'everything that's going', while another who said 'No', stated that she kept up to date by reading. Although they had not attended courses themselves, they were generally satisfied with the feedback they had received about courses provided for their staff, with only one believing that no good courses about reading were available.

Despite heads' lack of specific literacy training their expertise was recognised and respected by the post-holders. One head had been an LEA adviser and at least two had run courses for their LEA. Several more, especially among infant heads, had been literacy post-holders previously, while in some schools head teachers or deputies still undertook the role. This happened in small rural schools where the head had to teach a class and there were only one or two other teachers to cover several curriculum responsibilities. Sometimes, however, heads took full responsibility for literacy because they did not have teaching commitments and felt they could give more time than a full-time class teacher, or because they felt it was a very important role, or because of the difficulty of finding someone else to do the job to the head's satisfaction. Those few who did combine the jobs did not find it easy, with some describing it as 'fairly impossible'.

Most schools in our sample did have a teacher with designated responsibility for language, literacy or English. Some schools actually had two members of staff with this responsibility, either having one for each key stage of the National Curriculum, or separating responsibility for reading, or for the library, from other functions. These post-holders were much more likely than heads to have had some recent training in areas related to literacy and were often enthusiastic and willing to talk about the detail of the courses, which covered a wide range of literacy topics.

89

Several had been on ten- and twenty-day courses funded by the Department for Education and Employment, two had undertaken training in Reading Recovery, and post-holders in Authority A had taken part in an initiative in group reading which involved in-service training. They felt these courses were useful to them in their capacity as class teachers and in giving them the necessary knowledge for them to carry out their job as co-ordinator. Only one person, however, mentioned attending a course directly related to her role as leader and manager of the literacy teaching in school, although most recognised the importance of their managerial and leadership duties.

The thirty-five teachers in the research were also asked whether they had received any particular training in the teaching of reading. Fourteen indicated that their only training had been during their initial teacher training. For some this was over twenty years ago. Of these fourteen teachers, three also held the position of language co-ordinator in their school. Eight teachers said they had received *no* training in the teaching of reading and several others were highly critical of their initial teacher training in this respect:

> At the college reading was so poorly taught.... We said to them
> 'You haven't taught us how to teach kids to read. We don't know
> what to do.' And they said 'You have to sort it out yourself. You
> have to find your own way' which I thought was a dreadful cop out.
> It really worried me, so I did as much research as I could on
> reading.
>
> (Year 2 teacher with four years' experience)

For the rest training since they had qualified had taken the form either of attendance at LEA courses, or in-house in-service training led by the school's language co-ordinator. In some cases, individuals talked of benefits to themselves; in others, where schools had a system for disseminating information and experiences gained on courses, attendance could often result in changes in policy throughout the school:

> What's coming out of the Reading Recovery course is altering how
> we're thinking about how we're going to teach in Reception and
> Year 1 ... and also what we're going to do is we're actually going to
> give feedback to staff. So we're going to run some staff meetings on
> the Reading Recovery, so they know where we are, what we've done,
> and what we're implementing down here.
>
> (Early Years teacher)

I've found in school in-service training useful when people, like the language co-ordinator, have been on courses and have come back with ideas that we've sat down and discussed.

(Year 5 teacher)

School-based in-service appeared to be the most valued type of training, as it seemed to participants to be most relevant to the needs of the individual school. Few teachers talked in terms of having a philosophy of teaching reading, but for one who did, it was a session in her own school which had made her reassess her thinking, not only about reading but her general approach to teaching:

I think the in-service that we did here, when we changed from a whole scheme approach to a whole book approach and a whole literacy approach, if you like, that changed my thinking. And then I started to do it, you see, so that had an effect on how I was actually teaching, because I started to try out some of these ideas and I found they worked. I found I liked this more holistic approach and children being active in the process, rather than passive. You know, not thinking it was something that's been imposed on them from above, but they're already doing it, aren't they, when they come to school?

(Reception class teacher)

Given that so much emphasis was being placed on the need to improve literacy standards, it was surprising to find that only just over a third of teachers in our sample said they had received training in the teaching of reading since their initial training, though head teachers had said they thought there were plenty of courses available.

Definitions of literacy

It was clear from the time and thought given to discussing it, planning it and organising it, that the teaching of literacy was a very high priority for the heads, post-holders and the majority of teachers we interviewed. We were interested to discover, however, not simply how highly they valued literacy, but what it was that they valued, and, therefore, what abilities and attitudes they wished the children to develop. Questioned about their policies, teaching methods and organisation, our interviewees were fluent and informative, but our question 'How would you define literacy?' produced many shocked faces, embarrassed laughs and wishes that prior notice had been given. The definition of literacy was not something that appeared to have been given much direct thought, though no one refused to answer.

Their responses could be located along a continuum with those stressing a utilitarian view of literacy in school at one end and those adopting a broader perspective of literacy in society at the other:

> To be able to read sufficiently well to access the curriculum, to be able to talk and listen and discuss sufficiently well to explore and learn the curriculum and to be able to write sufficiently well, to express one's thoughts and interrogate the curriculum through one's writing.
>
> (Head teacher)

> I suppose in a basic sense you're literate if you can read and write to the sort of level where you can function reasonably in society, but I'd like to think of literacy as being wider than that – so ... um ... an appreciation of things through literature, children becoming real readers so that they can gain access to other worlds that they can't immediately be given access to.
>
> (Language co-ordinator)

Originally we anticipated definitions might fall into two categories: those which were utilitarian or functional and those which emphasised issues of personal development or culture. In the event, some interviewees covered both aspects, and moved from a narrow definition to one which included wider aspects, such as becoming equipped with the potential for lifelong enjoyment of reading, saying, for example:

> It's not just being able to read and write, it's enjoying reading too, and knowing it's important.

> Basically giving children a love of books and feeling that they want to read and they want to find things out from early on, something that's started off young that will hopefully stay with them, feeling comfortable with books and any written things around them in everyday life.

Most took for granted the view that literacy was about reading and writing or, having spoken of the need to understand the written word, they then went on to stress something beyond that, like the importance of spoken language as well. Many class teachers' comments stressed the functional aspect of literacy, talking in terms of being able to recognise letters, words and numbers, in order to be able to communicate with others.

It is interesting that, while some head teachers displayed a clear personal vision of literacy and what it meant for their pupils, this vision was not always being transmitted to their staff. In the cases below, the definitions of literacy offered by post-holders and the class teacher seemed less enthusiastic than those of their head teachers.

> I would say [literacy is a] love of language – to inculcate a love of language ... not just loving and appreciating the spoken word but the written word ... every aspect of language.
>
> (Head of school A)

> [Literacy is] things associated with reading and writing.
>
> (Language co-ordinator in school A)

> It's more than just being literate. It's not just being able to read. It's having a real love of books and the idea that print actually carries meaning. And that that meaning can be all sorts of things. You know, imaginative worlds ... it's very, very wide. And it's a way of understanding the world and a way of trying to get an understanding of what other people are thinking.
>
> (Head of school B)

> To make sense of the written word and be able to use it.
>
> (Class teacher in school B)

The responses were examined to find out whether teachers' beliefs about literacy seemed related to their length of service. No pattern emerged. Teachers with over twenty years' service were as likely as more newly qualified teachers to define literacy only in functional terms. The difficulties encountered by interviewees in addressing what literacy meant to them suggested that some teachers may be teaching reading and writing within a philosophical vacuum.

Teachers expressing a holistic view of reading and the child, which encompassed not only functional aspects of reading and writing, but also enjoyment and the acknowledgement of literacy as a pathway to greater knowledge and understanding, were more likely than those taking a purely utilitarian view to talk about providing their pupils with access to a wider range of reading materials and more opportunities to discuss the books they had read. However, rhetoric does not always match action. There were also teachers who had offered relatively narrow utilitarian definitions of literacy, yet our observations of their teaching indicated that they were, in reality, enthusiastic teachers of reading in a broad context, offering their pupils a wide range of opportunities to discover the world of literature and to make links with their own experiences.

Responsibility for literacy

Although post-holders were more likely than heads or teachers to have attended recent courses on literacy, this rarely meant that they took the lead in decisions about literacy policy. We asked head teachers and post-holders who held the main responsibility for literacy matters, and most agreed that it was shared between them, with some stressing the involvement of all members of staff. Both heads and post-holders spoke of dialogue. One post-holder, who had considerable teaching experience, said of the head:

> He's interested in it and wants to promote it. Theoretically the responsibility is his because he runs the whole school. He's very interested in what I do and he supports what I do, but of course I have to justify it.... He keeps up to date if ever I want to talk things over, I do talk things over with him.... I wrote the language policy and the reading policy and then we went through them together and discussed them and not just in a token way but a genuine involvement.

There was, however, a difference of emphasis, with heads and post-holders from some schools recognising that the main responsibility lay with the head, while others emphasised the delegation of powers to the post-holder. For example, one head who saw his role as supporting the post-holder said:

> It's not a strength of mine, but I recognise its importance and I've appointed key staff who bring the expertise we need.

whereas another claimed that after the 'usual dialogue' she had the final veto:

> I think that's my job really. There has to be someone who's reasonably autocratic, otherwise you get nowhere.

The expertise of heads who had themselves been post-holders or advisers, or had run courses, was recognised by the post-holders in their schools:

> The head has qualifications in language and she knows an awful lot about developing language in the school. We all respect her and what she knows, so we work together, though she leads the way, but I have my input as well.

and, from another:

> We get together and discuss things ... it's constant chatting it
> through. She's very good because she's very interested in the reading
> and writing – it's her baby.

In general there was no divergence of view, however, between post-holders
and heads from the same school. Whoever had the main responsibility for
literacy policy and teaching knew it, and this was recognised by his or her
colleague.

The role of the post-holder

The role of curriculum co-ordinators was considered in the Oftsed publication *Primary Matters: A Discussion on Teaching and Learning in Primary Schools*
(Ofsted 1994) and, according to HMI, the role of the 'subject manager'
(renamed because 'co-ordinator' was seen as too limited a description) was:

> a) to develop a clear view of the nature of their subject and its
> contribution to the wider curriculum of the school;
> b) to provide advice and documentation to help teachers to teach
> the subject and interrelate its constituent elements; and
> c) to play a major part in organising the teaching and learning
> resources of the subject so statutory requirements are covered.
>
> (p. 9)

We asked our interviewees to give their own description of the role of their
post-holders and then grouped them into broadly similar categories. Many
of the responsibilities they identified correspond to or are incorporated in
those mentioned by HMI, with several additions as well. It may not be
possible to legislate for enthusiasm, or to insist on the organisation of bookshops and literacy events and meetings for parents, but it was common for
our post-holders and heads to consider that this was part of the job.

There was widespread agreement in schools about the post-holder's main
tasks, and they mirrored almost exactly the findings of the national questionnaire described in Chapter 3, namely monitoring and evaluating
teaching, providing advice, leading in-service training and helping to
formulate and disseminate the school's language policy, giving practical
help. Interviewees gave many examples of this scope, when asked to describe
their role. One respondent described the essence of numerous other replies,
reporting a mixture of organisation, the personal modelling of practice, and
the deliberate involvement of her colleagues so they would not feel alienated:

> This isn't in any particular order, and there are lots of different
> aspects to it. I think it's very important to keep yourself up to date
> and to be aware of what is good practice and try to promote good

practice within the school through different means. I think one of them is you have to be a good role model. Another is that you have to share the expertise that you've got, and to use the expertise of others. For example, in Reception we've got two very experienced teachers and when I've been doing workshops about Early Years I've involved them. I do workshops for staff – group reading for example. The first thing I did was to demonstrate it in front of teaching staff and auxiliaries as well. I demonstrated it with children from my class and much younger children as well. It's no good just telling people, you have to share ideas and you have to involve them. It's important that people feel that they've got a great deal to offer and that you're building on their skills as well. Then, I had to update the language policy and the reading policy. I think also that part of my role is to initiate new ideas and make sure language has a high profile, that it's given prestige throughout the school, that it reflects the aims of the school generally – I think that's important. It's also part of my role to know what's going on in classrooms and I do that by working along – I don't mean checking up, but I do work alongside teachers in their classrooms. And I hope that by being approachable people will come along and say 'I've got this problem. How can we sort it out?' Sometimes we'll discuss it as a group and sometimes I'll come up with answers myself, but I try to involve others if it's appropriate.

Frequently, too, the comparison was made with secondary schools where pupils are funded much more generously than they are in primary schools, where post-holders have time allocated for management duties and are not expected to teach nine or ten other areas of the curriculum.

Literacy policies

Writing or developing policies to do with literacy was regarded as one of the post-holder's most important jobs, and all but one of our interview sample schools had literacy policies or were in the process of developing or reviewing them. The exception was a small rural school with a staff of two including the head who said they could only do one or two policies a year, and literacy was scheduled for later. Many schools had replaced or were in the process of replacing their old policies with new ones, and the trend, it appeared, was towards policies with more detail both over what was to be taught, and when and how it should be done. As most policies were quite new, the process of development was still fresh in the minds of heads and post-holders, except for the one head who confessed 'I haven't read it recently, but I can remember doing so.' The newness of the policies also meant that in most schools, there had not yet been time for them to have been evaluated.

In analysing the descriptions given by heads and post-holders of how they wrote their literacy policies, we noted the many purposes they wanted their policy to serve. Some were intended to invoke reflection and action in the classroom, others to inform key groups and individuals, such as teachers, parents and governors:

- Stating underlying values.
- Highlighting important themes.
- Setting broad guidelines of content for each age group.
- Making suggestions for targets.
- Helping teachers to plan.
- Ensuring progression and continuity.
- Aiding differentiation.
- Helping the post-holder to monitor teaching and learning.
- Setting out entitlements to resources.
- Giving practical suggestions.
- Informing new staff.
- Informing governors.
- Informing parents.

There was often a clear distinction between *rational* and *empirical* methods of composing policy. A few schools adopted a rational approach. These started the process of writing by articulating their aims and philosophy first and trying to apply it later. More schools, however, operated the other way round, using an empirical approach, trying to extract policy from what they regarded as their own 'good' practice, as in this example:

> It's very much based on what's going on in the school that is good. We've had a lot of workshops along the way, and in the area where I've got less experience – Reception – I've gone and asked them and they've talked me through what they do with a small child who can't write at all. There's been an input from all staff, and when I've written the draft, having based it on my expertise and reading, I'll put it back to them for comments.

Several heads and post-holders spoke of the need for a policy for the whole school, providing structure for teachers and ensuring progression for children. Mention of the importance of giving practical guidance was also common. They wanted a useful working document that developed, not something that teachers read once and then put on a high shelf. One post-holder described how she tried to help teachers clarify their own practice:

Well, it reflects what's good and also there are a lot of guidelines in it for ideas. Not prescriptive, but ideas of things that you can actually do. It highlights the stages that children go through when they're reading. It talks about the environment in a classroom that you need to promote. It talks about teacher expectation, learning objectives. It's differentiated. It's got continuity and progression from Key Stage 1 to Key Stage 2. It also includes information sheets about phonics … and then there's quite a large section about group reading and all the different opportunities for group reading…. I've tried to break down the objectives so they're fairly clear, to help people have a clear understanding of what they're doing and why they're doing it.

It was clear that the process of planning, developing and writing the school's literacy policy or policies had been a major undertaking in many schools, requiring a great deal of effort on the part of the post-holder and other teachers. In some schools small groups of teachers worked on the policy under the guidance of the head or post-holder, while in smaller schools it was not unusual for the whole staff to work together. A few schools had input from an LEA adviser, and occasionally governors were involved as well.

It was most unusual for the post-holder to work alone, and the involvement of all teachers was mentioned as important, not only because it gave a wider base of experience on which to draw, but because the exercise was seen as being beneficial in its own right. The view that teachers would be more committed to implementing the policy they had helped to develop was also expressed, and one head mentioned her concern that new teachers who had not been part of the process might not understand or get as much out of the policy as the others. Seeing the duplication of effort involved as we visited schools, however, we often wondered whether the writing of completely independent policies by each individual school represents the best use of staff meetings, in-service days and key teachers' time.

All the work that goes into the development of literacy policies is supposed to have an ultimate purpose, of course, beyond that of merely producing a document which will impress governors and school inspectors. We wanted to know how it worked in practice and we asked post-holders and heads how they thought it fulfilled its main function – the promotion of the teaching and learning of literacy within the school. When asked specifically about how the policy promoted the learning of literacy, many emphasised the 'structure', 'coherence', and 'continuity and progression' a policy could provide, minimising confusion. One head said:

We are working towards having an agreed school policy so that children don't get faced with very different expectations as they move through the school. Children can get so many mixed messages. Now we realise that we may never change some teachers' practices, and we're still going to have some hiccups ... but we're going to be an awful lot nearer than if we haven't even tried to tackle it. We're idealistic but not unrealistic. It's a long term view and we can come back to teachers and point out if they're not doing what we've agreed.

The cohesion a whole-school policy supplied was seen to be its main strength, followed closely by the practical guidance and information on resources it gave to teachers, especially new ones. When we interviewed class teachers, we asked them for their views on the school language policy, and though a few said it was too long or that they had not read it, the majority made positive comments such as that it was 'very useful' or 'has some good ideas' and 'is based on good practice'. It did not appear, however, that most teachers regarded the written policy as the first place they would look if they wanted guidance or ideas, with informal discussions with colleagues and the post-holder being the preferred option.

Post-holders' conditions of work

The many duties carried out by the literacy post-holders contributed to making this a time-consuming job, especially as it was almost always carried out in addition to full-time responsibility for teaching a class, and sometimes responsibility for other curriculum areas as well. The national questionnaire described earlier had revealed that fewer than half the post-holders had either an allowance or non-contact time for doing the job, though the figure was nearer 90 per cent in Birmingham schools. Commenting on the need for non-contact time, HMI (Ofsted 1994) said that little or no non-contact time was necessary for the duties of the subject managers mentioned earlier – developing a clear view of the nature of their subject, providing advice to teachers and organising teaching and resources – but that:

> The monitoring of teaching and learning and assessment practices requires non-contact time for subject managers.
>
> (p. 9)

Many of the post-holders also recognised the need for more opportunities to work in other classes to monitor teaching, and this was one of the ways they spent such 'non-contact time' as they had (and the reason this phrase is placed in quotation marks). In one school the head claimed such free time existed, but the post-holder herself thought not! 'Regular' sessions varied from once a week to once a term. Some heads required teachers to bid for time which was distributed according to the school's current needs. Others scarcely bothered with the bidding and just decided which curriculum area was the current highest priority – often an area identified on the School Development Plan.

Time to do the job was an important issue for some. One post-holder had even resigned because she felt she could not cope, and no other members of staff in that school could be persuaded to take on the job. Heads were aware that their post-holders could not carry out certain functions without class release, but stated that budgetary constraints prevented them from providing as much as they believed necessary.

Budgets, resources and support

Some post-holders said they had the main responsibility for holding the English or literacy budget, but regardless of who was in charge of the purse, the raising and spending of money for literacy was a subject that concerned all interviewees. Additional funds were available for some schools from LEA or government grants, including those for Birmingham schools associated with their projects during the Year of Reading, and 'Section 11' money for children from ethnic minority groups. One head said:

> I hate the phrase 'inner-city disadvantaged children', but I know it brings me money, so I use it.

Some schools were given extra money by outside agencies – the church, charities, parents' support groups. More active ways of fund raising were essential, however, if they were to have the resources they wanted, and a great deal of ingenuity and hard work was displayed. Many had an official 'school fund' which welcomed donations, and parents were involved running various events, and paying to attend them. Teachers organised competitions, sponsored silences and spelling tests. They ran bookshops and bookclubs, which not only brought in money, but also provided good-quality literature for the children. Two schools had obtained business sponsorship and one let the school car park to a business across the road, while one post-holder did proofreading in her spare time to provide extra funds for her department.

Most of the money raised was spent on equipment, but schools also used it to fund literacy events, such as inviting poets, authors and theatre groups in to visit the school, or to take the children out on visits. One infant school gave all the children a present of a book at Christmas. Most interviewees did not make a distinction between what they bought with their capitation and 'extras' paid for by their fund raising so they spoke of the need to fund additional staff – for Reading Recovery, to help children with reading problems or just to make classes smaller. Books were an expensive and essential purchase and the one mentioned most often. They also bought games, tape recorders and listening centres, furniture for the library, computers and information technology equipment.

We also asked about non-financial forms of support that schools were able to call upon. Some schools were good at finding help – from charities, publishers, local higher education institutions or reading centres, museums, curriculum associations, such as the National Association for the Teaching of English, and the Literacy Trust, local businesses as well as parents and the LEA. As was described in Chapter 4, the relationship between schools and the LEA had changed, and heads and post-holders were aware that services which had been 'free' now had to be judged according to whether they could be afforded and gave good value. They still turned to the LEA for help for a variety of purposes – advice and courses being the ones mentioned most often – and they sought advice when particular problems arose or when they wished to initiate changes in their policy or organisation.

Schools used the Library Service to supply books on a regular basis and to advise and give practical help in improving and updating the school library. They also drew on several health-related services, such as speech therapy, the School Health Service and the educational psychology service, and sought, with varying degrees of success, help and support for children with special educational needs or emotional and behavioural difficulties. Many heads mentioned the support they received from other schools in the neighbour-hood, with post-holders meeting, sharing ideas and sometimes working together to develop policies. It was collegial in style, rather than the competitive model favoured by the Conservative government in power at the time of the interviews. As one head said:

> It's important to work together in a cluster. We don't want to compete. We want to help all the children, not just those from our own school.

Assessment, monitoring and record keeping

We asked heads, post-holders and class teachers 'How do you assess and record children's reading abilities?' It was clear from the replies of the heads and post-holders that this was an area they believed was, or should be, organised to be consistent throughout the school, and to be monitored by the head. For some, achieving this uniformity was an ongoing problem they were still trying to solve:

> We are looking at whether we do need a record sheet for reading, and we've just got a fundamental split of views as to how useful that actually is. We'll try again on that.

Others felt they had improved on previous practice:

Two years ago when I said 'Show me what records you are keeping' some were in great detail and some were very skimpy, and everybody had their own idea of what format and what information ... so we did some work on that ... and eventually it led to us having a uniform set of records.

The responses to our question touched on both what schools sought to assess and how they did it, with many interviewees saying they were concerned to assess children's reading behaviour and attitudes as well as the more easily assessed decoding skills, sight vocabulary and phonic knowledge. The lists below, in descending order of frequency, show (1) what we were told was assessed, (2) the forms of assessment used:

What schools wished to assess:

1   Reading behaviour
2   Phonic knowledge/letter recognition
3   Sight vocabulary/key words
4   Individuals with specific problems
5   Comprehension

Forms of assessment mentioned:

1   Standardised published reading tests
2   National tests and levels of achievement
3   Miscue analysis
4   Statement Banks/highlighted lists of achievements
5   Checklists of sight vocabulary/high-frequency words
6   Checklists of sounds and letters

In Birmingham most interviewees referred to the use of a 'Statement Bank', a cumulative record on which they recorded children's reading strategies and behaviour. In Authority D a similar document had been produced which a number of the teachers said they used. The Birmingham schools' Statement Banks had been developed either by the LEA's English advisory team or by the National Association for the Teaching of English, or devised by themselves.

Many heads and post-holders appeared to be striving to find some elusive paragon form of assessment. They were aware of the shortcomings of the approaches and instruments they currently used, their narrowness, inaccuracy or the length of time they took to administer. There seemed to be a fervent hope that the equivalent of the philosopher's stone, that would turn all to gold, lay just around the next corner.

The frequent use of standardised, norm-referenced reading tests was accompanied by some mistrust of their value:

> People have felt they're unhelpful. You get a reading age but there are children who score really badly and read quite well, so that doesn't help us much. But we did use them to highlight children who we thought were failing.

Yet heads and post-holders were more happy to support test scores when they indicated that the reading of individual children or groups of children had improved, revealing a pragmatic ambivalence about such tests.

There was praise for the Statement Banks:

> [They are] very useful because they've saved a lot of time for staff who were already hard pressed.

> You can record positive reading behaviour and strategies and knowledge and understanding as well.

There was also some concern that, though they were recognised to be essential, assessment and record keeping may become too bureaucratic, incompatible with lively, inspiring teaching. After listing an impressive array of structured assessments covering a variety of skills, knowledge and attitudes, one post-holder said:

> The way I'm telling it now it sounds terribly, terribly formal, but this is the assessment, you know. This is the structure that has to be in place. But the activities are exciting and stimulating and the children enjoy them.

Those in managerial positions often showed awareness of a conflict between the importance of keeping useful records and the danger that too much time would be spent on them. The results of the various forms of assessment employed were usually recorded, but other frequently mentioned types of records were, in descending order:

1 Class teacher's notes
2 List of books read
3 LEA record
4 Pupil profile/portfolio
5 Children's own records
6 Individual reading diaries, home/school diary

In most schools the clear impression was that they were operating more formal, systematic record keeping than they had done in the past. In a few schools, while recording was still taken seriously, it appeared to have passed through an earlier regime of obsessive recording through the ticking of checklists and boxes, to one where greater discrimination was in evidence. There seemed little doubt that the prospect of external inspection had also concentrated minds on the need not only to teach and assess, but to have detailed documentation in preparation for it.

In Key Stage 1 it was common for teachers to undertake phonics and key word checks. Year 2 teachers often referred to national tests taken by 7 year olds in English and mathematics. Teachers in only a third of all classes studied said that they made use of miscue analysis. While only one teacher in Birmingham and two in Authority D mentioned the use of standardised reading tests, in Authority C all schools were required by the LEA to carry out the testing of pupils in Year 3.

The way in which many teachers described their approach to the monitoring and assessment of pupils' reading appeared to emphasise children's progress at decoding, rather than understanding, as illustrated by the teachers' comments below:

> We have a running record which, every time a child reads, we write a comment in. We also have a group reading record which shows the strategies that you're developing within the group and it gives you a chance to tick off and write a comment to show which strategies they're using. We also have a record which is only done once a term to show again the strategies that they're using for their individual reading and sometimes it's a seen and sometimes it's an unseen book and again it's a tick to show the strategies they're using. We have phonic records as well.
>
> (Year 1 teacher)

> We do phonics tests and sight vocabulary tests. We all keep running records and whenever a child is heard to read everybody makes a comment, whether it's the classroom assistant or a parent or just somebody who's come in.
>
> (Year 3 teacher)

Yet only one of the teachers interviewed talked explicitly about the need to assess children's understanding:

> I'd look at all the different spheres of what I think reading is. I'd look at their reading aloud as a separate skill and I'd make notes about that. And I'd look at their ability to understand what they've read and what they're actually writing about their book or able to

talk about. And with group reading I'd listen to what they were saying about the book and how they were able to respond when I read a class book.

This was a teacher of a Year 6 class of 11 year olds; however, none of the other Key Stage 2 teachers in the sample of sixteen talked of the need to monitor children's levels of *understanding*. This may merely constitute further evidence that decoding skills are the main focus in current assessment practice, but it may also reflect an overall lack of monitoring of Key Stage 2 pupils' reading progress.

Evidence from the teachers' interviews suggests that by the later stages of Key Stage 2, it is rare for children, other than those having specific difficulties with reading, to read to or share a book with the teacher. This may be due to a lack of support within the classroom, but there also seems to be an implicit assumption that this activity is no longer very necessary. It is difficult to see how teachers are monitoring their pupils' reading without some sort of regular contact.

There is no doubt that many teachers are incorporating the teaching of 'higher-order reading skills' into their planning, as will be discussed in the next chapter, but the interview responses suggest that the choice of reading material becomes very much an individual child's own responsibility. If teachers do not monitor the reading of these older pupils, there may be an unfortunate consequence. It is possible that pupils may indeed be developing the skills of information retrieval, but emphasis on personal choice of reading material may not give them experience of the more sophisticated texts and different genres which are needed to develop further their skills of inference, prediction and analysis.

Target setting

Interviews confirmed what the national questionnaire had shown above in Chapter 3: that the strategy known commonly as 'target setting' appears to be diffuse and ill defined. Questions about setting targets, first for pupils and then for the school, produced the widest range of different answers of all. 'Target setting' had many different meanings to different teachers. In twenty-three of the thirty-five schools studied, targets were set for children who were struggling with their reading, as part of their Action Plan or IEP (Individual Education Plan). Often parents were involved at this stage. As one post-holder said:

We bring parents in and say 'this is what we'd like to work on and we'd like your co-operation – it's a sort of contract – to work on that'.... It might be behavioural problems. It might be reading

105

problems. It might be concentration, but they're all relevant to reading and writing.

Views differed on the sort of targets that should be set for children with special educational needs in reading. The majority favoured breaking down what needed to be learned into small steps, which was particularly appropriate for learning letters, sounds or key words. The target was *when* it should be learned. Others set targets of particular skills they wanted to focus on, such as using contextual clues or initial sounds for unknown words, or of experiences they wanted the children to have, such as reading regularly with another child.

In a few schools efforts were made to involve the children in the setting of their own targets, and this was linked with the desire for children to have a clearer idea of the progress they were making and of the steps they needed to take next. In some cases this was done through writers' workshops or reading conferences at which the child's progress and current achievements were reviewed and new targets set.

Any distinction between targets for individual children and targets for the whole school cannot be absolute. The target to have all children in the school reading at or above the level of their chronological age, for example, can be seen as a target for the whole school or as a target for each individual child. Despite this blurring at the edges of definition and classification, however, there was a wide variety of practice in the setting of targets for individual children, and an even greater difference in setting targets for the whole school.

Head and post-holders spoke of 'whole-school targets', such as completing the school library, encouraging everyone to read more, or for staff to reach a consensus on common standards and record keeping. Others spoke of targeting a particular year group, or a different area of the curriculum each year. It could be argued that a question which could produce such a wide range of responses should have been framed differently, but we wanted to know how far the discourse and culture of 'target setting' had penetrated, and what, if anything, its effect had been.

Even in Birmingham, where heads had been asked to set targets to increase the percentage of children at the end of Year 2 who scored Level 2 and 3 in the national tests for reading, and decrease the percentage who scored W (working towards Level 1) or Level 1 itself, the number of diffuse answers was still high. When asked about setting targets for the whole school, the heads or post-holders in less than half of our Birmingham schools responded in terms of the form of target setting being promoted by the LEA.

Some heads and post-holders in Birmingham commented on the drive by their LEA to make year-on-year improvements in the national test scores at the end of Key Stage 1. One head said:

> I don't believe in the City's way of target setting where you say how many level 1 children you've got, how many level 2, and then say you're going to increase. I would much rather they had said 'Let's have a really good go at our 5 year olds'.... Well, you'd set the targets for the adults working with the children. It seems a bit unfair to me to put all the onus on the children, when in fact if they've got a really enthusiastic, well-motivated teacher they push the children on.

Another mentioned his concern that some schools might set rather low targets so as to make sure they could achieve them. One head and post-holder who were being interviewed together had recently attended a meeting about Birmingham's Primary Guarantee where the matter of year-on-year improvements in test scores had been discussed. They favoured a more sophisticated method, whereby they would set their targets for each year in relation to how that particular class of children had scored in the city's baseline tests, given at the age of 5. After accurately outlining the LEA's plan the head said:

> We feel that each class is different year by year. We would rather, therefore, set our targets against the children and what we would use is our baseline score.... We have one or two classes where there are a lot of children who need extra help with reading, and you do have good years and bad years.

Despite the reservations expressed, it was clear that the initiative in Birmingham had raised the profile of target setting, and, by bringing it to the notice of heads, had encouraged them to think of other ways in which it might more usefully or more successfully be done. It had also emphasised once more the need for congruence between target setting and action in the classroom, for as one head said: 'There's no point in setting targets if you don't change practice.'

The teachers, like the heads, meant different things by the phrase 'setting targets'. One teacher described her notion of target setting as giving children key words to learn. Their success was acknowledged within the school's reward system by the awarding of stickers or certificates in assembly. In another teacher's class, 7 and 8 year old children struggling with their reading were placed on a four-week reading programme:

> I feel the four week reading programme is a target, because you have an aim at the end, you have the child's confidence and enjoyment in reading and books and everything will have increased. That's the main target for that programme.

Two teachers with a narrow view of target setting indicated their antipathy towards it as a concept, largely because they feared children would become too competitive:

> I don't really like that, to be honest. I know that a lot of children in my class are quite competitive anyway and I can see it becoming a bit of 'You're not as good as me!' and them not actually enjoying their reading.

> We've tried, especially lower down in the school, to take out this competitive bit with children saying 'Well, I'm on level 8 and you're only on level 6' ... [Reading] is a very individual thing in this school.

The setting of targets was seen by many as being an elastic, portmanteau concept capable of embracing whatever anyone did, did not do, liked, or disliked. It could cover any existing or planned programme, could include processes, aspirations, measured outcomes, hopes or fears. In general, the findings of this research indicate that the systematic target setting for individual pupils is not generally considered by teachers to be a necessary tool in their portfolio of strategies for improving reading standards. What is striking, however, is that much sharper definition is necessary if any conceptual clarity is to be achieved.

The road to improvement

We asked heads and post-holders if they had any particular strategies they used for improving children's reading. Some highlighted the importance of the school's general philosophy, others picked up on organisational aspects, or identified certain teaching methods as being especially beneficial. Approaches to motivate children were both intrinsic and extrinsic.

One of the most frequently mentioned intrinsic motivators was the importance of encouraging a love of reading and literature. Interviewees spoke of the need to make reading fun, to 'surround children with print' and have attractive book corners, to highlight reading and give it prestige and status, to raise teachers' expectations of what children should do. One extrinsic motivator was to use specific symbols of reward and recognition: presenting bookmarks, stickers, or certificates, celebrating various stages of progress in reading. One school gave such extrinsic rewards to elder brothers and sisters who had helped their younger siblings.

Organisational and environmental factors which were believed to help children improve their reading included several references to resources. Many interviewees spoke of the need to have books of high quality which would appeal to children, including a good supply of non-fiction books, as these were often popular with boys who did not like reading stories. Two schools had recently introduced reading schemes in place of or to supplement a 'Real Books' approach, and appreciated the structure this gave to reading within the school. Several heads mentioned that they did not like the term 'Real Books', with one adding: 'All books are 'real' books. They should all be valued.'

Other organisational factors which our heads and post-holders mentioned as important to raising standards were careful planning, monitoring and record keeping, encouraging parental involvement, and setting in ability groups or classes for specific teaching. There were many references to the need to plan for progression in the development of skills and to match teaching strategies to the needs of individual children. In order to achieve that, most schools in three of our LEAs made use of ability grouping within classes, and, in a few cases, of setting within year groups. In one school, two parallel Year 2 classes were set in three groups for phonics teaching. Only three heads mentioned the traditional method of helping low achievers to catch up, withdrawing groups of children who were falling behind, the 'remedial group', as a means of improving reading standards, and one of those arranged for groups of able readers to be withdrawn also.

The few schools where Reading Recovery was used were most enthusiastic about its effect on the children, though less so about the financial and organisational problems it caused. The financial help which LEAs and schools had received when they introduced Reading Recovery had been withdrawn, and the intensive input needed was very difficult to sustain without it. Some schools were adapting some of the principles of Reading Recovery, either for teaching the whole class or for children who had fallen behind, and several interviewees stressed the need to screen early for children with potential problems. The need to start structured teaching of reading early was mentioned, while one head was insistent about the importance of every child in Key Stage 1 reading to an adult every day. The seven most favoured responses are shown below, though the majority of respondents stressed the importance of not relying on a single approach:

1   Reading scheme/schemes
2   Structured phonics teaching
3   'Real Books'
4   Shared/paired reading
5   Sustained silent reading/ERIC (Everyone Reads In Class)
6   Group reading
7   Individual children reading to adults

Some interviewees stressed the importance in the reading process of the ability to appreciate rhyme, and the linking of reading and writing was also mentioned. We did not investigate to what extent our interviewees were aware of recent research into reading, but asked them to answer from their own experience, as we wanted them to tell us what they had found to work, rather than whether what they had read ought to work. Nevertheless, many of the aspects of the teaching of reading mentioned as important have been the subject of research. It seems probable that they had been introduced to these ideas through courses, reading or word of mouth from others who had tried them, rather than through the original research, as they were often changed, and adapted, not always in ways which appeared to be a deliberate or conscious development of the original.

6

TEACHERS' BELIEFS AND CLASSROOM PRACTICE

The thirty-five case study teachers

This chapter and the next three all describe the views and practices of the thirty-five case study teachers whose lessons were observed over a full school year. The classroom observation and interview data, derived from studying their practice, constituted Study 3 in the Primary Improvement Project research. It is important, before proceeding any further, to look at their pedigree, asking the question: were they really more than usually proficient teachers and therefore worth studying? In view of the uncertainties in the research literature about what constitutes 'competence', as was described in Chapter 1, more than one criterion needs to be applied. The following three criteria were generally positive for the whole group, though not for every single individual, so it does appear that they can be seen as better than average practitioners:

1   *Approval of superiors*   Some had been selected by the heads of their schools as being teachers who were thought to be particularly effective in teaching literacy, others had volunteered and were in the main also well regarded. Only one was not esteemed by the head.

2   *Higher pupil achievement*   We analysed the test scores of 416 pupils in fifteen of their classes who had been given either the NFER Group Reading Test or the France Primary Reading Test, or, in the case of Reception class children who were not yet reading, the LARR Test (it was not possible to test all pupils for reasons cited earlier). Of these, some 355 pupils completed both the beginning and end of year tests, and the following results were obtained from the two sets of standardised scores:

Over the year, 62 per cent improved their score, 28 per cent obtained a lower score and 10 per cent recorded the same standardised score (in theory all pupils should obtain the same standardised score if they have improved over the year at the 'average' rate). This

111

sizeable majority of 'improvers' over 'sinkers' and pupils who recorded no change, was statistically highly significant. On both a correlated *t* test (which tells of the extent to which a difference in beginning and end of year mean scores could have happened by chance), and the Wilcoxon Signed Ranks test (which checks whether such positive and negative movements could have happened by chance), these changes for the better were significant at beyond the 0.001 level. In other words they would have happened by chance less than once in a thousand times.

3 *Better application and behaviour* When the 'on-task' and 'deviancy' scores were computed from observation data, children were more involved in their work and less likely to be misbehaving than in research projects we have previously undertaken in primary schools. The average on-task score of 80 was higher than the figure of 71 found in a comparable study of primary teachers, and the average deviancy score of 3.5 was lower than the figure of 5.0 obtained in the same comparable study (Wragg 1993). There are several different ways in which such results could occur, but in a class of thirty pupils, an on-task score of 80 would be obtained if, for example, twenty pupils were paying a very high degree of attention to their task, eight were medium on-task and two were off-task. A deviancy score of 3.5 in a class of thirty might be obtained if twenty-eight pupils were behaving well and two children were engaged in mild misbehaviour, such as moving without permission, or in talk to each other that was not about their work. It must be remembered that (1) the criteria were strictly applied by researchers, (2) some of the classes studied were of very young children who find it more difficult to concentrate all the time, (3) all children have to come off their task on some occasion, for example if they go to the toilet, or are waiting to see the teacher.

These thirty-five teachers, therefore, do seem to be worth studying in more detail, as in most, though not all, cases their teaching scores well on several criteria.

Classroom organisation

Talking to teachers about their practice gives one kind of insight, but observing them at work can offer even more. Sometimes there is congruence between what people say they do and what one observes. On other occasions there can be a gap between aspiration and actuality. Observation of lessons over a whole school year allowed researchers to check out what actually happened in classrooms when literacy was the central focus. There were several aspects of practice that were identified from statements in interviews, critical events we observed, or general field notes observers made when in classrooms.

Group reading

Teachers in our case study schools held different views about how reading should be organised, with a fairly even split between those who felt that children should read to an adult on a one-to-one basis and those who had embraced 'group reading' as their main method of organisation. Many of the methods mentioned, such as group reading, paired reading, ERIC (Everyone Reads In Class), or the apprenticeship approach, are compatible with each other and with the explicit focused teaching of specific reading skills such as phonics. There was considerable enthusiasm for group reading in the schools where it was used, with one post-holder going so far as to say, 'Group reading is the thing I've been waiting for all my life', which may reveal as much about someone's life as the efficacy of the approach.

The advantages of this method were seen not simply as saving valuable time by allowing someone to hear five or six children together, but that it gave the teacher the opportunity to teach a variety of skills explicitly, either as the need arose, or by design, as when the teacher gathered a group of children who all needed help in the same area. The need for 'explicit teaching' was mentioned frequently, often in specific contradistinction to simply 'hearing readers'. In group reading the children's attention was focused on many different aspects of the text, and it was used equally successfully in Reception classes and in Key Stage 2, giving opportunities to teach anything from phonics to information retrieval skills and from rhyme to character analysis.

The head teacher of one infant school insisted that every child must read to an adult every day, and that the class teacher must personally hear each child on a regular basis. To ensure this was happening a daily record was kept and different colour pens were used to denote who had read with a child – red for the teacher, black for the classroom assistant, blue for parent helpers. The head teacher's philosophy had been embraced by the majority of the class teachers, although one confessed that it was sometimes an impossible target. In contrast, another infant school in the same region had shunned the practicality of hearing every child read and had turned to group reading as a means of organisation. A class teacher there explained the school's thinking:

> The only way that we see that we can deliver what we want to deliver is by using groups. The idea of hearing individual children read.... You would spend 9.00 to 3.15 hearing one child read in 5 minute sessions and we don't really believe that would do any good anyway, even if we had the time to do it.

In Birmingham, where group reading has become a major method of organising the teaching of reading in primary schools, one Reception class teacher
described how she intended to make use of group reading sessions:

> We're going to start group reading next term where they read four
> at a time and they're reading the same book. They each have a copy
> of the book in front of them and read it with each other and with
> the teacher, to get to know the characters and really get to know the
> book and do an activity together on the book.

Other Key Stage 1 teachers mentioned the use of group reading to highlight
letter sounds, key words, and punctuation. By Key Stage 2, the emphasis has
shifted further towards analysis of text, characters, plot and the style of
writing. A Year 3 teacher explained how it worked in his class:

> The group reading will involve reading the book, looking at words
> that are found difficult – you know, actually teaching strategies or
> reminding them of word attack strategies. And all the way through
> we'll be working on expression. Sometimes groups will do play
> readings or take a piece of narrative text and convert it into a play.
> And then there's what I was doing here this morning which was
> quite a sophisticated level of analysis and comparison of text with
> two poems.

The group reading described by the teachers in this study was not seen
merely as an alternative to hearing an individual child read. It provided the
opportunity on a regular basis for children to support each other in their
reading. In its simplest form this meant helping each other with unknown
words in a shared text. At a more sophisticated level children were together
developing their skills of inference and analysis, either through discussion of
texts in a formal setting, or through the way they decided to interpret the
text in the plays they performed.

The observation and interview data showed that group reading was a
common activity in two authorities (Birmingham and A) being popular
with children and teachers, but utilised less frequently in the other authorities visited. When used in Birmingham with the younger children it shared
many of the features of class work with big books, described later in this
chapter, being led by an adult, while other children got on with other tasks
requiring less help. Older children were more often meant to work together,
or alone in seating groups, and were given some task other than simply
reading the text.

Like many of the terms used in interview, however, 'group reading' was
an elastic concept that lent itself to many different interpretations, so we
observed quite contrasting practices under what was ostensibly the same

generic heading. The following three examples illustrate different manifestations. The first is a *consistent individual interpretation*. When Mrs Cuthbert's class was observed, the children read round the group in order. All the pupils had their own copy of the book and each was expected to follow the text closely while another pupil was reading. From time to time the teacher stopped the story to ask what might happen next, drawing attention to the pictures, punctuation, and asking for speculations on characters' feelings.

By contrast, Mrs Davies's lessons showed a *varied individual interpretation*, with no single predominant pattern. Several groups were meant to be reading together. The group working with the teacher actually did what was expected, reading and analysing the text together, but the other unsupervised groups did not appear to work as a unit. Indeed, the most able group in the class was meant to be discussing and predicting what would happen in the story, but they simply read ahead and wrote down what actually *did* happen. In practice, therefore, the 'group' was merely a collection of individuals on a common but separately undertaken task, working around the same table.

Mrs Frank's practice was different again. In her school there was a *strong corporate interpretation*, to which all the teachers in the school were expected to subscribe. An observation from one of Mrs Frank's lessons illustrates how group reading was used, and there were similar manifestations in a number of the schools studied:

> Groups of children were working in various locations with classroom assistants on a teacher-directed task [Reading Time session]. Five children were reading books to each other. Six children remained with the teacher. All were seated on chairs and they each had a copy of *The Train that Ran Away*.
>
> Teacher: 'Turn to the first page and read it by yourself.' After a minute or so ... 'Pinch the word that says "that". Has everybody pinched it? Right now turn over ... read quietly to yourself.' This they all did. 'Now let's read it all together.'
>
> The teacher did not wait for the children, she just read at a steady pace with lots of intonation. She also pointed to the text as she read and the children followed the text in their own copy with their fingers. They did this for all the pages of the book. The teacher used the term 'pinch' a great deal, inviting children to put thumb and forefinger around the target word, e.g. 'Can you pinch the word that says "track"? What does it begin with? Michael?' Michael replies 'T' [uttering the letter sound]. 'Well done, Michael.'

Mrs Frank explained that words such as 'pinch' were used to focus children's attention on a word's properties and were part of a common school vocabulary. Equipping children with the school's own terminology of language learning was seen as an important outcome of its precisely conceived policy:

> There's almost an in house style. If you listen to me do a reading group and then you go and listen to somebody else, you might even hear the same sort of inflections and same language to encourage, to bring out the child's own strategies, because it's been talked through so much and so carefully.

Whole-class reading sessions

'Quiet reading'

Three-quarters of the teachers interviewed indicated that quiet reading opportunities were provided for their pupils, which was substantiated by the observation data. Of these, over half explained that sessions were timetabled to take place every day at the same time, and in one LEA area studied it was common for this to be a whole-school activity, although it was not clear whether this was an LEA suggestion.

From the descriptions given by teachers of their quiet reading periods, it was apparent that there were differences in perceptions of 'quiet reading', both in terms of content and organisation. For many teachers the term simply meant a session when everyone in the classroom was involved in some kind of reading activity. As was described above, it was a feature of most of the teachers in this sample that their lessons were very orderly; that is why we recorded some of our lowest 'deviancy' and highest pupil 'on-task' scores, so the word 'quiet' or 'silent' usually meant just that. In other research projects, where we have observed less well-ordered classrooms, we have witnessed supposedly 'quiet reading' sessions that were anything but quiet or silent. There were some teachers who recorded nearly 100 per cent of their class on the task in three different lessons where individual pupils were studied, and perhaps one single act of mildly deviant behaviour. Since this climate of attentiveness was usually achieved in a benign and businesslike, rather than unpleasant, intimidating or threatening, manner, skilful classroom management and social control do appear to be a significant factor in these teachers' success.

In some classrooms, more especially in Key Stage 2, there were opportunities for longer sessions of silent reading. The overwhelming orderliness of this sustained period allowed concentration over a significant period of time. One teacher of 10 and 11 year olds explained how she endeavoured to make the act of reading a top priority, with no distractions from pupils talking or moving around the classroom. This required a degree of forethought and a clear classroom rule, so as to ensure a noise-free environment:

Sometimes I say, 'No-one's going to get up today, so make sure you've got enough reading material because nobody's getting up for anything'.

It was much more rare for silent reading to take place in Key Stage 1, but one teacher felt very strongly that it was important that children should learn at an early stage how grown-ups behave, and she stressed the importance of her own contribution, both in providing an explanation of the reason for the activity and acting as a role model of the adult reader:

I think by the end of Year 2 there should be at least one session a week where they have silent reading, but I would explain to them why they're doing that – because I want them to read like adults. And I would sit down and read as well.

In other classes children were expected to read individually, but low-volume talk was permitted so long as it was on-task. In all the instances described above, the principal purpose of the session was to provide children with the opportunity to develop their enjoyment of books in a fairly exploratory and unstructured way. In a small number of Key Stage 2 classes, however, the teachers took a more interventionist stance, setting up a wide range of different and systematically focused reading experiences for their pupils every day for half an hour after lunch, as this Year 5 teacher explained:

They get a different diet at those times, so they'd have five activities which they'd rotate during the week. One of them might be reading from the poetry box, one might be at the listening centre, one might be browsing in the book corner, one might be reading their group book for that week, and then we'd rotate them, so that they're reading at all times but they've got different things to look at.

In over half the cases observed, the 'quiet reading' sessions doubled up as a block of time during which children read their books to adults, so moving the emphasis of the session from pupils' individual enjoyment of books to a situation in which their reading was being monitored and assessed.

There were some instances of lack of congruence between intention and outcome. One example was in classrooms where the 'quiet reading' session involved children reading books while sitting on the carpet, either before or during the calling of the morning register. It was almost impossible for a truly quiet environment to be sustained at this particular time in the day, as children and parents arrived at different times and often parents needed to talk to teachers. Teachers relying on this time alone for quiet reading need to monitor the quality of the actual experience they are providing for children.

What was read also varied. Some teachers wished the children to read a

117

prescribed book, while others asked them to read a variety of books, or encouraged any type of written text. The effectiveness of this ERIC time varied, in particular according to a combination of the teacher's class management skills and the nature of the reading matter involved. A number of writers on the topic agree with the teacher above, who believed that teachers should act as role models during silent reading (McCracken 1971, Gambrell 1978, Berglund and Johns 1983). Indeed, research by Wheldall and Entwistle (1988) and Wheldall (1989) suggested that pupils spent more time reading if the teachers were also reading, although Campbell and Scrivens (1995) point out that a range of teacher roles were noted to provide support and encouragement for children to become or remain active readers. However, despite the occasional assertion in interview that teachers should act as role models, we never witnessed it actually happening during any ERIC period. It was a prime example of the gap there can sometimes be between what someone wishes to believe and observed practice.

In those classes where ERIC was a regular feature, the children were generally allowed a free choice of books from the class library, the school library or from home. In some classes children were then allowed to change their books freely during the reading session, but a few teachers, like the one cited above, had implemented a system where children had to take sufficient books to their desk at the start of the activity to avoid them having to get up again. In some schools certain sessions were designated for free choice reading and others were a time for the pupils to read books from the reading scheme. A number of schools always adopted the same approach, whereas others varied it. One Year 5 teacher who had silent reading in the morning and free choice reading in the afternoon explained the difference:

> In this [silent reading] session the least able have free choice of reading, but read from the Oxford Reading Tree to the teacher or an ancillary. A number of children are using *Wide Range* scheme books. We are phasing this out and I am in the process of moving children from this to 'guided choice', i.e. books that are manageable but suffi- ciently challenging. [In free choice reading] children have a completely free choice from class library books, topic collection books or books made by other children ... [it's] not necessarily a completely silent session, as children may discuss, or read in pairs etc.

ERIC was popular with and thought to be valuable by all the teachers who did it except one, who believed that children wasted time and 'messed about'. One teacher followed up the session by asking individual children what parts of the story they had liked, why they had enjoyed it, and then read some of the extracts to the rest of the class. In another school it was decided that their Key Stage 2 pupils were not optimising the two and a half hours a week they had allocated to silent reading. They altered it by requiring pupils to discuss their book with the teacher when they finished it, also introducing a 'class recommendation book', a sort of consumer guide, in which pupils recorded what they felt about the book for the benefit of the whole class.

Paired reading

'Paired reading', the process whereby children read to each other, usually involving a class of older pupils being asked to read with a class of younger children, had been mentioned as an approved and useful approach to improving children's reading by several heads and post-holders. It was often found to be difficult to organise, especially when it involved moving whole classes of children at fixed times, but several schools did use volunteers from the top of the school to help younger children.

The more strict manifestation of paired reading, in which an experienced reader reads until the less experienced reader joins in and then indicates readiness to take over, was not used in any of our schools. As with Reading Recovery, schools adapted the approach, either because they thought their own way was better suited to their circumstances, or because they were not aware of the original interpretation of the title. In many cases what the teacher labelled 'paired reading' appeared to mean nothing more than two children sitting together sharing the same copy of a book. Most commonly the pairings were within the same class. In a number of schools carefully organised paired reading sessions had been arranged between Key Stage 1 and Key Stage 2 classes. One Year 5 teacher explained how it was working in her school at the beginning of the year:

> On a Thursday morning half of the Year 2 class come to me and half of my class go to her class and they share any sort of reading mate-rial they like – story books or information books. The children completely run it themselves. They decide what they want to take, what they want to read. We've also started having a selection of younger children's books in this class as well, so that when the little ones come up they can choose those as well to read to my class.

Organisational problems were sometimes encountered where two different classes were involved. Indeed, the Year 2 teacher at one school admitted that it had 'fizzled out' by the February half term because of other timetable pressures. In one school where there was a 'Young Teachers' Club', older siblings were trained to support their younger brothers' and sisters' reading not only during the daily ERIC session after lunch, but also in the home. The Young Teachers received certificates when their younger siblings had learned to read twenty, forty, sixty or 100 words. The older children involved were all volunteers and the school was particularly pleased to report that the Young Teachers' Club contained a balance of girls and boys. Not only was this seen as providing positive role models for boys in the school, but they hoped the experience the male Young Teachers were gaining would encourage them to play a fuller role in their own children's education one day in the future. Indeed, they believed it was an important part of 'training for parenthood'.

Overall, however, the observation data showed that although there were many examples of informal paired reading during ERIC sessions in the schools studied, in only a few schools was paired reading formalised. The researcher's account below of two teachers' lessons gives the flavour of what happened. Mrs Ernest had initiated paired reading between her Reception/Year 1 class and the Year 5/6 class. Mrs Jenkins used it within her own class:

Mrs Ernest The Reception/Year 1 teacher, Mrs Ernest, told pupils at the start of the session that today they were going to read their book to their junior school person and she had therefore put little baskets of books and big books out on the tables. The pupils had each saved a chair for their junior to sit next to them. The Year 6 pupils arrived and started reading without any further instructions from the teacher.

When one of the infants had finished her book, the Year 6 pupil sitting next to her dutifully told Mrs Ernest, who asked whether she had had any difficulty with any of the words. 'Only "look" ', was the response. Mrs Ernest then told the pair that they could choose another book. At one point, one of the Year 6 pupils needed the help of a classmate, turning to him and asking, 'What does that say, Martin?' He readily told her that the word was 'Toadstool'. Martin himself was reading a book to his Year 1 partner.

There were varied approaches used by different pupils. One 11 year old read to his partner, but the 6 year old pupil paid him little attention. A different 11 year old pupil selected a book and then asked the 6 year old pupil to read it to her. When the younger child could not manage a particular section she asked the older pupil partner to read to her. Another 11 year old pointed to the words and the 6 year old read them. Whilst the paired reading continued, the teacher heard certain children reading and the classroom assistant filled out reading record cards.

After ten minutes Mrs Ernest started to move about the room. She stopped to ask how one of her pupils was getting on. She was told that he got every single word right. She celebrated the achievement by saying publicly that it was 'brilliant' and the two children should now go and choose a new scheme book. This time the 6 year old asked the 11 year old pupil to read it to him first. After twenty minutes of paired reading the pupils were asked to put the books away and the juniors were thanked for their help. This class also operated paired reading amongst themselves and pupils were encouraged to look at the words in their reading scheme books together.

Mrs Maple Just before playtime Mrs Maple asked her Year 2 children if they could remember what they would be doing after playtime. Hands shot up ... Sharon said, 'Sharing our book with our partner.' Teacher: 'That's right, just like you did yesterday. So when you come in from play, find your book and start straightaway. Remember that one of you should read one page, and then the other of you the next one, so you're taking it in turns.'

After play, without further prompting from the teacher, the children came in, got out their books and sat at various locations around the room. All the children had partners. All pairs, except one, were of the same sex. Most pairs appeared to be working well together, taking turns as told.

One pair of boys was off-task, flicking pencils. The teacher noticed this pair and moved them to her table. In some pairings a dominant partner could be identified. These commonly kept hold of the book even when their partner was reading. In the only boy/girl pairing, the girl was clearly dominant – she kept the book and read to the boy. He did not read at all. In one pair of boys, one pupil, Brad, did all the reading. When the researcher asked the two of them about this, he said, 'Tim doesn't like doing it.' Tim didn't comment. The paired reading session lasted for fifteen minutes.

The teacher had found that quiet reading – by this she meant 'silent' – didn't work with the class. 'It's almost impossible for them to be quiet for any length of time.' She had therefore decided to try paired reading. The children had chosen their own partners, except in a couple of cases where the teacher said she had 'manipulated' the pairings.

In the first session of the year she had chosen one child and demonstrated to the class how paired reading should be undertaken. She felt that the paired reading was successful. Her own role during the fifteen minutes was to monitor the different pairs and to encourage them not only to read to each other, but also to talk about the text and pictures.

In one case study school, the paired reading programme was extremely well organised. At a regular time each week, pupils read with children three years younger than themselves. The purpose had been explained to them, and the sessions were orderly and businesslike. Although this school sustained its programme throughout the year, there was, inescapably, a problem with the quality of the model offered when one child read to another.

Children learn a great deal by imitation. Not all older pupils are themselves fluent and interesting readers and competent models. An interview with Charlotte, aged 5, neatly reveals the dilemma. Charlotte was one of the biggest improvers we tested during the year. When asked who read to her, she replied that there was her teacher, the classroom assistant 'and Darren'. 'Who is Darren?' the researcher enquired. 'Darren is my Year 4 reading partner,' she replied. The researcher began to wonder if the efforts of Darren might have contributed significantly to her spectacular improvement. However, she continued: 'the trouble is he just goes: "Buzzy buzzy buzzy, gabble gabble gabble".' When subsequently observing Darren's halting and unarresting reading of a story to her, the researcher could find no better form of words to describe the maelstrom than 5 year old Charlotte's own natural language. Paired reading may well be effective for many children, and the act of public sponsorship may convey an important message, but the stilted reading of a relatively unskilled 8 year old seemed to have little real impact on this bright 5 year old.

Teacher reading to the class

There was an interesting example of a notable difference between what teachers said in interview and what actually happened in their classrooms. During interviews, surprisingly few teachers in Key Stage 1 and only one Key Stage 2 teacher talked about the value of reading out loud to the children and sharing books with them for pleasure. Yet observation of classroom practice indicated that this was a strong feature in many of the lessons observed. This junior school teacher, who discussed reading regularly to her class, expressed her surprise at their enthusiasm for this type of session:

> I teach reading ... through my own reading of stories and poetry. I let them choose what they want me to read. They really like it and I'm really surprised, because when I've taught Year 5 children before, they've tended to find it a bit babyish. And what I love doing with them sometimes is: I read a page and then one of the others decides; they want to read the next, so we swap round. And if there were voices they'd take over the voices of the characters. Or they'd just read a couple of lines or guess what the next line will be.

In the schools studied, teachers used stories both as a stimulus for writing and for reading to children for pleasure. In Key Stage 1 classes, it was more common to see a teacher read a picture book in one session, although occasionally a longer book would be read every day to the class over a week or so. In Key Stage 2 classes where the teacher was observed reading to the class, it was more likely to be a 'chapter' book. One teacher who read to her class every day, but only when the lower-ability group had been withdrawn to receive additional language support, commented:

> I don't think it's appropriate for those children. The vocabulary is quite advanced, and the themes ... they're quite involved. It's complex and it's also pretty scary too, towards the end.

This teacher did not read a story to the entire class until March, so it was not until the end of the second term in the school year that the lower-ability children had their first opportunity to participate in such whole-class teacher reading. It did seem a notable omission in their literacy experience that year.

Other teachers made reading to the whole class a priority and junior school classes were likely to try and link the fiction they were reading with one of the class topics. Interviews with the pupils showed that a number of them were able to recall the story that their teachers had read to them in class more readily than those where teacher and pupils had been observed reading separately. This teacher regularly read to the whole class, including pupils of lower ability.

> For the first term Mrs Bates had instigated group reading, but in the second term she had decided to use one session a week for a whole class novel. The teacher explained to the class why she had chosen that particular book, saying that she had enjoyed reading it as a child and that it had also engaged her three previous classes. She pointed out that it was a fairly long book, which would be nice for those children who did not normally read long books. Although it would be useful to their topic work, she also commented that it was a good book irrespective of this.
>
> The teacher then read to the children asking them to listen carefully as they were going to talk more about the book later. After reading for twenty minutes the teacher stopped and asked the pupils to give her one word descriptors of the book's two main characters, which she then wrote on the board.
>
> One child took the initiative to predict a change in character, for which he was praised by the teacher. The teacher then set an exercise on the book, stating beforehand that the book was full of dialogue and descriptors. The exercise was based on a plan of one of the rooms described in the book, which the children had to complete using the descriptors in the text.

Mrs Bates encouraged children to develop higher-order reading skills by giving the pupils an exercise with a purpose. Individual observations of pupils in the class showed that they listened quietly and with apparent interest in the novel and worked diligently in groups on the subsequent task.

The pupils in Mrs Turner's class of 10 year olds were clearly aware, in interview, not only of what their teacher read to the class, but also why:

> She reads *Lady Daisy* and we follow it along and sometimes the teacher reads us a story before we go home or before a lesson if it's got something to do with it, to start us off.

> Ten minutes before we go home, we have this book, *Lady Daisy*. We have a book each and read every evening, it's also to do with our topic.

The teacher had explained about what she did and why:

> All the children have a copy of the text and are encouraged to follow, whilst I read. We are currently reading *Lady Daisy Chain* by Dick King Smith, which links nicely with our topic, 'The Victorians'. In this session we read for shared enjoyment, read to demonstrate fluency, expression, intonation and expression by the teacher, I hope. We use text to substantiate fact and opinion and to predict and discuss characterisation and the plot.

Reading stories at the infant stage generally took a different format, consisting of one or more texts at a time. Teachers used various strategies when telling stories, but one common approach was to ask children to predict what was to happen next. One Year 1 teacher, Miss Brown, made reading to the class a high priority and seemed particularly effective, not only making it a pleasurable occasion for the children, but also using the opportunity to develop children's vocabulary about books, as the following account reveals:

> The teacher holds up *Little Bear's Story*, by Jane Hissey. 'I don't know whether you can remember, but I read this book to you when you were in the Reception Class. Can anyone remember the name of the author?' Child puts up hand: 'Jane.' Teacher: 'That's right. Jane Hissey.'
> She holds up a second book – *Ruff* by Jane Hissey. 'This is by the same author. Can you see her name here?' A child puts up his hand: 'The pictures look the same.' Teacher: 'Yes, they look similar, don't they? Why do you think that is?' Child: 'Because they're drawn by the same person!' Teacher: 'Yes, that's right. Well done for spotting

that! Can anyone remember another word which means pictures in books?' Sam: 'Illustrations!' Teacher: 'That's right. Well done, Sam.'

The teacher reads the *Ruff* story to the children, using different voices for the different animals and occasionally stops to ask the children questions: 'What do you think the dog might be called?', 'What do you think will happen next?' In the story, Ruff has never had a birthday and the teacher asks the children 'How do you think you'd feel if you'd never had a birthday?' allowing considerable time for discussion of this.

At the end of the story Matthew, who has been working in the library with the classroom assistant, returns and she gets the children to retell the story to Matthew. One child asks if there are other books 'by the same author'. The teacher tells them she will find some more to read them.

Miss Brown did not see reading a story as a means of 'filling up' the last twenty minutes of the day. She described herself as having 'a great love of books' and felt that engendering this in her pupils was a crucial part of her teaching role. Reading the story to the class was only one of the strategies she used to achieve this objective. Following the episode described above, she collected a large selection of Jane Hissey's books and placed them in the 'Author Corner' where, for a couple of weeks, children could browse through them and borrow them. Authors featured in this 'Author Corner' were changed regularly and the children enjoyed a wide range of authors. The combination of her considerable personal enthusiasm and meticulous follow-up organisation seemed to act as a powerful motivator.

Big books

Although there were many similarities amongst the schools in the different authorities in the way that Key Stage 1 teachers organised and approached the teaching of reading, one noticeable addition to teachers' range of strategies in two of the areas in which we observed, namely Birmingham and Authority A, was the use of the 'Big Book', which could be a larger version either of a reading scheme book, or of a 'real book'. The teachers' awareness of the possibilities offered by big books had been raised at courses organised by their LEAs. Teachers felt the sheer size of picture, text and punctuation allowed them to share features of text publicly in whole-class teaching that would be too small to highlight in a normal-sized or small book. Big books were often observed being used with a small group or with the whole class, to share a story or to make a variety of teaching points. One Birmingham Reception teacher talked with enthusiasm of the opportunity big books gave her to teach reading in this way:

We're going to have a big book focus every day – same book for the week – and what we do most days is read a book together and every day pick out a different thing, like large print that makes you say the word louder, looking at the shape of words, trying to *feel* the sounds in the words, and thinking of other words with the same sounds.

In other Key Stage 1 classes, big books were also used as a tool for 'drawing children's attention to capital letters, full stops, sentence structure and speech marks'. Two teachers also featured a 'book of the week', subsequently basing other activities on them, such as worksheets. One teacher sometimes had a Poem of the Week which they all read together, as well as a book. She took great care to ensure all could see and were looking at the key features in the text. Most teachers held the book half sideways, so the children could see the text and pictures, but this teacher put it on a stand and pointed to each word with a stick. She drew attention to initial sounds and the shape of words and invited children to come up to point to particular words.

Another purpose of big book activity was to introduce children to certain books, sometimes from the reading scheme, and familiarise them with the characters, the rhythm of the text and, indeed, to get to know the books by heart so that they could then 'read' them to themselves. One newly qualified teacher said she had been on a Reading Enrichment Course run by Birmingham LEA which had been very useful, and from this had started to pay more attention to individual features of the text, as well as to the author. She claimed to have had no such instruction about teaching reading in her initial training, beyond 'just hearing readers'. This course had informed her group and big book class work.

Interestingly not one single teacher in the case study schools in Authority D mentioned using big books as a teaching strategy, nor did analysis of the observation data reveal examples of their use in the classroom. Unlike Birmingham, Authority D, at that time, had adopted a largely non-interventionist stance in literacy matters and saw its role as reacting to schools' individual needs, rather than taking a leading position on policy and practice.

Reading as a stimulus for writing

Many teachers deliberately linked reading, writing and speaking. A number used a piece of reading, fiction or non-fiction, as a stimulus for children to write their own story or factual account. This linking strategy was observed in use with varying degrees of success. One particularly successful version was observed in a class of 8 year olds, where the teacher capitalised on their own knowledge of a certain type of story before moving on to a carefully planned piece of writing:

The teacher and the children are sitting on the carpet. The teacher starts the session with, 'Can you think of any stories to do with vegetables where they grow, or where there's more of them?' Suggestions are made: *Jack and the Beanstalk* and *The Enormous Turnip*, and these are enthusiastically received. '*Jack and the Beanstalk* was the one I was thinking of. Can you remember how the story went?' Most of the children put their hands up.

The teacher asks various pupils to recount the plot, moving around the class to involve several of them. Her manner is relaxed and conversational and she shows great interest in what the children are saying. She uses praise frequently: 'You've all got much better memories than me.'

She then empties out a container of small potatoes on to a tray in front of her: 'Just suppose that one of those potatoes, and we don't know which, is not an ordinary potato, just like the bean that Jack had. Close your eyes and imagine what might happen if one of these was not quite an ordinary potato.'

After a short period for reflection, she takes out a pen and says, 'Has anyone got any ideas about what might happen if one of these was not quite an ordinary potato?' Various suggestions are made by the children and the teacher writes them all down on two large pieces of paper in front of her on the carpet where all the children can see. Occasionally she asks a prompting question to stimulate further ideas. When the white sheets are full the teacher turns them round so they are facing the children and gets the group to read what she has written. 'Let's see what the "ideas machine" has come up with.'

She points to the words as she and the children read them at the same time. The teacher reads with great expression in her voice, conveying a message of excitement. 'Gosh, we've got some amazing ideas. Now I want you to choose your potato which might, just might, not be an ordinary potato. Sarah, close your eyes and choose one.' Each child does the same, selecting a potato with closed eyes. 'I'm now going to ask you to write some ideas about what might happen to this perhaps not so ordinary potato.'

The children were fully prepared for their task, and in addition they also had an individual potato in front of them as a continuing stimulus while they wrote their story. The writing produced seemed to be of good quality for the age and background of the class. Many stories were based on the suggestions that had emerged during the brainstorming session, but some of the more able children developed their own new ideas.

Not all reading–writing links were as successful as the one above. One lesson with a class of 7 year olds was nowhere near as effective.

The teacher is sitting on a chair. The children sit on the carpet in front of her. The teacher is holding the book *Sally – Sky Diver* by Polly Noakes on her lap. For most of the time she has the book towards her, only occasionally holding up the book to show the children the pictures, which some of them cannot see. She allows the children to comment as she reads and they are clearly involved with the story, but the teacher's responses to their comments seem ineffective and ill-focused.

Pupil: How could she stay in space that long? She can't breathe!
Teacher: Well, it's a story, isn't it?

At the end of the story she says, 'That was a strange tale. This morning we're going to have a go at writing a strange story.' She then holds up an addressed envelope. 'You're taking this letter to the post and suddenly the wind takes hold of it and takes it away. The letter has an adventure. Who has some ideas about what might happen to it?' The teacher takes three suggestions from children and then says: 'All eyes closed. Think how your story is going to start.... If you think you're ready, you can go and start writing.'

All the children stand up immediately and start writing. The work undertaken by the majority of children during the morning was of modest quality, mostly retelling the original story by Polly Noakes. There had been little engagement or stimulus to provoke much else. Productivity levels were low, with some children writing no more than three lines in an hour.

This less stimulating use of story to link with writing was observed on a number of occasions in this class and in another class at a different school. The teacher's own apparent lack of enthusiasm for the original story, as well as the children's lack of preparation, meant it became a tedious and, so far as the researcher could judge, unenjoyable activity for them.

Children's own personalised and self-made books

A large number of teachers mentioned the importance of children making their own books, both fiction and non-fiction. In Reception classes self-made books, often written in the first person, were used to enable children to become familiar with key words through repetition. 'I can' and 'I am' books were used by a number of teachers. One Reception class teacher demonstrated a very structured approach to personal books. The first book created was about the individual child and their family and introduced a small number of key words. The second contained a series of fictional events involving the child and the characters from the Oxford Reading Tree scheme. Some children were then judged to be ready to make a start on the reading scheme, while others had to create a third fictional book. All the words used in the individual books were listed on the child's own 'word wall'. When the teacher thought the time was right, the words were copied onto card and taken home in a tin for practice. The teacher judged this approach to be very successful but commented, 'It does take ages!' It was, however, time she was willing to spend.

As children moved up through the primary school, they were observed more frequently to be engaged in writing their own fiction and non-fiction. In Birmingham this activity had been formalised as an official target in the authority's Primary Guarantee: 'Each child in Key Stage 1 and Key Stage 2 will make a book for others to read', but the practice was common throughout all the local authority areas studied. One Year 5 class teacher tried to replicate as accurately as possible the writing of a real book by a real author. She asked her pupils to research a topic of interest to them and then use this information to write their own book on the subject. The final copy would be as close to a published book as they could make it, incorporating a contents page, index, glossary, biographical details of the author, ISBN number and sale price. Books made by the children themselves were often displayed prominently in both infant and junior classrooms.

Individual practice varied amongst the teachers observed encouraging self-made books. In some classes, particularly those with older children, all their written work was pasted into a book when it had been corrected and written out 'in neat'. In other cases it was creating a book for a particular purpose that was the end product. In Reception classes, as mentioned earlier, the 'first person' type of book was very common, where children draw pictures, tell the teacher the sentence they want to write, and then copy out or trace over the teacher's sentence. This frequently involves the repetition of key sentence components, such as 'I can see ... ' or 'I like ... '.

In the earlier years, it was more common for teachers to gather together several pieces of children's work on a particular topic and present them in a class book. Miss Brown produced class books on 'Hot and Cold' and 'Opposites' amongst other topics. She was especially keen to show how much she valued the children's work, as this episode reveals:

> Miss Brown holds up a large self-made book with a strong laminated cover for the children to see. 'We've got a lovely book here.' Can anyone tell me what the title is?' Several hands go up. Pupil 1: 'Hot and Cold.' Teacher: 'That's right. Well done.'
> She opens the book and inside there are pieces of children's work. She reads the first few pages, naming the child whose piece of work it is. 'I'm going to put it in the book corner so you can read it all, if you'd like to.' She then picks up another book of children's work

'The Book of Prayers' and reads some of these pieces, selecting different children's work.

She makes sure that all the children can see the pictures, holding the book up high and showing it to each side as she reads. 'Shall I put this one in the book corner as well? Aren't you all clever to make such lovely books?' She then moves over to the shelves in the reading area and shows the children where she is putting the two books.

Like many of the most successful teachers observed, Miss Brown made reading important and celebrated achievement as it occurred. She explained how 'class' books allowed her to do this publicly, saying, 'I feel they are very important because they show I value the children's work, and they enjoy reading each other's work as well.'

Writing for an audience

The term 'writing for an audience' has become a familiar expression in documents on literacy, but some of the most effective teachers observed were keen to translate rhetoric into action. This often involved first of all thinking about the audience when writing and, second, the act of reading out one's own writing publicly. In one school the 'audience' was able to buy the self-made books made by 8 year old children in two Year 3 classes. These pupils produced books for sale at their school book fair.

There were many stages to the activity: drafting of the story; a 'conference' with the teacher or classroom assistant to discuss the story and check spellings and punctuation; taking the revised draft and word processing it on laptop computers; printing it out; cutting out the printed text and sticking it into the 'books', made up of A4 sheets of paper folded four times; the drawing of illustrations; and the design of the front and back cover. A number of photocopies were made of each book so that more than one could be sold of each. The children seemed very excited at the idea that others within the school could buy books they themselves had written. The teacher said that the intention of the task was 'to provide the children with a "real" activity so that they were writing for a "real audience"'.

In a class of 10 year olds the audience was fellow pupils, of the same age or younger. This class was also involved in paired reading sessions with a class of 7 year olds in the same school. One of the activities undertaken during the first term was that Year 5 children had to write a book for their Year 2 partner, after consultation with that younger child about the type of story they liked best and the sort of characters they would like to be included. The Year 2 children contributed to the illustrations in these books and the final products were then displayed in the Year 2 class.

In another school, 7 year olds were asked to make a book for the

Reception class on their topic 'The School', which the class had done earlier in the year. The teacher took the opportunity to launch an exploration of different genres that writers use:

> The teacher says: 'We've got to imagine that we are the authors, a great big class full of authors.... What shall we ask the Reception children when they come up? We need to write some questions up on the board. Let's think of the sort of writing we can do. We can do stories ... '
>
> The teacher then looks to the pupils for ideas: 'What is your favourite thing about the school?' Mary asks: 'Would you like non-fiction?' The teacher responds to this idea by saying that they may need to explain to the Reception children what this means. 'What I want you to think about is how we can write it down. Mary said 'non-fiction'. What other sorts of books are there?' Pupils volunteer: 'fiction', 'poems'. The teacher comments, 'Now you are getting the idea of what I am asking.'

On some occasions children's own writing took a very dominant position, in terms of both the time and esteem accorded to what they had written. Mrs Hutchings, described in more detail in Chapter 9, illustrates well the way in which self-made books were valued and the audience for which they were written was reified. On a regular basis children, on their own initiative, continued writing when they were at home, often bringing in books they had written either individually or with a friend, to share with the rest of the class. In interview Mrs Hutchings said she encouraged the children to write at home and in spare classroom time, and to bring in their writings to share with other children. She noticed that if one child used a particular word in a story it tended to appear in others. She found that styles of writing in published books were often noticed and adopted by the children. At that time, the favourite was 'The End, or is it? No, it isn't ... '

Teachers adopted different approaches to writing for an audience. Some were extremely systematic and made clear what they expected. One teacher, Mrs Turner, had instigated a 'writing pathway' which laid out what was expected from children-as-author in the presentation of their written work.

1   Planning – plan what you are going to say.
2   Drafting – write your first draft.
3   Revising – read your writing through.
4   Make any changes to your writing. You can cross things out, add bits or change the order of what you have written.
5   Read your writing through again.
6   Make sure there are no mistakes in your writing – check that you have spelled all the words correctly, put in all the capital

letters, put in all the other punctuation like full stops, commas and question marks.

7   Editing – take your work to the teacher for a final check. It has to be absolutely correct before you copy it out to print it.

8   Publishing – write it out in your best handwriting or print it on a word processor.

The act of public reading of one's own writing was observed in several forms. Children might read it to an adult, to a partner, to their group, or to the whole class. There appeared to be many reasons for getting pupils to read out their work: to provide a good example of writing to the rest of the class; to offer an opportunity for children to develop their skills of appreciation by saying what they liked about, or thought worked well in, a particular piece; to use the piece to suggest ideas to those who were finding it difficult to think of any; to allow the rest of the class to suggest further directions for the piece of writing; to allow the teacher to pick up on teaching points, such as grammar, punctuation, use of words such as adjectives; to show that the teacher valued the pupils' writings.

Information technology

The use of information technology in the classroom was not a particular focus of this study, but records of the lessons observed provided an insight into the use of computers in primary classrooms. In the majority of classrooms there were one or two computers. Where there were two, one of these was usually an old BBC computer, the second one a more up-to-date PC. One school had purchased a number of laptop computers in addition to the three PCs shared between the two Year 3 classes observed.

There was a tendency for the less able children to have access to computers for certain activities, although sometimes teachers paired a less able child with a more able one so that they would be able to provide help. While this reduced the number of times a teacher was called to the computer, the quality of the learning experience for the more able child has to be questioned, especially as, in two of the classes observed, the same two able children were given this responsibility on a number of occasions, so it occupied quite a deal of their time.

Broadlands Primary is exceptionally well equipped with computers. As well as having two computers in most classrooms, there is a room with about a dozen machines where children can be found working at play times as well as in groups during lessons. The language co-ordinator stressed the importance of reading across the curriculum and was very enthusiastic in interview about the use of IT for improving literacy. The children in the Reception class we observed used computers for writing and drawing, while the older children had individual floppy disks so that they could do extended writing and graphics projects. They used CD-ROM programs for projects and for English – keeping records of their own progress in spelling, vocabulary and comprehension. They had e-mail links with schools in other countries, and were also used to demonstrating their skills to the many visitors the school attracts. There was also evidence of their extensive use of computers in one of the classroom displays seen during an observation visit, in which computer designs of bridges, word-processed factual information about how they had designed them, and poems about bridges had been combined.

In some cases, by contrast, there was a danger that 'working on the computer', far from being a high-status activity, had labelled a child as a poor achiever in the eyes of fellow pupils. This extract from an interview with a dyslexic child who was of above-average general ability illustrates the point. A special needs teacher worked with her about half an hour a day, mainly using the computer:

Interviewer: So how do you think you are getting on in your reading this year so far?
Pupil: Well, I thought I was doing quite well, but I can't be.
Interviewer: Why's that?
Pupil: Because I'm on the computer.

The use of computers for word processing stories was widespread in the classes observed and across ability ranges, but usually involved children merely copying up their final draft. In a few classes children also used the computer to compose their story. In the classes where only one or two computers were located, individuals had very few opportunities to undertake this type of task. In the school in which several laptop computers had been acquired, up to eleven children at one time were able to compose their own stories on their own personal computer. These children displayed a much better knowledge of word-processing techniques and could confidently delete text and move text. They also made more use of the text design and layout possibilities offered by the computer. Henry, a high-ability 8 year old, incorporated capital letters and underlining for emphasis, centred his headings and put all spoken text in speech marks.

Children in Henry's class had frequent opportunities to use laptops, and their experience with computers showed in the quality of their work. However, in common with all the children observed using a computer, their inability to 'touch type' meant that often composing or copying stories was a slow and laborious task, and this issue needs to be addressed. Indeed, when a Year 1 teacher was questioned about the fact that word-processed work displayed on the walls contained typing and spelling errors, she replied: 'The children take so long to do the piece of work, I haven't got the heart to make them go back and correct all their mistakes. It just takes them so long!' In only one class was the computer never switched on. This was due to the teacher's lack of confidence with computers, an issue which had been raised during her staff appraisal the previous year but which so far, she admitted, she had managed to avoid addressing.

Author studies

Some teachers had organised the opportunity for their pupils to examine particular authors in more depth. This could involve setting up an 'Author Corner' – a section of the reading area in which there were displayed a number of books by the same author. One teacher, Miss Brown, the Year 1 teacher described above, had created an attractive display, with the front of each book clearly visible. Some books were placed open on stands, so that children could see the pictures and text inside. Written questions, such as: 'Have you read any books by Roger Hargreaves?' and 'Which is your favourite Mr Men character?', were pinned to the back wall on colour cards. Where artefacts or toys relating to the books were available, these were also displayed. A selection of the current author's books was read by the teacher to the class during the period of their display. Children were encouraged to choose from the selection of books to read at other times and the teacher reported that they often asked to take the books home to read with their parents.

This approach seemed very successful in engaging children's interest in books and gave her an opportunity to talk about illustrations and styles of writing, even with infant-age children. However, in another classroom we observed, one of the few in the sample to register very little improvement in reading test scores over the school year, a different picture emerged. Although the teacher had stated her intention to the researcher at the beginning of the year to 'make more use of author boxes, probably changing authors every half term instead of every term', the same two authors' books, those of Margaret Mahy and Gene Kemp, remained in the author boxes throughout the whole school year.

Children were indeed observed working on the two authors' works, comparing their styles of writing, the subjects of their books, the types of characters they wrote about, but there was no opportunity at any stage of the year to develop children's awareness of other authors and other styles. In addition, the teacher rarely monitored the children's reading materials, and this may help provide some explanation of the lack of improvement in many of the children's reading test results between October and the following June. While there seemed to be progress in their ability to analyse text, there was little evidence of the teacher striving to move them on to more sophisticated books in their personal reading.

Celebration and rewards

A notable feature of many of the episodes described in this chapter has been the importance attached by effective teachers of literacy to the celebration of achievement wherever and however it occurred, and in many cases precise targeting and focusing on particular aspects of literacy. Related to this issue is the nature of rewards, incentives, recognition and reinforcement. Praise for children's work by teachers was a common feature of nearly all the class-rooms studied, much more commonly observed than either disapproval or punishment. This may, to some extent, have been influenced by the presence of an observer.

In one school extrinsic rewards were considered a very effective incentive for good work and behaviour, although some teachers operated the system to a greater extent than others. While one of the teachers in the school was rarely seen to praise or reward good work, another teacher used rewards, such as stickers and stars, regularly to raise children's self-esteem and to motivate them. The event described below is typical of those observed in her classroom:

> The teacher is sitting with Jonathan, a low-ability child with little self-confidence. She has selected a number of books of a similar degree of difficulty and allows him to choose which one he wants to read. 'Shall we have a look at it together?'
>
> The teacher talks about the picture on the cover and tells Jonathan the title of the book. Without prompting, he identifies that one of the words in the title, 'jumps', starts with the same sound as his own name. 'Well done, Jonathan. That's very clever of you to spot that!' She then reads the text to Jonathan, pointing her finger at each word.
>
> After she has discussed the story with him, she takes out some flashcards to test Jonathan's sight vocabulary. These are five of the first twelve key words and he reads them all. The teacher takes out her page of stickers and gives him a star 'Because you've done really well, Jonathan!' Jonathan blushes and looks delighted. He then wanders off to show his star to his friend.

On the wall in the classroom was a chart with all the children's names and the stars awarded to them. It was clear from the observations that the system was used consistently throughout the year and that children were given stars for achievement and effort in both work and behaviour. It was also part of the school's routine for each class teacher to nominate a child each week to receive particular recognition in assembly, who was then publicly rewarded with Maltesers. At an end of term assembly, certificates were handed out. Such explicit use of material rewards was rare, however, and most recognition was in the intrinsic form described several times above – enthusiasm and celebration over something well done for its own sake, though this kind of reinforcement is close to becoming an extrinsic reward. The *discriminating* use of either extrinsic or intrinsic rewards seemed to be another noteworthy feature of some of the more effective teachers. They struck a balance between blanket approval of and enthusiasm for anything children produced and making recognition a rarity. Celebration was regular, but earned.

Displays

One common means of recognising and rewarding children is to display their work publicly. The standard of displays in the classrooms observed varied between very high-quality art work with an emphasis on learning and valuing children's work at one end of the spectrum and a complete lack of interest in display at the other. The norm seemed to be reasonably attractive wall displays changed at least once a term containing samples of children's work, relating to that term's topics, often labelled with statements written or word processed by the teacher or children themselves. In most of these classrooms, there were also displays of books or artefacts related to the current topics.

In some classrooms displays were of a very high artistic quality and were changed at least every half term. The wall displays often included teachers' own statements and questions. Children's writing was regularly put up on the walls and normally included pieces of work by all the pupils in the class, rather than a selected few. Poems, stories, letters to characters in books and factual writing all featured regularly. In one class where display was a notable feature, both parents and children seemed to value them. On a number of occasions children were observed pointing out new displays to parents on arrival at school in the morning. Particularly popular were those which incorporated artefacts which could be handled and the author displays.

Although wall displays were highly esteemed in many classrooms, there were a few teachers for whom display was manifestly not given the same priority. In one class the maths displays during the year far outnumbered language-based ones, there was little use of challenging questions or statements and a few pieces of the more able children's writing were selected for exhibition. Only during the visit of a team of external inspectors did the displays in this teacher's classroom become attractive and interesting with more children's work shown. After this visit in early May the displays were not changed again before the end of the summer term.

In another school, in the two classrooms observed, although large wall areas were available for display, these remained virtually empty for the whole year, and when work was exhibited it tended to be a few pieces of the children's art work, poorly mounted and unattractively set out. As a result the classrooms had a bleak and uninviting appearance. The lack of display of children's own writing must raise questions about the messages this sent to children concerning how their work was being valued. Not only was no work exhibited on walls, but in neither of these classrooms were there any 'class books' of children's writing – a common feature in most of the other classes studied.

There is no doubt that good displays make a more attractive environment to work in, but the evidence from the reading test results suggests that they are not a predictor of improved reading standards. When we analysed the children's test scores at the end of the school year, a greater improvement had actually been made in the two classes where display was apparently neglected, than in some of the classes where display was clearly considered to be extremely important. It might equally be argued, therefore, that the large amount of time some teachers spent creating attractive walls for their classroom might have been better spent planning and evaluating their teaching of reading. Although wall displays are often greatly esteemed by children, teachers, heads and visitors, on the basis of test score improvement, at any rate, we did not find any clear evidence that they either helped or hindered progress.

Teachers' perceptions of successful and less successful activities

At the end of the year of observation, teachers were asked what they felt in their teaching of reading had been particularly successful during the year. Their responses covered strategies which they believed had benefited individual children, the acquisition or reorganisation of resources, and school policy issues:

> Some very strong phonics work – that's made a terrific difference to three children in particular.
>
> > (Year 3 teacher)

> Big books – everyone joined in and it made every child think they were a reader.
>
> > (Reception class teacher)

> Getting the Scholastic boxes – we didn't have any group read novel type of books before. There are multiple copies and they also come with a great big book of suggestions and information about the books, themes etc.
>
> > (Year 3 teacher)

[We've] made a reading corner in the corridor. All the books are on the shelves and no longer in boxes. We've also put bean bags out there – that's made a difference.

(Year 6 teacher)

Using ability groups for teaching skills.

(Year 5 teacher)

Reading meetings for parents. We only got six at first, but then we nagged and got about 50%. It allows us to explain what we're doing and cuts out adverse comments.

(Reception class teacher)

The responses of the thirty-five teachers were analysed to see if any general trends could be identified either within schools in the same region or within key stages. In most cases, however, the replies were individual and personal to the teacher and school concerned, each particular strategy or activity being mentioned by only one or two teachers, though several mentioned group reading or other strategies that appeared to focus children's attention on some aspect of a text. The particular focus varied with age and ability: for example, punctuation and letter combinations with classes of 5 and 6 year olds; book reviews and work on language in a Year 2 group; the introduction of a wider range of materials, discussion of meaning, characters and plot as appropriate to different age levels.

Praise and encouragement were mentioned by a third of teachers as particularly important tools for improving children's personal self-esteem and confidence in their own reading ability. It was common for teachers to express this encouragement in the form of smiley faces in home/school reading diaries. One teacher of young infants used other adults to express further approval:

If they've read really nicely to me, I'll take them along and ask Mr G. if he's got five minutes to hear them, which they think is wonderful – that they've been asked to be heard by the Year 2 teacher.

Most teachers agreed that it was *regular* rather than sporadic reading activities that were important and that children should have access to a wide range of quality fiction and non-fiction materials.

It was a commonly held view of class teachers that the most successful approach with less able or reluctant readers was closely aligned to what they believed worked well with beginning readers. Phonics teaching and the structure of a reading scheme with its repetition of key words were features frequently mentioned by teachers. Paradoxically this was sometimes the very approach that had failed the children so far. A related problem commonly identified by Key Stage 2 teachers was the lack of appropriate reading scheme materials for the more mature child. Many teachers said they had personally spent time searching for material with a more sophisticated content but in accessible language which would appeal to the interests of their reluctant Year 5 and Year 6 readers and suggested that there was a need for more commercially published reading schemes aimed at this type of child.

From the teachers' accounts, it appeared that their current beliefs and practices had their foundations in several sources: the framework provided by the school's reading policy; their own experience of what types of approaches and materials worked well for them and their pupils; a sharing of expertise with colleagues. A number of teachers talked of finding ideas for reading activities in educational publications. There was also evidence that distal factors such as LEA initiatives could have an impact on practice in the classroom. In two of the authorities in which our case study schools were located, it was clear that the LEA had taken a high profile. Teachers in Birmingham referred to the Year of Reading, Reading Recovery, big books, methods of assessment, and receiving funding for reading projects within their schools, as successful macro-strategies by their LEA, while in the second authority collaborative group reading was mentioned enthusiastically. In the remaining two authorities, however, this type of strategic role had not been adopted. Over three-quarters of the class teachers interviewed in these authorities said they were unaware of any recent LEA initiatives to do with reading. At case study level this confirmed the very varied perception of the quality of LEA support which came through so strongly in the national questionnaire.

7

TEACHING READING SKILLS

Accounts of primary school teachers in the mass media have sometimes suggested that they are divided into two camps: the 'traditionalists', who esteem structure, put a premium on accurate grammar, spelling and punctuation, prefer to teach phonics, and the 'progressives', often labelled 'trendies' in some newspapers, who eschew structure, use 'Real Books' rather than reading schemes, and ignore formal features of language when teaching children to read. We did not seek to assign teachers to any preordained categories in this research project, but rather to interview and observe teachers, analyse the data, and then report practices from the thirty-five case study classrooms in Study 3.

There were some similarities in the approaches adopted by the infant teachers in our case study schools. Reception class teachers had usually said in interview that they concentrated on familiarising children with books and how they work, teaching them that pictures tell stories and that print carries meaning. Most of the teachers of 6 and 7 year olds talked of building up children's reading confidence, providing a wider range of reading materials and introducing them to basic research skills which would translate reading competence into action. This last aspiration included learning how to use the school library. Almost all talked specifically of particular reading skills they sought to introduce and develop.

Phonics teaching

Almost all the infant teachers in the sample spontaneously mentioned in interview the importance of developing children's phonic awareness, and all of them taught it, though the way in which it was done varied. A number of schools used structured reading schemes with a phonics component, like *Letterland*, in the early years, while others had devised their own structured phonics programme. Phonics teaching usually took place as a timetabled lesson once a week:

[We cover a] weekly letter for initial sounds.

(Reception/Year 1 teacher)

[We have] a formal session each week. Started with single letters, now doing word patterns.

(Year 2/3 teacher)

Letterland, an hour a week, writing and matching sounds.

(Year 1 teacher)

In only a small number of cases did the phonics teaching display an *ad hoc* approach. In these cases teachers were more likely to concentrate on the learning of initial letter sounds. Although systematic phonics teaching continued in the junior school, it was clear from the teachers' comments that, in Years 4, 5 and 6, it was mainly employed as a strategy for helping less able readers who had not yet acquired sufficient mastery of letters and sounds, often through the use of a phonics-based published reading scheme such as *Fuzz Buzz*.

A notable feature of teachers' own descriptions of phonics teaching was the absence of technical terminology. Terms such as 'phonemes' and 'graphemes' were almost never used. Teachers usually referred to 'initial letter sounds' or 'blends', but employed little of the formal language of the literature on reading. However, there was no evidence that knowledge of the correct terminology was necessary for effective phonics teaching to take place. Examples of phonics teaching were observed in approximately two-thirds of the classes studied, with the majority taking place in infant schools. Developing children's phonological awareness was considered a key strategy in the teaching of reading, writing and spelling and structure. In most cases progression in phonics teaching formed part of the school's written language policy.

In one school, where 'phonics' was a timetabled session once a week, differentiated activities were provided for children of all abilities, supplemented by phonics games with classroom assistants or sessions that took place 'on the carpet' with the whole class. At the back of each of the Year 1 children's home/school reading diary was written the complete alphabet. The adult to whom the child read was supposed to check the children's knowledge of the letter sounds at regular intervals. As a reinforcement of the phonics work in this class, parents were asked to 'sound out' the word lists sent home. The teacher felt this was an important way of developing children's spelling.

Children's awareness of phonics had sometimes commenced before they even started school. In one of the infant schools studied, *Letterland* formed the basis of the phonics teaching. Several of the children who had attended the local playgroup had been introduced to the *Letterland* characters in the two terms before they started school. They had visited the Reception class one afternoon a week, during which time they undertook activities related to the *Letterland* scheme led by their playgroup leader within the classroom. When they started school, the Reception class teacher built on knowledge they had already acquired and parents were encouraged to buy *Letterland* books and videos for use at home. By contrast another teacher in the sample had given up the use of *Letterland* and felt the children had done just as well without it.

One teacher was enthusiastic about seeking out new ways to make learning phonics enjoyable. She was observed trying out an activity she had seen in *Child Education*.

The whole class is sitting on the carpet.

Teacher: Who can remember from yesterday what a tongue twister is?
Pupil 1: Something which, if you say it fast, twists your tongue up!
Teacher: Absolutely right, Tom. What was special about the tongue twisters you made up yesterday?
Pupil 2: Each word started with the same sound.

The teacher asks one child to read hers out, then gets her to read it out faster and faster. Great hilarity in the class as they all try to say it faster and faster. She then organises the different groups' activities and retains a group of six lower-ability children on the carpet.

Teacher: Ruth, think of an animal that you might like your tongue twister to be about.
Ruth: Mouse.

The teacher takes out the *Letterland* card of 'Munching Mouse' and shows it to the children. She writes the word 'mouse' on an easel stressing the initial letter sound. 'Now we need a name.' She takes suggestions from all the other children and then lets Ruth choose 'Mama', which she writes on the easel, again stressing the sounds.

Teacher: The next word must start with 'm' (*Sounded out*) too.
Various children suggest 'met' and 'made', before the group decides on 'met'. Then Ruth chooses 'Mary' to round off the sentence.

Teacher: Can you say that really fast, again and again?

There is great mirth as children do this. The teacher then goes through the same process for each child in the group.

With the more able children, the teacher said in interview, she had worked through a couple of examples with them and then let them develop their own tongue twisters. At the end of the school year, when the children in this class moved into Year 2, the large majority of them were reading confidently and competently for their age.

With junior-age children phonics teaching was most commonly employed as a form of remediation for those who had not made good progress in the infant school. In Marshlands School, amid general concern about the reading standards of children, the approach had been formalised. In an attempt to address the reading problem, a 'Language Rescue Group' of the least able readers in the two Year 3 classes had been set up, which was taken in the first term by one of the Year 3 teachers and later on in the school year by the head teacher. According to the Year 3 teacher, the intention was to give these children a quite specific phonics input every day for half an hour. Part of such a session, observed early in the school year, is described below:

The teacher writes 'th', 'sh' and 'ch' at the head of three columns on the blackboard.

Teacher: Can anyone tell me anything about these?
Pupil: (*Indicating a word on the blackboard*) She.
Teacher: Very good Luke ... which letters on the board start the word 'she'?

Luke points to 'sh'. The teacher then stresses the sound 'ch' makes 'ch', not 'cher'.

Teacher: [There's] no 'er' sound at the end ... let's all practise saying it.

They do so.

Teacher: Now what words can I make for each of these columns?

As children suggest words, she writes them in the columns on the board, highlighting the difference between 'sh' and 'ch'. When four or five words have been written under each sound, the teacher asks the children to choose one word and, without looking at it again on the board, to write the word they have chosen and then check it against the word on the board. She asks them to do this for four more words.

In the same school, another Year 3 teacher was observed taking a phonics session with a middle-ability set of pupils drawn from two parallel classes. They were looking at initial consonant blends, working through a scheme. The teacher recalled the previous week's blend 'bl' before introducing the one for that session 'cl'. Children suggested various words, he asked them about the meaning of each one before writing it on the board, and afterwards they had to choose six words to put in sentences, so as to display their awareness of meaning.

A later session observed with the same Language Rescue Group mentioned earlier, but on this occasion taken by the head teacher, seemed inconsistent with the 'reading in context and with understanding' approach of the other Year 3 teachers:

The head teacher is sitting on a chair next to a whiteboard easel. The children sit in front of her on the floor with their clipboards, paper and pencils. She says: 'OK, see if you can write this four letter word – "glad".'
    The children write on their paper.

Head teacher: Sarah, what did you get for your first two letters?
Sarah: g – l (*Sounding letters*).

The head writes these on the whiteboard.

Head: Michael, what did you get for the last part of the word?
Michael: a – d (*Giving letter names*).

She then does the same with four more words: 'flick', 'club', 'plan' and 'blob'.

Head: You can't sound out every word you read. I'd rather you learn the words, rather than sound them. If you don't know a word, you can guess it sometimes by reading what's before and what's after it.

She then takes out flashcards with single unrelated words written on them.

Head: Right, what do you notice about this word?' (*Holding up the word 'class'*).

Children's responses include: 'It starts with c – l' [giving letter names]; 'It has two s's in it' [giving letter names].

Head: Right just say the letters of the word.

> The children do this in unison. She then runs through the other words to see if the children know them. When they get stuck on 'touch' she says: 'When you're guessing, your first sound can help you, not to sound it out, but just as a hint.'

The aim of this lesson was difficult to understand in relation to the school's stated policy and the practice and beliefs of the class's regular Year 3 teachers. Having emphasised in interview the usefulness of context to read unknown words, the head teacher then produced single decontextualised words on flashcards. She did not attempt to find a phonics context, for example by identifying similarly configured words, in which children could have identified a pattern, as in an 'onset and rime' approach. The head and the teachers took pride in what they believed was a co-ordinated approach towards the teaching of reading in general, and in the work of the Language Rescue Group in particular, but the perceived consistency was not always observed in practice.

Although this school had a very structured scheme and organisation for the teaching of phonics, it seemed to have produced a culture of dependency, rather than one of independence. When the researcher interviewed the children in the class and asked what they would do if they met a word they did not know, they all replied 'ask the teacher'. Yet in other classes it was common for children to say they would sound out unfamiliar words phonically. Unless children can make the transfer from the artificiality of blackboard work to the reality of reading and understanding text, structured phonics work may be wasted.

This lack of consistency and the children appearing not to transfer the word attack skills they had supposedly developed to their own reading may partly explain why the second end of year reading test of the majority of children in the Language Rescue Group revealed no relative improvement on their first test score. In the sessions of group reading observed in the Year 3 classes it was rare to hear a teacher suggest to a child using 'sounding out' as a strategy for working out an unknown word. Children's dependency was seen regularly by the researcher. On most occasions when pupils could not recognise a word, another child would supply it, so their progress towards becoming autonomous readers was slower than in other classes observed.

Look and say

As a deliberate strategy in the teaching of reading, 'Look and Say', the process whereby children learned to recognise whole words, was mentioned in interview and observed in practice less frequently than phonics. It seemed more likely to occur in Reception and Year 1 classes to develop sight vocabulary. This was usually done in one or more of three contexts:

1 with frequent-use key words, commonly linked to the early stages of a school's reading scheme, where teachers monitored children's progress through the first 100 key words;
2 with words significant to individual children;
3 (less often) with words related to topics.

Teachers sometimes extended the basic skill of look and say from reading to writing. Accurate spelling was added in by those teachers who developed a sequence whereby children had to scan the word, cover it over, make an attempt at writing it and then check their accuracy – 'Look, Cover, Write, Check'. While some teachers made use of flashcards, a number of teachers explicitly rejected their use in the learning of key words and placed emphasis instead on learning words within context, sometimes around a theme or book they had been reading:

> I would say it's almost always contextualised, so it's maybe within colours, or days of the week, within a topic or story.
>
> (Year 1 teacher)

Several teachers cut up sentences and got the children to rearrange them and then copy or stick them in their books. Sometimes they linked this with phonics by drawing attention to initial letters, so the approach was not purely look and say. The active teaching of sight vocabulary was observed in fewer than a third of the classes studied. In one teacher's Year 1 class, where she endeavoured to make everything a 'fun' activity, she used a game to remind children of the first twelve key words in their scheme:

> The teacher sits on a chair, children sit on the carpet in a circle. She takes from a box the first twelve key words on cards shaped like stones and places these in a row starting at her feet and moving away from her. The cards are face down with the words hidden.
>
> *Teacher:* Who wants to have a go at moving along the stepping stones?
>
> Lots of hands go up. Beth is selected and turns over the first card 'a' and reads it out. She then turns over the next one and reads 'and' but gets stuck on the third word 'he'.
>
> *Teacher:* Well done, Beth. That's really good! Who else would like a go?

Once more many hands are raised. John is selected. He too gets stuck on 'he'. Seven children have turns, but three are unable to read 'that' following 'the'.

The teacher puts her hand over the 'e' in the word 'the' and the 'at' in 'that'.

Teacher: These two words start with the same sound – what is it?

Hands are raised and the child selected says 'th'. The next child then reads 'that' correctly. More children take turns at moving along the stepping stones.

The teacher also chooses a couple of children who have not volunteered and gives them a lot of praise when they read the first word. Where children do need help the teacher offers this by mouthing the initial letter sound. Eventually two pupils manage to do all the twelve key words and they are each clapped by the whole class.

Although there was obviously an element of competition in this activity, no pressure was put by the teacher upon the children. The teacher explained her approach:

I like to make use of language games as much as possible. I use them not only to check the children's sight vocabulary but also to reinforce their phonic awareness. Most of the children find them great fun.

In this class the first 100 key words were written in the back of the children's home/school reading diary and their recognition of these was regularly checked by adults who heard them read. Spelling tests were a weekly feature in this classroom as they were in a number of others. Reception and Year 1 teachers often used games as a vehicle for teaching sight vocabulary. As children moved up the school, there was much less emphasis on learning words in this manner. Where it did feature, it was normally related to vocabulary for a specific topic, and often linked to spelling.

Hearing children read

Two of the interview questions we asked teachers before observing them teach were designed to elicit information about their practice when children read to them. The two questions were: 'If you are listening to a child read and s/he stops at a word, what would you do?' and 'If you are listening to a child read and s/he makes a mistake, for example reads the word "boot" instead of "book", what would you do?'

The responses to the first question suggested that teachers considered it important for children to have a range of strategies for coping with unknown words. A typical reply came from a Reception class teacher:

> You suggest the strategies they could use like: read the part of the sentence again; read on to the end of the sentence; look at the picture; look at the sounds if all else fails, see if they can decode it, look at the shape; does it rhyme with any of the other words? – that sort of thing.

Twenty-nine of the sample of thirty-five case study teachers indicated that they would suggest the use of some sort of phonics-related strategy, usually asking the pupil what the initial letter sound of the word was, and often, if this was not sufficient for children to decode the word, getting them to 'sound out the word'. Context cues were the next most common tool mentioned by teachers. Twenty-three teachers talked of asking children either to re-read a sentence, or to read on to the end of the sentence and then to make a sensible guess. However, observations of teachers and other adults reading with children revealed this was not a frequently used tool in practice, nor did children talk about it either. Expediency and the need to keep track of several children, or maintain the pace of the lesson, meant there was little time for such exploration and perusal.

The importance of encouraging children to make use of pictures cues was highlighted by just over half the teachers interviewed. Children were encouraged to look carefully at the illustrations accompanying the text to see if these could help them identify certain words. Many teachers sought other means of individualising what they did, explaining that the strategies they would use and encourage their pupils to deploy would depend on the child's own stage of reading development and confidence:

> With Jonathan, I would probably mouth the first sound to see if he can get it right because, that way, he feels he's got it right – I haven't told him. With children who are a bit further on, I'd perhaps ask them what it started with, see if they could start to sound it out themselves and then start to blend it, or guide them to the picture if there's something in the picture that would help them.
>
> (Year 1 teacher)

> If it's a struggling reader, you use those things (like) breaking up the word, but if it's a more able reader, you tend to use contextual clues.
>
> (Year 5 teacher)

In some cases, teachers said they would provide the unknown word at once, either because they felt it was important for the child to retain the meaning of the story, or because they felt that struggling with unknown words undermined self-confidence and caused children to take a negative view of reading.

Almost all teachers indicated that if a child read a word incorrectly, but it made sense in the context, they would ignore it. This raises the important issue of whether it is wise to condone errors, as well as the extent to which accuracy is to be sought at all times. Where the word was contextually incorrect, most teachers said they would ask the child 'Does that make sense?' One teacher explained why she felt it was so important to draw their attention to any misread word:

> I certainly pick them up on it because it means that they're not paying attention to what they're doing and they're just decoding stuff and not really understanding it.

Some teachers said they would stop the child almost immediately; the majority said they would wait for the reader to finish the sentence and then if the child did not automatically self-correct, they would ask for the sentence to be read again. Only a very small number of teachers talked of praising children for the part of the word they had read correctly.

Hearing children read is a key means by which the skills of an individual child can be assessed and a time when strategies to help the child can be given on a personalised basis. It is not surprising, therefore, that hearing children read was a regularly observed activity during this research project. Yet the way in which this was undertaken in different classrooms varied considerably, in terms of whose duty it was to hear pupils read, how long pupils read for, which children were chosen to read, and the nature and quality of the reading experience. Important class management issues also emerged from this part of our study, especially in the way that teachers shared out their time. Some teachers handled this aspect well, others less effectively.

Most teachers commented in interview that reading was an invaluable part of the teaching of literacy and many strategies were articulated as being important in helping children read. However, time constraints and the other pressures of hearing pupils read on a one-to-one basis meant that teachers hearing pupils read was not observed to constitute a *major* part of the school day, even though it was regularly observed as an activity. Often the predominant responsibility was passed on to classroom assistants and occasionally to parent helpers. Teachers themselves heard children less frequently, especially in the case of the more able readers. In some classes studied, children interviewed at the end of the school year could not even recall when they had last read to their teacher.

The way in which children were heard to read varied considerably. Indeed, in our observations there was no single entity that could be called 'hearing children read', such was the range of purposes, contexts, strategies and people involved. In one local authority classroom assistants and parent helpers were typically given a list of readers to hear and worked their way through these. In some cases hearing a child read commonly involved the child bringing along their reading scheme or other school book, sitting beside the adult, often at a table where other children were working, and reading for five minutes on average. In other schools pupils would take their books to the teacher who would be sitting at a desk, or in some cases the classroom assistant or special needs teacher would be located outside the classroom, or in another room, and would sit and listen to them read elsewhere.

The adults concerned, particularly in the case of classroom assistants, would prompt the child to use reading strategies such as phonic cues and picture cues. Context cues were less frequently suggested. Little in-depth discussion of the text was observed, although the introduction of reading diaries in some classes was intended as a forum through which children could analyse the text. The child's reading was sometimes recorded in a home/school reading record. What was recorded varied considerably, however, sometimes with nothing more than a brief comment, like 'read well' or 'needed a little help with this', often just with the date on which the book had been completed or the page numbers. In other cases an effort had been made to write meaningful comments and to use symbols such as smiley faces, to indicate that children were progressing well.

Interruptions and distractions were a significant constraint for teachers. By contrast, classroom assistants and parent helpers were less likely to be interrupted by other children when hearing a child read. The observation notes reproduced below exemplify what can happen in a class while a teacher is attempting to hear a child read:

> Robin is reading his book to the teacher. The teacher points to the text with a pencil as he reads. Without warning, the teacher gets up to deal with boys misbehaving at another table. Robin continues reading out loud. ... He stops ... waits for her to come back. She returns to him and says 'I'll be back in a minute.' She then goes over to see another child who is doing some maths work.
>
> After two minutes she returns, sits down, and points to the text again, to the piece Robin has already read out loud to himself. She asks him what a particular word means and explains when he says he doesn't know. She then disengages once more to ask another child to come over and see her, as he was misbehaving. Robin has to wait. ... A girl comes over to see the teacher with her maths work.

Robin still waits. He eventually, without being asked to by the teacher, starts reading out loud again.

The teacher is still engaged in monitoring the misbehaviour of two boys and gets one of them to sit by her. She is again interrupted by a child having problems with her maths work. Robin is still reading out loud, though without an audience. Finally the teacher gives him her attention, listens to him read one page and then says 'That's super, Robin. Well done!' and writes down a comment in her own reading record file.

Though the considerable demands on teachers' time and attention can put a strain on their classroom management skills, it is possible to avoid the poorer-quality reading experience described above, as the following account demonstrates. This event took place in a different classroom during the daily after-lunch session when every child was involved in some kind of reading:

The teacher asks Tom to get his book and come and sit down beside her.

Teacher: Tell me what's happened so far.
Tom: The lion's got the mouse.
Teacher: I wonder what's going to happen. Let's read on and see.

Tom reads slowly, carefully pointing at the text with his finger.

Teacher: Do you think the lion will let the mouse go?
Tom: Yes, I know he will!
Teacher: You've read this story before! (*Laughs*).
Tom: No, I heard Alistair reading it! (*Both laugh*).

Amy [a child new to the class] comes over to show the teacher her book. The teacher says firmly: 'I'm sorry. I'm hearing Tom read. I need to be on my own with Tom. Sorry, Tom . . .' Tom continues to read, self-correcting when he makes a mistake. The teacher sometimes draws his attention to the pictures and they discuss the story as they go along. The teacher gives him lots of praise.

After six minutes, the teacher says: 'Do you mind if we leave it there for today, Tom? I have to hear some other children read too.'

Tom: No, that's all right. Can I read it by myself?
Teacher: Of course. Well done, Tom. You've done really well.

The contrast between the two accounts above reveals the importance of many features, if children are to be heard reading with any success. Crucial ingredients appear to be:

1 *Orderliness* – disruptive behaviour by other pupils is a powerful distractor.
2 *Focus* – it helps if there is a strong focus on reading as the major activity of the moment, so that maths or other problems do not take the teacher away from the principal domain.
3 *Independence* – children not being heard read need to be able to make many of their own decisions, so they are not overly dependent on the teacher; equally, those being heard need independence too, so they can guess intelligently at unfamiliar words.
4 *Priority* – the child being heard needs to have top priority, except in emergencies.
5 *Importance* – reading needs to be made important, so that interruptions are frowned upon.
6 *Worthwhileness* – the book needs to be engaging and worth talking about.

Another teacher observed, by using the half-hour daily ERIC session when the rest of the class were fully occupied with reading, and by reinforcing her rule that she was not to be interrupted while with a child, she was able to give each one an individualised and focused reading experience. She also ensured that when the classroom assistant or parent helpers read with a child they were seated away from other children and not interrupted.

Infant-age children were likely to read more regularly to the teacher than those in junior schools, where it was generally only the less able readers who did so. Several teachers mentioned that it was better to hear children less often but in a more concentrated fashion, diagnosing their mistakes and discussing their progress with them. Many kept quite detailed records of the child's progress, and these were filled in by whichever adult heard the child. Two teachers had found that they were not hearing the better readers and so arranged to give children a special day when they would guarantee to hear them. Most children knew which book to read, or could easily find an appropriate one, but occasionally children in some classes would pick something way beyond them, or others would pick the easiest one they could find.

Writing and spelling

Meticulous attention to accuracy was also an issue when it came to children learning to write, especially in the case of spelling. Approaches towards the teaching of spelling differed in the classes studied. In a Year 2 class, when writing, children were told by the teacher 'Don't worry about your spelling. I want you to get your ideas down on paper. We can worry about the spellings later.' In a Year 3 class, children were asked to 'Make your best guess now. Then you can check your spellings later for when you're writing up your final copy.' In a combined Reception/Year 1/Year 2 class, children were encouraged to use a 'magic line' if they did not know how to spell a word. This involved writing the initial letter followed by a line, a strategy which for some children resulted in nothing more than a succession of lines which they could not possibly read back.

One Year 2 teacher initiated 'I can try' books in an attempt to increase the pupils' confidence in their own ability to spell. Each time they did not know a word they were expected to try it for themselves before the teacher would write the correct version in their books. This was a stark contrast to practice in another class, where a Year 3 teacher was regularly surrounded by pupils holding their small personal word books which were divided into the letters of the alphabet. They would merely state the word they required and the teacher would write it in their books. The same teacher also conveyed the message to the pupils that they should not worry about their spellings, but just get their ideas down on paper.

Many children, however, did want to know how to spell a word. One Year 1 teacher had tried to take a more effective approach, providing a larger 'word book' in which each page was divided into three columns. Pupils had to write down how they thought the word should be spelled, and then the teacher either ticked their version if it was right, or wrote down the correct spelling in the second column. The child would then have to cover the correct spelling and write the word down from memory in the third column, before including the word in a piece of writing. In this class children were also encouraged to make use of the large picture dictionaries and these were laid on the desks by the teacher before most writing activities.

In a Year 5 class the teacher was very keen on children learning to spell correctly, but tried to avoid restricting their vocabulary if they thought they would be unable to spell the word correctly. When engaged in writing they were told to check their work through and have it read by the teacher before it was printed, if they were unsure of words they were told to look them up in their dictionary. To balance this she told the children in one lesson: 'Don't worry about the spellings at this point. … Spelling is important, but don't let it put you off using exciting words.' She then told them that she herself often had to make sure about things by going and looking them up in the dictionary.

In some classes children learned spellings on a regular basis and were tested. In Mrs Munroe's class children took a list of spellings in a word book home to learn and were tested on these on a set day each week. She believed it was important for children to learn words in phonic families, so on one weekend the list of words for the older children to learn had been 'moon, spoon, soon, noon, loop, hoop, shoot, boot'. In other classes, the words were taken from the first 100 key words in the reading scheme.

When a Year 2 child in one school, however, was asked by the researcher what he did about spellings he did not know, he replied 'Spellings don't matter in this class'. The stress placed by some teachers on the need for children's creative writing to be allowed to flow needs to be balanced with an emphasis on developing their understanding of the importance of accurate spelling. Teachers of young children in particular should be aware that this attitude could become entrenched and difficult to counter in later years.

Observation of teachers and spelling raise two important issues, therefore. The first is to do with effective classroom management. Some teachers allowed themselves to become buried beneath queues of pupils in quest of correct spellings, while others encouraged the use of dictionaries. Pupil independence is an element which figured more than once as an important factor in effective teaching and learning, and the high degree of dependency on the teacher in some classrooms will reduce the opportunities for autonomous thinking and action. The second issue is that of emphasis and learning. If accurate spelling is perceived to be unimportant, then the danger is that children use, and therefore learn, inaccurate forms. It is then extraordinarily difficult to graft on 'correct' forms at a later stage. Unlearning is often much more difficult than learning itself, as two components are needed: deletion and insertion.

Punctuation

In those classes where spelling was emphasised, there was also a tendency to stress the importance of punctuation. Sentences starting with a capital letter and ending with a full stop were the main principle observed being taught. In one school, the head teacher prided herself on the school's thorough approach to the teaching of language, and from Reception onwards the children's attention was drawn to spelling and punctuation in their pieces of written work. The event described below was typical of the Year 1 teacher's approach to punctuation:

> The children are undertaking a writing activity as part of a science topic. They have to draw pictures of something being 'pushed' and something being 'pulled'. Under each picture they have to write a sentence.
>
> The teacher is moving around the classroom monitoring the children's work. She notices that someone has not started a sentence properly.

Teacher: Right, can everyone stop for a minute, please? Can you tell me what a sentence starts with?

About three-quarters of the class put their hands up. Teacher selects a boy.

Boy: A capital letter.
Teacher: Good boy! That's right. It starts with a capital letter. (*To class*) Does it always start with a capital letter?

All those children who call out say, 'Yes!'

Teacher: That's right! Well done! And who can tell us what a sentence ends with?

Again lots of hands go up. Teacher selects a girl.

Girl: A full stop!
Teacher: Well done, Sally. So, as I move around the classroom, I want to see you all using a capital letter at the beginning of your sentence and a full stop at the end.

The teacher explained her approach:

> I feel it's really important that children learn early on about punctu-
> ation. I was really pleased when we were talking about what they'd
> done at half term, getting them ready to write about it, that when
> I'd asked them what sorts of things they had to remember, when
> writing, they knew about the capital letters and full stops, and they
> talked about letters 'sitting on the line' and doing neat writing.

In another school, a Year 3 teacher was still having to remind children about the nature and structure of sentences, but her humorous animation of punc-tuation features seemed rather more engaging of children's attention than most of the ways in which we observed punctuation being discussed:

Teacher: When you're telling me about the characters and the story, make sure your writing is in proper sentences. What do I mean by a 'proper' sentence?
Girl: Capital letter at the beginning.
Teacher: Yes, all sentences have a capital letter at the beginning. It's a way of saying 'Hello, I'm a new sentence'. What about the end?
Boy: Full stop.
Teacher: That's right. The full stop's another message. It's saying 'Right, I've finished now!'

In another class well-presented writing received public recognition and reward, just as was reported earlier in the case of reading:

The teacher is sitting on her chair, the children are on the carpet.

Teacher: Catherine, are you feeling proud today?

Catherine looks at her.

Teacher: You should be! Catherine has done lots of work and she's put in all the things I wanted her to, like capital letters and full stops and she hasn't used 'And then ...'. Catherine, I think that this is the best work you've ever done!

The teacher gives Catherine a sticker.

By contrast, one teacher was less willing to take the time to explain grammatical and punctuation mistakes. She chose instead to reprimand a child for attempting to use paragraphs when he did not understand how to do so:

A Year 6 class was doing language work. One child, Martin, who had earlier been moved by the teacher for misbehaving, took his book to show the teacher. The teacher studied the text and asked him why he had been missing lines out. Another child intervened and told the teacher that in their previous class they had been told to miss lines out for a new paragraph. The teacher turned and told Martin that she had not told him to miss lines out and then sent him back to his seat.

She later told the rest of the class: 'Some pupils are trying to use paragraphs and they don't know how to use them. So if you don't know how to use them, don't. A paragraph is not a sentence or a few words, so don't use them if you don't know how.' Nothing further was mentioned about paragraphs in that lesson.

In this example pupils are told what a paragraph is *not*, but are given no means to help them understand what a paragraph actually *is*. Clearly their previous teacher had gone some way to exploring the use of paragraphs, but not far enough for the children to be able to apply them correctly. Unless their new teacher addressed the issue, it was unlikely that they would be able to before going to secondary school. The policy of this teacher was that pupils worked in their jotters first, then they had their work corrected and finally their text was neatly rewritten out. The teacher commented that she always corrected all their mistakes, although this was not always evident.

Correcting mistakes is not, however, the same as explaining them and it is not surprising if confusion arises.

In one school where they used a 'Real Books' approach to reading, many of the Reception and Year 1 pupils had difficulty decoding words in their reading books. When questioned about punctuation they were clear that sentences started with capital letters and ended with full stops. Some pupils, however, had not learned rules properly and became confused. One pupil commented authoritatively that a sentence started with the word 'The' and ended with a full stop. He knew this because 'we do work with full stops'. The other pupils who were interviewed in this class were equally confused about how a sentence started, but were clear about a full stop going at the end.

It was surprising, however, that we observed very little correspondence between punctuation and reading. Many children, when asked to read out aloud, read their text in a halting, staccato manner. This was partly because they did not always understand what they were reading. In one Reception class, however, the teacher actually asked children to speak the words 'full stop' when one occurred in the text. It seemed strange to hear a pupil reading, 'My name is Imran – full stop', but by June most children were no longer reading them aloud and were using them accurately in their written work.

It was relatively rare for teachers to point out that punctuation can offer important cues about units of meaning and inform the reader on when to take a breath, insert a pause, or give emphasis. Punctuation seemed to be something that was taught or commented on when children were writing, but not a topic that figured so strongly when they were reading. Giving children a second chance to read a phrase or sentence once more, but this time with meaning in the light of the punctuation cues, was also infrequently observed.

Making progress in reading

Once children have made a start on reading there are many strategies teachers employ to move them on to higher levels of competence in the later stages of infant schools and throughout the junior stage. We observed a wide range of activities which teachers devised in order to give meaning to reading, to cover different genres, to offer children texts that would help them to improve their writing, or otherwise to improve their individual skills as readers.

In the literature about reading, discussions concerning 'higher-order reading skills' have often implied that these are approached when a child has become a competent reader. Some commentators have questioned whether the ability to scan, skim, slow down when necessary, make notes of summary, use reference works and libraries, should even be called 'higher order' at all. The majority of infant and junior school teachers in this study did not actively discriminate any putative 'higher' or 'lower' levels, as the

teaching of decoding skills often operated in parallel with providing opportunities to discuss books, to enhance the children's understanding of text
and to develop their information retrieval skills. A teacher of a Year 1 class
explained how the 5 year olds in her class were becoming familiar with the
school library which operated a simplified Dewey system:

> They have a library skills session, once a week, and I concentrate on
> fiction and non-fiction and where they are in the library and how
> they would find, say, a book on dinosaurs, if that's what they were
> looking for.

Junior school teachers, responding to the question 'How do you teach
reading?', revealed differences in their perceptions of what teaching reading
to older pupils involved and the level of priority it was given. Many teachers
talked enthusiastically of extending children's information retrieval expertise
and teaching the skills of skimming and scanning. One Year 3 teacher, who
was an English literature graduate, had particularly strong views about the
need for children to analyse and compare texts and emphasised more than
others the need to introduce the children to a wide range of genres. Another
teacher mentioned how she developed children's own use of expression
through the reading of scripted plays.

Not all junior school teachers talked with the same degree of knowledge
of children's literary and language competence. For some teachers, once a
child could decode fluently, reading became a peripheral concern:

> It's incidental because they're reading all the time, so it's not taught
> to the same extent as it would be with younger children.
>
> (Year 6 teacher)

Reading materials and resources

In the large majority of schools studied, as was the case in the national questionnaire results reported earlier, infant-age children gained some familiarity
with at least one commercially published reading scheme. In some schools
this was a single scheme; in the majority of schools a number of different
schemes had been grouped together in colour-coded stages of difficulty. In
most schools children were allowed to choose freely within a colour band,
but in a small number the teachers took a more interventionist stance and
insisted that children read through the books in numerical order, only
allowing them to move on when they could read each book competently.

'Structure' and 'progression' were identified as the key advantages of
schemes by this sample of teachers, and a number commented on the useful
repetition of key words, although other teachers saw this as a disadvantage,
making the text stilted and boring. Three teachers admitted that they liked

having a reading scheme because it was easy for them to use. These tended to be teachers who had qualified more recently and did not feel they had sufficient personal knowledge to structure their pupils' reading themselves. Some teachers, much to their surprise, had found that their children really liked the commercially produced reading scheme books and would choose them even when they had free choice. There was a general consensus that reading schemes had improved over the last ten years, both in content of story and in the quality of illustrations.

The most commonly articulated disadvantage was that graded reading schemes encouraged competition. However, one teacher rejected this:

> I suppose if you go back to the old criticisms, it was that children were competitive and they weren't learning to love books, they were learning to climb the book ladder, but I think children still compare their own reading skills with other children and I think it's really about handling books and children's abilities sensibly and sensitively.

In another school where concern about its reading standards had led to the introduction of a reading scheme, the teacher of a Year 2/3 class disliked the competition this had engendered but acknowledged that there had been some benefits:

> The children have become very competitive about it, which I don't really like, but at least it's got them reading!

Consciously or intuitively teachers tended to minimise the disadvantages of reading schemes by treating schemes as if they were 'Real Books' and reading the stories, introducing and discussing the characters, and by using several schemes or schemes and supplements. Junior schools in our sample used reading schemes more flexibly, selecting them for certain children.

Although commercially published reading schemes were in place in all but one of the case study schools, teachers were keen to explain that children were given access to 'Real Books' (any book not part of a commercial reading scheme). Schemes alone were thought to be too narrow and it was considered important that children felt able to tackle all sorts of reading material and not just materials that looked like 'a reading book'. Nearly all the class-rooms studied had some sort of 'book corner' containing a variety of fiction and non-fiction materials. Although more rare in Reception and Year 1 classes, children would also have access to the school library and were able to take home books usually once a week. In all of the schools studied, once children had reached a certain level of fluency, they were weaned off the reading scheme and on to 'Real Books'.

The resources in the classrooms had been selected in a number of different ways. Topic book loans from the Schools Library Service (SLS) featured in all schools as an important contribution to teachers' resources. Some teachers had personally visited their local SLS and selected their 'exchange books' for their class libraries and their half-termly boxes of books, but this was fairly rare. It was more common for teachers to put in a request stating the term's topics and to leave it to the SLS to make up the pack. Other reading materials were drawn from the school's own library collection. In some classes the teacher had asked the children what sort of books they would like in their classroom. In others children had been directly involved in the selection of books from the school library. In the majority of classrooms, the main collection of books remained static throughout the year, only topic books being changed. In a few, the materials were changed by swapping with others from the school library on a termly basis. The external services used by teachers, like the SLS, are discussed again in Chapter 8.

Only a few teachers were seen using, or mentioned in interview, materials other than books – for example, newspapers, magazines and comics – although Miss Brown, a Year 1 teacher described more fully in Chapter 9, made them a regular feature of her 'home corner' during the first term. In subsequent terms, as the corner became a shop and then a travel agent, appropriate reading materials such as catalogues and brochures were included. Given the limited variety of type of text available in some classrooms, other teachers might consider extending the type of reading material available in the ways that some of the more ingenious did here.

Analysis of text

Teachers in interview often talked of trying to instil a 'love of reading' in children and most used this or similar phraseology when describing their perceptions of literacy. It was seen as a major motivating vehicle for improving reading in a 'natural' way. During observation researchers saw several examples of teachers trying to instil this positive attitude to reading through analysis of the skilful use by authors of written language, as in the following event:

> Mrs Simmons reads a poem to her Year 5 class. At the end she comments: 'The English language is so rich, it's so full of words to describe. Sometimes we have six words that nearly describe the same thing, I want you to pick the best word.'
>
> The pupils are then set an exercise where they have to write a poem that starts 'I would like to paint ...'. The pupils are asked to sit quietly and think of images. After a while the teacher stops the class and suggests it would be nice to share their thoughts with others.

One boy appears to have captured the essence of the exercise, concluding: 'I would like to paint a bee buzzing, squeezing, ducking through the golden daffodils, gathering nectar on its way. I would like to paint the satisfaction of finishing a book a thousand pages long. I should like to paint the excitement of the moment a baby is born.'

Whether or not teachers can instil 'a love of books', or merely foster it, is difficult to say. However, this teacher's lessons, featuring as they did the explicit analysis and exploration of text, did appear to nurture a positive attitude to language, books and the written word.

Poetry

Although the *writing* of poetry, often linked to the current term's topic, was observed in over half the classrooms, the *reading* of poetry, other than children's own work, was less evident. In one school it was often included as a group activity during the Year 3 daily 'Reading Time'. In one session observed, a classroom assistant worked with a group of medium-ability children with a poem from *Please Mrs Butler* by Allan Ahlberg. Each child had a photocopy of the poem. When they returned to the classroom, they read the poem to the rest of the class, half the group taking one part, the other another part. After the group had performed the poem, the teacher said: 'Would you mind if I read it now? I love that poem!' As she read the poem with lots of expression the rest of the class joined in.

In a second session a teacher worked for half an hour with a group of higher-ability children, all of whom were girls, encouraging them to analyse and compare two poems with an interrelated theme. Part of that session went as follows:

> The teacher reads a poem called 'The Mystery Creatures' by Wes Magee. His voice is expressing shock.
>
> *Teacher:* Why do you think I was reading it like that?
> *Anne:* Because you were scared.
> *Teacher:* Yes. Why was I scared?
> *Anne:* Because you'd never seen the creatures before.
> *Teacher:* Good, that's right. What do you think the poem is describing?
>
> It is, in fact, describing human babies but the girls think it's referring to pigs.
>
> *Teacher:* Hadn't you realised the poem was describing human beings?
> *Katy:* Human beings don't grunt!

Teacher: What sort of human beings do you think it's talking about?
Anne: Babies!
Teacher: Yes, well done.

The teacher then gives out photocopied sheets of another poem and asks the girls to read this to themselves. He then tries to draw out how they think the second poem is different from the first. The group finds this difficult and the teacher re-reads a couple of lines of the poem.

Teacher: Who do you think is speaking in each of the two poems?

In fact, the first poem is written by an alien about human babies and the second is written by a human about aliens. After more prompting by the teacher, Anne, who has dominated the discussion, eventually realises this. The teacher then gets them to read the poems again to themselves. The session ends.

During the interview following the lesson, the teacher stated that he was pleased with the activity, saying it had gone very well.

It's great to have the space to give the brighter ones a chance to get to grips with some real thinking about poems. We spend so much time worrying about the less able children, it's important to provide activities which extend the brighter ones.

The researcher's observations of the activity included a study of individual pupils. There seemed to be a lack of interest in the task amongst the group, except for Anne, who was particularly enthusiastic. It may be that the activity was simply too difficult, or that the poems themselves did not capture the pupils' interest and imagination. While it is no doubt important that children should engage in more demanding text-related tasks, there is a need to ensure that children do not become disaffected with poetry by activities which do not engage them. A different teacher, described below, seemed to be more successful in gaining the attention of a greater number in poetry:

It is a quarter of an hour before lunch time.

Teacher: Oh good. We've got some time this morning for some more poetry. … (*Holds up Shel Silverstein's 'A Night in the Attic' from which she has used a poem earlier in the morning as a stimulus for the children's own poetry writing.*) Would anyone like to read 'Mrs MacWitter'?

A large number of children put their hands up, one is selected and reads it confidently to the class. After this another child volunteers and is selected to read a different poem, which she reads with great expression.

Teacher: Well done. That was really good, reading it out like that. OK, now I'm going to read you my favourite poem. It's called 'The Bridge'. Close your eyes and see if it gives you any pictures in your head.

When the teacher finishes reading, a child asks 'Can we see the picture [the illustration in the poetry book]?' The teacher explains why it is her favourite poem: 'It's a bridge which doesn't quite span a river, so it's like teaching. We can only teach you so much, the rest you have to do yourselves.'

The poems selected in this class seemed to be better suited to the children's interests, and the regular use of poems, allied to the teacher's own enthusiasm, made a powerful combination for grasping and then sustaining the class's attention.

Story tapes

Story tapes and tape machines were seen in many of the classrooms visited, but were only observed being utilised in nine of the classes. In one classroom books and tapes containing fairy stories were displayed in the reading corner during the summer term and were used as a stimulus for the children writing their own fairy tales. In another classroom, the tape machine was used to play a taped book to which the whole class listened. The teacher explained that she had taped this story from the radio because it provided an opportunity for her to address with the class the concept of 'truth'. She said she had been unable to find a book to read to the pupils which was 'as powerful a story'.

Those teachers whose pupils did use story tapes were more likely to employ commercially produced ones, but one Year 5 teacher made a point of recording her own. In this classroom there was a high degree of meticulous organisation and autonomous pupil self-management. A rota for pupils to listen to story tapes had been established, and every pupil was allocated to a story tape group. The story tapes were regularly observed in use and when the pupils listened to the tapes they all appeared keen to sit and listen quietly, systematically following the story with an individual copy of the book to which it related.

One typical lesson observed saw the children enter from the playground and immediately get out the books for ERIC time. Four children who were on the rota to do story tapes went straight over to the tape corner and sat with their copies of *When My Naughty Little Sister Was Good*. When they had finished, one child, whose responsibility it was, put their tape away and got out the tape for the next group. The next group sat quietly and listened to the first chapter of their tape. When it was finished, one group member asked the teacher if they could listen to another chapter. When told they could, there were gasps of excitement and then the next chapter was listened to quietly by all the pupils, whilst following the story from the corresponding books.

On another occasion when the children were told to pack the story tapes away, two pupils were overheard commenting: 'Ah, I was enjoying that. Weren't you Mark?' The teacher overheard this exchange as well, and told them that they could finish listening to it after lunch. She was the school's language co-ordinator and her use of story tapes was the most meticulously planned we observed anywhere, clearly an enjoyable event for all the children. As language co-ordinator she also encouraged other teachers in the school to do the same:

> Children can listen to taped stories whilst following the text and then discuss aspects of their reading with the teacher. Should any suitable books of short stories be available at the Book Fair (or from any other source) it would be helpful if teachers would select four identical copies and make a tape of these. At the moment most commercially produced taped stories are very long and cannot be used practically.

Plays

Simple plays featured strongly in some teachers' lessons. In some cases they were plays that the teacher had chosen, in others they were part of some published scheme used in the school, as in the case of the *Story Chest* reading scheme. In one school, the teacher gave a high priority to this aspect of children's reading and pupils were encouraged to perform plays not only to the class but also in the school assembly, suggesting that this was part of the whole-school culture. Those performing plays were given time during 'Reading Time' sessions to rehearse and they had access to the school's stock of fancy dress costumes for their performances. A typical event is described below:

> Three children, two boys and one girl, stand at the front of the classroom. The teacher and the rest of the class are their audience. The three are quarrelling over who should introduce the play.
>
> *Teacher:* Why not all say it together?

They do this. One of the boys is a spaceman, the girl is a granny, the role of the second boy is unclear. All are dressed up in costumes. The children perform the play, reading the script from their own personal copies of the *Story Chest* play. All children perform with great confidence, using sound effects and facial expressions.

When it is over, the teacher says: 'That was really good, Dan, the expression you used in your voice. Can anyone think of a word that describes Kylie's character?'

Hands go up, a child is selected: 'Fussy'.

Dan: She sounded really old.
Teacher: Yes, she did. That was very convincing, Kylie. Well done, you three, great. Take a bow.

As they do so there is enthusiastic clapping from the audience.

Pupils were also asked in some classrooms to adapt books into plays. The example below shows how this task was used with a Year 2 class:

One group are going off with a parent to read a play. Before they go the teacher discusses the play with the class. She holds a book up and asks them which parts they would not read. She then explains to them that the 'slopey' writing is an instruction. She suggests that they should have one read through first as a practice.

After the group have left the teacher gives the rest of the class instructions on what they are to do. One group are asked to write a play. The teacher makes suggestions, such as: 'It is easiest to tell a story you know well, like *The Three Little Pigs.*' The teacher comments that they should write what they think the person would say. She suggests that they can look at any of the books in the book corner to remind them.

The pupils start work on their task, discussing what they have to do. The teacher goes over and checks on their work. When the children have finished their writing they act out or read out their plays.

Pragmatism in practice

As in the previous chapter, the accounts in this chapter have shown teachers using a range of strategies, often determined by the interaction between their personal beliefs and the detailed context in which they found themselves operating. When asked to discuss the place of phonics teaching, 'Look and Say', reading schemes and 'Real Books' in their teaching of reading, teachers were invariably reluctant to identify one strategy as being particularly important, either because the approach taken depended on an individual child's needs, or because they felt that all teaching strategies were equally important.

The crude picture of two distinct groups of 'traditional' and 'progressive' teachers sometimes depicted in the mass media did not seem a relevant description of the teaching of reading in primary schools as witnessed in this research project. The national questionnaire data, the responses of teachers interviewed in the case study schools, and the live observation of lessons confirmed that no single strategy for teaching reading was used to the total exclusion of others. Teachers seemed to be of one mind about the need for pragmatic eclecticism, recognising that reading is a complex process requiring a balance of methods. This teacher of 7 year olds stated what many others believed:

We use all the approaches (reading schemes, real books, phonics, look and say). The children work though the reading scheme individually and it's a mix of reading schemes and that works very well for us. It's structured and we can introduce the vocabulary. Alongside of that they get lots of opportunities to use real books and they take them home as well and that just broadens their perception of what books are all about.

We have library times and there's always a reading session during the day when they use real books rather than scheme books. And then look and say ... with Year 2. I don't do that as much as you would with younger ones, because a lot of them have already got their 100 key words, but with those who haven't I use the 'word monster' idea. They have a little stand-up card monster with a big mouth and, as they get the words right, they feed him breakfast, dinner and tea. It just makes it a bit more fun.

And then we do phonics once a week. ... It varies – they're all differentiated. I've got about four different groups. I usually do some sort of introduction to the sound with each group and then there's a follow up activity to reinforce it. So I might be drawing pictures or I'll do a quiz and I'll say 'This is a word beginning with "ch"' and describe it and they have to guess the word. And we also tie it in with the handwriting. There's a variety of activities. There has to be.

8

SUPPORT FROM PARENTS, CLASSROOM ASSISTANTS, LIBRARIANS

Reading, in contrast to other curriculum areas in the primary school, is rarely the unique preserve of the class teacher. While history, geography, art, technology, science even, will normally be planned, executed and evaluated by the class teacher alone, various adults, some of whom are paid, others unpaid, are often involved in the process of reading in school, particularly in the infant stage. The use of classroom assistants was widespread in our sample schools. In addition, parental help at home was encouraged by most primary schools, as our national survey reported in Chapter 3 showed clearly. Most schools had access to some kind of external library service. In this chapter we shall consider some of these additional sources of help and support.

Support personnel in the classroom

The majority of teachers in the sample received additional help in the classroom with reading, although a number felt it was important to distinguish between 'teaching', which was what they believed to be their domain, and 'support':

> In the actual *teaching* of reading, no, not really. I mean, I try and encourage adults to come in and read with the children, but actually teaching them, no. They share books with the children.

The four most common forms of adult support available to teachers in this sample are shown below, in descending order of frequency. They are very close to the national survey picture reported in Chapter 3:

1   Ancillaries including classroom assistants, integration assistants, etc.
2   Parents
3   Student teachers/trainee nursery nurses
4   Special needs teachers

167

Two-thirds of the thirty-five teachers observed had a classroom assistant or ancillary for at least some of the week, while about a third had parent helpers or students. A quarter were assisted by special needs teachers.

A particular study was made of two of these four groups, namely parents and classroom assistants. We did not study special needs teachers or trainee teachers in any detail. Where special needs teachers were observed working alongside class teachers, their role was in all but one case to work with less able children, often on phonics and other reading-related activities. In the remaining class, the special needs teacher was engaged in extending the skills of more able pupils. Other adults who were present included miscellaneous volunteers from the community and meal-time assistants. Three teachers were assisted by the head, while only two teachers had no other adult present at all.

There was little difference in the four local authorities studied, apart from the conspicuous absence of parent helpers in the eleven Birmingham schools, a point that was mentioned in Chapter 4. Given the special efforts being made in Birmingham schools to improve literacy, this was certainly surprising. Only one Birmingham teacher had secured any parental help, in contrast to schools in another more rural authority studied, where all but three of the eleven class teachers had at least one regular parent helper. One Birmingham head teacher believed, whether correctly or not, that, in many families where English was not the main language, the level of literacy was generally low, so he arranged English classes for parents:

> One of the problems we find here is that many of our parents are not only not literate in English, they're not literate even in their own language.

We studied a number of schools in multicultural areas where parents whose mother tongue was not English did become involved in classroom helping. The 'illiterate parents' belief, unsupported by action, could easily become an obstacle to greater involvement. Efforts made by several Birmingham schools to encourage parental help included the provision of Parents' Rooms and the organisation of English classes, but although these were considered to have been valuable in establishing contact, fostering understanding between home and school, and improving the quality of help given to children at home, there was no immediate pay-off in the form of actual presence as helpers within the classroom.

Differences could also be identified in the pattern of support between year groups in the same school. Teachers in Reception through to Year 3 received much greater reading support in class than Year 4, 5 and 6 teachers. About 90 per cent of the ancillaries and parents seen in classrooms were helping teachers who worked in the first four year groups, up to the age of 7 to 8 year olds. The lack of parental support in the classes for 9 to 11 year olds was mostly, teachers felt, due to mothers entering employment as their children became older. The presence of paid ancillaries almost entirely in the younger classes, however, suggests that schools also make the judgement that this is where adult help can be used most effectively.

There has been a great deal of concern about the underachievement of boys in education, particularly in literacy in the primary school and later in secondary school public examinations like the GCSE and A level. Secondary schools have commented that boys often enter their schools with a lower level of literacy than girls. As will be discussed later in Chapter 10, boys are not being provided with appropriate adult role models in the early years. Only one part-time classroom assistant in the schools studied was male, and teachers' comments and our own observations suggest it is extremely rare for those 'hearing children read' in the classroom to be fathers or other male adults.

The role of parents

Some schools in this sample made an early statement about the importance of parents by arranging home visits, often before children started school, while a few were involved in family literacy schemes, or arranged language classes for parents who wished to learn English. All the schools sent books home for children to read to parents, parents to read to their children, or for both to share, and some tried to make it clear to parents which of these things they should do by the use of different colour bookmarks, or comments in a home/school diary, as described later in this chapter. In a few schools, allowing books to go home was a fairly new departure, while in others it seemed to fade out towards the top of junior school.

In interview heads and teachers often said that links with parents were important, so that schools could respond quickly to any problems that might arise. Actual examples of responding to parental concern which we encountered, however, were almost always of teachers recognising the need and taking the opportunity to explain why certain actions were being taken, rather than of them reconsidering the area of concern, or by changing practice. Most heads and post-holders seemed to see the home/school diaries, for example, as part of their missionary work to parents, providing an opportunity to explain what the child had been doing and enlist parents' help in tackling any problems that had arisen, rather than as a communication between co-equal partners.

This may be unavoidable, and not necessarily undesirable. After all, teachers have expert knowledge about the teaching of reading and young children's intellectual development which it is valuable to share with parents. Several schools sent parents detailed and carefully conceived booklets and leaflets explaining ways in which they could help their children become confident and skilled readers who loved books, and there were a few examples of changes brought about through heads responding to the concerns of parents.

One head described a situation in which a parent had complained about a specific matter:

> She said 'My child has only been heard once this week by the teacher' and we knew that the teacher sitting with the child was only one strategy for encouraging them and teaching them to read. So why was the parent complaining? And it dawned on us that when we were at school, possibly the only way we were taught was when the teacher sat and listened. That's not the only way, but parents perceive it to be, and we hadn't told her there were other ways.

Following this realisation, the school decided to guarantee a weekly reading interview for each child in the junior stage, and to explain to parents what they planned to do.

In order to overcome the problem of parents who lack the skills to help, some schools ran meetings, workshops and courses. The most common approach was to invite parents to a meeting specifically devoted to the teaching of reading in the school, something which occurred in two-thirds of the sample schools. There was obvious disappointment when the response was low, as it sometimes was. Most parents seemed more willing to attend a traditional parents' meeting to discuss their own children's progress, rather than one which focused exclusively on a particular aspect of the curriculum or on school policy. Head teachers felt they had to be quite firm with parents and press them hard to come to these meetings. One school even offered free raffle tickets to parents who arrived at the start of a meeting, but most relied on persuasion plus light emotional blackmail.

Schools with a large proportion of parents who spoke little English felt a double responsibility to ensure these parents felt welcome and to help them with their language skills. First, the children would benefit if their parents were helped, but there was also a feeling of the need to provide something of value for the whole community. One head described how their efforts to help parents improve their own English had even, if looked at purely from a selfish perspective, been too successful:

> We eventually encouraged quite a number of our parents to come into school to be parent helpers and we ran various groups for them. It was so successful we linked it to one of the local colleges who ran Access courses ... and this developed, so they now run City and Guilds and other courses here in school for the parents. Consequently all those parents who used to come in and help us voluntarily have now focused on their own development and so don't come into school any more, except to attend their courses. I

suppose it's all right, because we are supporting the community, but we've lost that body of support.

The reasons for inviting parents into school for meetings, workshops or courses about literacy were twofold. The main one was to ensure that all parents knew about the way the school taught reading so that they could help their own children at home. In addition, schools often wanted to recruit a smaller band of volunteers who would help teachers in the classroom, either in their own child's class or in any other classes, as unpaid classroom assistants. This was done in a fairly informal way, either with the class teacher explaining what was required, or a few parents coming to a meeting where general principles were explained. Occasionally schools were involved in more formal training programmes:

> [We do] a thing called 'Schoolwise', which is a college-based programme which links in with schools, that encourages parents to find out about schools and the parents actually get accredited with an Open College.... The idea is that they come into school and do some school experience, working as volunteers.

Class teachers were often expected to invite parents into school to discuss any problems that their children were having, and in some cases, the school had a policy of making home visits if problems had been identified. One school was particularly determined:

> We do home visits and we say to parents 'You've got to come in and get involved' and if they don't turn up for the sessions, Maria goes and fetches them. Or if the parent doesn't turn up and the child doesn't turn up, we take the session to them.

Although heads were aware of the problem of parents who cannot or will not help, they saw it as part of the school's responsibility to try to remedy this situation. Over and over again we were told 'We need to find ways of getting parents involved' or 'We would like to have more parents involved'. To a certain extent this is enlightened self-interest, in that they would like more adult help in the classroom, but it also seemed to be illustrative of a widespread recognition of the importance of involving parents in the development of their children's literacy. Even those wholeheartedly committed to involving parents, however, admitted that hearing their child read could prove stressful for both parent and child:

> The difficulty is if it gets to be an anxious time where a child doesn't like doing it and it gets to be a battle. That's the difficulty for some parents.

It was not only heads, but also the majority of teachers, apart from a small number of sceptics, who appeared to believe that parents in the home played a crucial role in encouraging and supporting their children's reading. As one Year 3 teacher put it:

> They're the prime mover. They've taught their child to speak. There's no reason why they can't teach their child to read with a bit of help from us.

Some teachers were concerned that parental effort would be inhibited by insufficient knowledge and expertise to tackle the complicated task of teaching a child to read, particularly in terms of being up to date, or sharing beliefs with teachers, as this Year 3 teacher explained:

> They have an enormous role to play but they don't have the training. I think the understanding of how children learn to read and the teaching of reading has changed so much in the last ten to fifteen years, that a lot of parents can only base it on their own experience of school and things have moved on since then.

A number of teachers commented on the clash of beliefs and ideologies that could occur, particularly if parents failed to grasp, or rejected in some way the school's approach to reading. This was particularly likely to happen over the way the act of 'reading' was interpreted, broadly by some teachers, more focused by some parents:

> We've sent letters home.... I think we've had a reading evening. In the little books that go home with the children, there's a sort of sheet at the front suggesting ideas of how you can help your child when they bring a reading book home and it's things like: letting them look at pictures; letting them relate the pictures to the words; but you still get parents who don't do that. If they're [the children] not reading the words to them, they're not reading.

> Some of these parents really don't understand what we're trying to do and how we go about it. Parents still think that the book needs to have words in it.

Many of the teachers saw efforts to establish a partnership in literacy as a means to building good relationships with parents in general, especially if it was a genuinely reciprocal and equal relationship:

> I think it's all to do with the ethos of the school really. It's all very well saying 'We expect the parents to do this'. If you've got a very

closed door and the parents aren't particularly involved in the school life, then it's going to be very difficult to get them to back you up and help in what you're doing.

[Teachers need to] offer support, encourage and praise. Say 'X has done really well. What have you been doing with him?' Show you can learn from them. Give them confidence in their role.

Teachers hoped that parents would understand the need to provide interesting and exciting experiences of books in the home, reading to their children, not just hearing them read when they brought home books from school. Pleasure rather than technique was stressed. They emphasised the need for parents to *enjoy* books with their children in order to instil in them a love of reading:

They should enjoy books with them, make it a priority in the evenings, at weekends and in the holidays ... go to the library, read themselves, show children what a wonderful world the book world is! To read, read, read!

One teacher articulated very clearly the advantages to a child of a quality literacy environment at home:

The more supportive they are at home, the better. If they've got lots of books at home or if they belong to a library, it just makes our job easier, because children come to school understanding what literacy is all about. And I think it's great if adults can set an example, not consciously, but if they're reading or writing.

Yet this emphasis on the importance of parents being reading role models for children contrasted sharply with the evidence gathered during our classroom observations, as reported in Chapter 6, where teachers were rarely seen reading themselves during ERIC sessions. Understandably they preferred attending to their pupils. Furthermore, as the next section shows, parents did not always share schools' views concerning the amount and quality of information provided to them about reading.

Parents' perceptions of schools' information and advice about reading

While all the teachers and heads interviewed said that they informed parents of how reading was taught at their school, either at meetings for new parents, or in the form of letters or booklets, nearly half of the parents interviewed said they were not aware of any information having been given. This must be a worrying finding for schools, although the explanation for this difference in perceptions is not clear. In a small number of cases the children in the study had joined the school after the Reception class and therefore the parents may have missed the meeting, although this raises the question of whether schools need to have a rolling programme to meet the needs of such parents. Where parents of children in the same class were interviewed, it was not unusual for them to hold different recollections of whether they had received information. Of course, it may be that those parents who said they had not, had not attended the pre-school or other meetings for parents, but perhaps schools should try other ways of communicating this vital information to them.

There was also evidence that the quality of information offered by schools varied. In a small number of cases parents said they had been provided with detailed explanations of the school's methods of teaching reading; in the majority parents reported that they had simply been told what was expected of them and it was clear they had no real idea of the philosophy of reading underlying the school's approach. There was some evidence that there is a reluctance in some schools to give parents detailed information. During interviews we conducted with class teachers, some had emphasised that teaching reading is a complex activity and considered parents were not trained to 'teach' reading, as was mentioned above. In only one school, according to parents, had there been any attempt to offer parents information on the way in which some children learn to read, and one parent had found this quite a startling revelation:

> We had a meeting for new parents.... The only thing I do remember was the fact that you think a child would recognise the small words like 'in' and 'on' but to them that's as hard to read as like the word 'elephant' – that's got so many ups and downs that they would recognise that word ... that was quite an eye opener.

Perhaps if more information like this were given to parents, they would be much better able to understand some of the processes involved and therefore be more effective when sharing books with their children. There seems to be a real dilemma here for some teachers who are very keen to get parents to 'hear children read', but are not prepared to share with them ways in which children actually learn to read, or indeed offer advice about what parents should do if their children make errors when reading. Perhaps it is the threat to their own professionalism that knowledgeable parents might bring, which causes this reluctance to offer more detailed insight for parents.

The evidence that most parents had only a superficial understanding of how their children were learning to read was further supported when parents were specifically asked how their child's school taught reading. Some said bluntly in interview that they did not know. Other responses could be divided into two groups: (1) those who talked about organisational aspects, and (2) those who concentrated on the way in which the reading books and materials were structured. The comments below illustrate these two types of parental observation:

1   *Organisation*

They get helpers in and they sit in little groups and they all take turns, I think, at reading their book.

I assume they have set tables that would do some reading with somebody.

I presume that they just sit there and listen and, I think, just read to an individual. And we're asked to listen to them every night.

2   *Books and materials*

First of all they have books without any words and they just go through the pictures and say what they think they're doing in the pictures. Then they have a book with basically the same word in it, which goes through the whole book. They get used to the words and then they build up till they know more and more words.

They start off with books with strong pictures. The actual writing isn't so much but they use a lot of the pictures as the basis for the reading.... And they brought home the cards with the words on and the words they're learning on the cards seem to be tied up to the books.

As was the case with the last parent speaking above, many of those interviewed were often drawing on their observations and experiences with their own children rather than referring to any explicitly explained school policy. Another parent said: 'I couldn't tell you whether they are hot on phonics. It's simply a reading book that comes home.'

Taking books home

Twenty-nine of the thirty-five teachers interviewed stated that the children in their class took home books to read. In almost all these cases, the teachers also mentioned a means of communication between the school and home commonly called the 'home/school reading diary' or 'reading record', in which adults hearing a child read would typically record the date, title of book, page reached and a comment about the child's reading. The most important contribution most parents could make, in many teachers' view, was to share their child's reading book with them when they took it home. As one teacher put it:

> I always say to parents, 'We can only do so much with reading. Reading is the most important thing your child can possibly do. If they don't get that right, they're not going to get anything else right, really. And you have to help us because we can't do it on our own.' I had 31 kids last year in Reception. I can't possibly get it done on my own and I tell them that. 'You have to help me and if you don't help me, your child's not going to learn as quickly as he or she is able'.

Home/school diaries were kept up with varying degrees of enthusiasm and perseverance. They were usually intended as two-way communication, with a space for parents to write their comments. As one head explained:

> There's a space for a comment at the side so that mum can write, 'This book was too boring', or 'He's brought the same book home for five nights', or 'Why can't he have a harder book?' So there's an opportunity for the parents to write and then a space for the teacher to give a comment, not every night, but maybe at half term the teacher will put a general comment. Obviously if messages are coming back that 'The child isn't ... blah blah', then it's an opportunity for the teacher to make an appointment to see that parent and maybe to follow up and explain what's happening.

In one Birmingham school, in an attempt to involve parents more in their children's reading, this process had been formalised through the drawing up of a 'reading contract' between pupils, parents and teachers, but the two teachers interviewed at the school had reservations about whether it actually led to more or better reading, or whether parents always understood what they were signing, as one explained:

> We have a reading contract which the parents have to sign – that they'll hear their child read every day and that they'll bring their book back every day. I'm sort of unconvinced by that. I think it's a nice idea, but it doesn't really work.

The other teacher had given up asking for comments by the parents and asked them merely to record when the child had read and to what page, but she acknowledged that the parents' lack of English made this task problematic in some cases. Often when books were sent home from school, it was older siblings who took on the responsibility of listening to their younger brothers or sisters read and commenting in any home/school reading diary.

Concerns were expressed by teachers in the different LEAs studied that parents at all socio-economic levels were finding it increasingly difficult to fit hearing their child read into their busy schedules. The increase in the number of mothers in full-time work and the growth in one-parent families had, in many teachers' opinion, resulted in this activity being squeezed out of their daily routine. However, the evidence we collected during the pupil case studies, reported in Chapter 11, suggests that teachers' fears may be misplaced.

In most cases the home/school diary was the major means of effecting communications between teachers and parents. Although no systematic study was undertaken of the detailed content of these, there did seem to be evidence that the parents of lower-ability children were less likely to complete them. The way in which the teacher used the home/school diary was usually reflected in the parents' use. Where teachers did no more than write the date, title and page reached, parents would copy this format, although occasionally parents of more able children might comment if their child had found a book too easy, or had read it before. In one class, however, the teacher valued the home/school diary as an opportunity to communicate more fully with parents, to explain her approach and to involve them more in their child's reading. The following comments seen in one child's diary were typical of this teacher's written interactions with parents:

> Elizabeth read well today and at the time of reading remembered the key words. I am sending home her book with the same key words in, so that she can practise them.

Her mother had written in response:

> I've practised the book with her, but she's still having problems with 'that'.

Although this Year 1 teacher was always keen and available to talk to parents before and after school, she acknowledged that she could not always speak to everyone and she felt the home/school diary maintained the link between the parents and herself.

Teachers often based their perceptions of parental support on parents' contributions in the home/school diary, believing a lack of comments to indicate a lack of support. However, our interviews with parents suggest that this may be a misconception. A number of different reasons emerged from the interviews as to why some parents had not completed the diary. These included the following:

1   they had not known what to write;
2   they felt they were just saying the same things over again;
3   they felt the teacher did not take any notice of their comments;
4   they could not write very well themselves.

Parents' accounts of their experiences sharing the school reading book with their child

Most parents said in interview that they were happy with their child's progress in reading. There were one or two aspects, however, that are worthy of further scrutiny. When talking about what happened when their child brought home a school reading book to share with them, it was very noticeable that parents' comments tended to focus on their child's decoding skills. There was evidence that parents of younger children did discuss pictures and also the story in books with little or no text, but once a child could read some words, in many cases 'sharing a book' merely became 'hearing them read'.

This was further confirmed by parents' answers to the question: 'What do you do when your child reads to you?' The responses revealed that many parents viewed reading with their child as an assessment exercise, rather than as an opportunity to develop a love of books, the explicitly stated expectation of their children's teachers. The picture of this process derived from the interviews is of parents sitting with their child encouraging them to sound out letters, or to 'guess' words and then revisiting the text until the child can read it 'correctly'. The two comments below were typical of many:

Sometimes he reads on his own, but I still go back and test him.

Polly can be a bit sloppy in her reading, like she will change the definite article into the indefinite article. The school's never mentioned this, but I actually do make her go back and read the sentence again.

Perhaps, unsurprisingly, the lack of emphasis on enjoyment of the text had, in a number of cases, led to the child becoming alienated:

She is so slow that you find it so frustrating to listen to and she'll go 'What do you think this word is?' and I go to say it and she'll say 'I wish you hadn't told me that. I'm supposed to break it up', and I'll say 'I've given you the opportunity to break it up, you're struggling like mad. I'm trying to help you.' But she does get very, very frustrated.

I try to get him to make the sounds of the letters, but Nick has not got an awful lot of confidence and he gets a bit aerated at times. When he gets like that, I tend to leave it and go on, because otherwise he gets upset and then he doesn't want to do it at all.

Both of the children described above were low-ability readers for their age group, but the overriding emphasis by parents on accurate decoding, rather than understanding and pleasure, could be found across the ability groups. While schools may be giving parents information about reading, there appears to be a need for a fundamental rethinking of the type and manner in which advice is given, with perhaps more modelling of 'sharing a book'. There was sometimes a real conflict between what the school expected and what parents actually did. When teachers intended reading at home to be about meaning and enjoyment and not decoding individual words, some parents felt frustrated at the dissonance. In other cases too much pressure from home became counter-productive.

Parents were asked whether they had received any training or advice concerning sharing a book with their child in the home. Nearly half said they had not. Of those who said they had, a few indicated that the advice was nothing more than:

Please spend as much time reading with your child as you can.

We're sending a book home with your child and we'd like you to read it with them.

Parents from only one class reported being advised by the class teacher not to make the sharing of books with their children a tense experience: 'We had a pep talk to say "Don't despair, don't pressurise, don't expect miracles overnight. Let us know if you have any worries." ' This advice was given at a meeting for new parents and the teacher later made extensive use of the home/school reading record to communicate more detailed information to parents concerning their child's reading. In many cases, parents said they liked the opportunity bringing home a book provided for them to monitor their child's progress, and some talked explicitly of making sure the school was doing its job properly.

It gives us an idea of how they're progressing or whether they are progressing.

Because it's keeping you in touch with what's going on at school and obviously you're getting feedback from the teacher as well (in the reading record).

Only a small number spontaneously referred to the pleasure the event of sharing a book with their child gave them, and usually it was the physical proximity with their child that they valued, rather than the sharing of a good book:

> I like to know what they're reading. And it's nice just to have that little bit of time sitting together too.

It was not possible to interview all the parents of children studied, so it would be unwise to draw any firm conclusions from these findings. Nonetheless, a number of issues have emerged which appear to need addressing. Unsurprisingly perhaps, the majority of those children who had had a literacy environment provided for them in their pre-school years by their parents appeared to have had a head-start over their peers in learning to read. Many schools had strong links with pre-school groups and this provided an important avenue for advising parents on how to begin to develop their young children's literacy skills. The parents who had given their children 'a good start' also continued their interest and support as their children progressed through the school, providing a range of literacy experiences for them.

One important message from the interviews with parents, however, is that schools should examine the *type* of information they are offering parents. A number of parents do say they want more specific information than what they currently receive. Some find that what they are given now is too superficial if they are to be effective in helping their children. This is not solely a middle-class professional issue. Most parents are baffled about what to do, for example, when a child is stuck for a word. One of our target pupils, Charlotte, aged 5, even showed her own mother, a poor reader, how to split up words to make them easier to attack. Lack of congruence between a teacher's and a parent's methods and expectations may lead to frustrations and tensions in both home and school.

It can, of course, also be argued that some reading scheme or other books are boring or devoid of any real story, and so discourage parents from trying to enjoy the text and pictures with their child. Our interviews suggest that, for one reason or another, reading a school book may become a separate event, detached from any enjoyment of reading which might occur at other times in the home.

The intention of this section was to highlight a small number of areas which schools might like to address, not to give the impression that the parents interviewed felt negative generally about their relationship with their child's school. This was not the case at all. When questioned as to whether they felt their child's teacher kept them informed of their child's reading development, over three-quarters of parents interviewed felt they did and, with one exception, all believed that the teacher would contact them if there was a problem with their child's reading. Furthermore, every parent felt able to talk to the teacher about their child and, of the parents interviewed, the large majority expressed themselves as 'very happy' with the progress their children had made with reading.

Parents in the classroom

In a number of the classes studied, particularly in the infant schools, the parents came into the classroom in the morning with their children. In many cases, this was purely pastoral: simply to see them hang up their coats and put their 'book bags' in the appropriate place. Some parents took the opportunity to have a quick word with the teacher. It was very rare for parents to be involved in selecting a child's reading material for that day. This mostly took place after a child had read to an adult during the day.

In one school, however, prior to the start of the morning, teachers wrote the day's 'Early Work' (i.e. work children were to do at the commencement of the day) on the blackboard. The activities set would be either a maths investigation or a language-based task, such as 'Share a book, please', or 'Finish writing up your video instructions'. Many of the parents stayed while their children undertook this activity, though, according to the teacher, there was not a specific intention that they should stay to help out with it: 'We have this Early Work – I write it on the board for the children ... the parents somehow feel that they have to do it.' Despite so many parents being keen to be involved with their children's learning, the school did not take a more proactive stance in this area.

Parent helpers were not always present in the classes observed and as the age of the children increased, many mothers, who were the most common parent in the classroom, seemed to go back to work or find other things to do. Their role was not always clearly defined, but some parent helpers observed had been encouraged to use phonic strategies and picture cues. One teacher explained how she carefully monitored a parent's suitability for sharing books with children:

> Usually the first time they came in I'd let them do painting or something like that and once they'd been in a couple of times, so that I could see how they were with the children, then I'd perhaps hand them over to Lyn [the classroom assistant] and get her to show them exactly what we were doing with the reading and let them have a session and see how they were going. I had one mum who was very, very good last year, but with some of them I've felt it's perhaps not as useful for them to be doing reading, that they'd perhaps be better doing art and craft.

In all classrooms where we observed volunteers hearing children read, it was invariably on an *individual* basis. On no occasion did researchers witness any *group* reading session involving a volunteer. In almost all cases, the adult and child would sit away from the rest of the class in a 'quiet' corner. This was in marked contrast to what was observed with classroom assistants, who in many classrooms heard a child read while sitting at a table with a group of children, often monitoring their work at the same time. On no occasion was a volunteer adult observed making any real attempt to talk about the book being read with the child. Unlike the case of classroom assistants, with parent volunteers the process was more mechanical, akin to a factory production line: the child read the book; the volunteer noted down that fact in the home/school diary; the child then selected a new book, the title of which was written by the volunteer in the home/school diary; the next child was called to read.

Parents helped the children with many activities, including some to do with reading, though heads' ideas of what were suitable activities for parents varied. In several schools parents, almost invariably mothers, mainly provided an opportunity for children to read to interested adults, but occasionally were a little more ambitious, as one head explained:

> The mums who come in to work in school have a little bit of training ... to talk them through what our approach is and to answer any of their questions so that they're following similar lines. Obviously, with regard to the activities they do, although largely they may sit and listen and give the child the opportunity for one-to-one, they're working under the direction of the teacher. It really depends on the mum, but if they show initiative, then it may be that the teacher can ask them to do some word games, phonic games or perhaps help with writing.

Usually there was no reward for parent classroom helpers, other than the personal satisfaction of helping the school, but some schools did offer more extrinsic rewards. One head, who was very keen on acronyms, had a team of SMART mums (Super Mums Ancillary Resource Team) who helped in classes and were presented with certificates and badges at a special assembly in recognition of the work they did. Two other schools gave financial rewards, 'though not very much'.

In some schools teachers said they felt under pressure from parents to make sure children were heard reading every day. It may be the case that this pressure resulted in the very act of hearing reading being given prominence with parent helpers, in that teachers sometimes set up 'quick-fix' reading times, where decoding the text was paramount and where time constraints prevented exploration of the text and the child's understanding of it.

Classroom assistants

The amount and quality of support provided by classroom assistants varied. In some classes, a classroom assistant was present on all occasions observed and undertook, in addition to hearing children read, language games with lower-ability children and general classroom support. In some Birmingham schools the assistant's name appeared on the classroom door alongside the teacher's. A number of teachers preferred to use the classroom assistant's time for intensive work with children who had difficulties in their reading, assigning them to a statemented child, for example. One assistant spent most of her time with a single child, though she was available to monitor neighbouring children's work. A major role was often to hear children read and to work with small groups on maths and language activities. In two classrooms the assistant worked only with one or two low-ability children for about twenty minutes each, reading with them, monitoring their knowledge of sounds and key words.

In another classroom, the assistant, Cynthia, played a large role in the teaching of reading. A typical session with a child would last fifteen minutes, during which time often more than one book would be shared and much discussion undertaken, as well as monitoring of the child's sight vocabulary. In addition to this daily monitoring, she had been given responsibility for administering a diagnostic test with some children and then planning appropriate reading activities for them. When the teacher took delivery of two new reading schemes, it was Cynthia who was given responsibility for reading through the books, assessing their level and slotting them into the stages of the existing scheme. She had also set up and administered the school's own 'book track' scheme, designing the 'diary' to be used by the children and parents.

The unusually high profile and important role played by Cynthia in this class was in part due to the class teacher's own admission of lack of knowledge and confidence about teaching children to read. The teacher had qualified as a mature student three years previously after doing a postgraduate certificate in education and felt she had learned nothing about the teaching of reading on that course. She had based all her early teaching, she said, on her experiences with her own children. However, the insights gained on a course run by the LEA during the year we observed, as well as the acquisition of further book schemes, to provide greater breadth of reading across the various levels, made her feel more positive about her teaching of reading.

Cynthia was able to operate at a high level of competence partly because she had benefited from training, which was far more available to classroom assistants than to other volunteer helpers. In all schools in Authorities A, Birmingham and D, classroom assistants had been given training. Teachers at three schools in Authority C, however, said they were unsure whether their classroom assistants had received training in reading support. Some Urdu- or Gujerati-speaking Birmingham classroom assistants had undertaken courses to help them support children in their home language in the classroom and communicate with parents.

It is in the area of training that there is such a stark contrast between classroom assistants and other adults we observed in classrooms. Parents, for example, received virtually no formal support, so in turn the help they could give was bound to be limited, compared with what classroom assistants could offer. Although parents in Authority D in particular were important contributors to the reading process in school, even here those parents working in the classroom were rarely provided with anything that could properly be called 'training', leaving teachers to take an individual approach. The majority of teachers seemed to rely on parents' experiences of reading with their own children to guide them in their reading with others when they helped out in the classroom.

Given that parents' accounts of hearing their own child read at home, as we described earlier, emphasised attention to decoding skills and rarely mentioned the need to read for meaning and enjoyment, this may be an unwise strategy. Indeed, there was some unease in schools about the informal nature of this approach and one teacher confessed that she felt that such informality was probably inadequate for some of the tasks parents might now be asked to undertake:

> I certainly think we should do *something*. Maybe just with those coming in to help – just to talk it through. Certainly with group reading, because that is such a good experience if it is done well and often it is not.... Yes, I feel there is a need for it [training] and I don't think we address it.

Library support

Many classes had timetabled sessions in their own school library. In some classes teachers used this time for changing children's books. This was another activity often supervised by classroom assistants, when they were asked to supervise these visits to the library, though the school librarian, if there was one, would also play an important part. In one school, it was parent helpers who ran the library on two afternoons a week, discussing books with the children and guiding them in their selection of reading material. In some schools the whole class or small groups would go to the library for specific library skills training: for example, learning how to use catalogues and the Dewey system, or being taught about contents pages and indexes. This was common in junior-age classes, but in one school 6 year olds were receiving this type of session. In smaller schools, access to the library was often restricted. This was because the library area had multiple uses, such as for television programmes, music lessons, even medicals.

The major external support service in all the schools studied was the Schools Library Service (SLS), although it became apparent from teachers' comments that the quality of the service provided differed in the various LEAs. In one authority the SLS staff assembled 'topic boxes' (collections of books on a particular theme, like 'dinosaurs' or 'the Romans'). They also offered sales of books at a discount, and these services were considered to be an important factor in ensuring high-quality resources in classrooms throughout the LEA. The SLS was spoken of by teachers and heads with great enthusiasm and appreciation. In other LEAs, although the library service was mentioned, it was clearly not so highly regarded. Indeed, in one of the LEA regions, as the number of schools deciding not to buy in its services continued to rise, there was a possibility that the whole library service would be disbanded.

Some teachers made use of other external organisations and individuals to supplement their own reading activities and to provide rich literacy experiences for their pupils. In a small number of the schools studied teachers talked of taking their pupils to their local library, to familiarise them with public libraries and what they have to offer. In some local libraries, pupils were also given the opportunity to attend authors' sessions, where they were able to listen to authors reading their own work and to question them about their writing experiences. Several schools engaged the services of visiting story-tellers and poets, often as part of a special 'book day' or 'book week'.

9

CASE STUDIES OF INDIVIDUAL CLASSROOMS

The beliefs and accounts of practice of the thirty-five teachers who were observed over a whole school year as case studies in Study 3 have been examined in the last three chapters. In this chapter we focus on six teachers from the sample in more detail, in order to explore what factors appeared to be influential in improving levels of literacy. Teachers have been selected from across the primary age range. Inevitably there are differences in context and observed behaviour, but this does not mean that there are no common characteristics, even if these are varied in their interpretation. What these might be will be discussed at the end of the chapter.

The six case studies in this chapter will be described in ascending order of age group taught, starting with a Reception class of 4 and 5 year olds. Two of the teachers were members of staff at the same school, while the others came from different schools. Three of the teachers held the post of language co-ordinator in their school. Three of the four LEA areas studied in this research are represented by these six histories. Inevitably, of course, the teachers manifest features which are indicative of their effectiveness as teachers not just in the field of literacy, but more generally as well.

Miss Dobson – Reception teacher

Miss Dobson had been teaching for eight years at Beverley Road Community School. It was her first teaching post and she had gained experience of teaching each of the infant-age groups, from 4 or 5 up to 7 year olds. Her Reception class had thirty-two children, all of whom started in the September after their fourth birthday, in keeping with that LEA's policy. Her classroom was full of colourful displays of children's work on walls, doors, windows and hanging from the ceiling (at children's height), plus alphabets, questions and challenges, and signs written in different languages. The corridor was used as an extension of the classroom, housing a workbench, sand tray, work table and a book corner with seats and carefully laid-out displays of fiction and non-fiction books.

Only one pupil had English as his first language, the others speaking

Punjabi, Bengali, Urdu or Gujerati as their mother tongue. Miss Dobson worked closely with her multi-lingual classroom assistant, who translated when necessary, but English was used as much as possible in the classroom, the classroom assistant adding just a few words of explanation in Urdu, Gujerati or Punjabi when needed, or making reference to cultural differences, as this incident shows:

> Miss Dobson is reading a story about a family with a new baby. She reads slowly and shows the pictures to the children as she does so. The classroom assistant looks around the class, seeking out those whose attention seems to be wandering, or assessing who may need help. From time to time she asks a question in the child's home language, or gives a word of explanation. When a 'tea cosy' is mentioned, she laughs and tells Miss Dobson, 'They aren't all that common in Gujerat'.

Miss Dobson was able to describe clearly the many different activities and strategies she used to teach reading, but had not been on any courses since leaving college, and did not display knowledge of what she called 'literacy jargon', or the latest theories. The children first learned the letters of their names, then other letters, and worked on initial sounds. Beverley Road School used the Oxford Reading Tree scheme and this was introduced gradually as the children were considered ready. Before starting them on the scheme Miss Dobson familiarised the children with the characters by reading the stories and by calling the children's work groups after the characters – 'Floppy', 'Kipper', 'Biff', etc.

The very first reading book each new pupil had was a personalised book dictated by the child and written by Miss Dobson, about the child's family and the things they liked doing. Making these individual books for thirty-two children consumed a great deal of time, but Miss Dobson believed it was worth it. For their second book she made a story about the child, which also included a character from the reading scheme. After that she decided if the pupil was ready for the first scheme books, or needed another one specially made.

Each personalised book had a 'word wall' on the back cover, with all the vocabulary listed, so pupils could read the words out of context as well as in. The children did a lot of sentence work using these words from their personalised books and in other contexts, with Miss Dobson writing down the children's own words, cutting the sentences up into individual words, getting the children to replace them in the right order, and finally to stick them in a book kept for that purpose. Each pupil built up a personal sight vocabulary of words to do with themselves and their families, plus high-frequency words which they used in and out of context. When their sight vocabulary had reached a certain standard she allowed them to take words home in a tin to build sentences at home. The word 'allowed' is her choice of vocabulary when presenting the idea to the class. She regarded it as a privilege, and consequently that was how the children saw it.

Once children had started the reading scheme they became involved in a group reading method, taking turns to read and also being involved in discussions about the story, vocabulary, characters and illustrations. In one observed session the children all read several times. The story prompted discussion about: whether fathers should help with the washing; 'feeling poorly'; a child whose father had diabetes and what this meant; what a cheque was. Miss Dobson was able to concentrate on one group at a time because of the way she organised the session and the help she received from the classroom assistant who dealt adeptly with other children.

Miss Dobson combined energy and enthusiasm with meticulous organisation. The reading work was structured and monitored closely, so that, without looking at her records, she could tell the interviewer about each child's progress: that Bilal now knew fourteen sight words, for example. When the researcher visited the school to hear the six selected children read for the first time, she was presented with a folder by Miss Dobson. This included a timetable for when the child should be heard, a copy of each child's 'word wall', the school's policy on reading records, the Assessment Statement Bank, a Phonic Assessment sheet and the Oxford Reading Tree book list.

In reply to the interview question about differences between Key Stage 1 and Key Stage 2, Miss Dobson referred to the teacher's attitude, saying that with younger children the teacher could go 'a bit over the top' with enthusiasm and praise. When asked what she would do if a child miscued and read 'boot', instead of 'book', her first comment was: 'Give praise for a good try and point out what was right', before saying: 'Point to the end and ask if it made sense.'

Certainly there was considerable and regular public recognition of approved work and behaviour, as she frequently told children how clever they were, commented that she could see a group 'working so hard over there', or that she had noticed 'some brilliant readers in the corner'. The children appeared to respond favourably and seemed to make more progress than the norm in classrooms in similar circumstances. They themselves believed they had made a good start at reading, as Reception class children often do, and "cos Miss Dobson says' was sufficient answer to the interviewer's questions about why they thought they were good at reading, why they should learn to read, or, indeed, why they should do anything.

It may appear that Miss Dobson made her pupils too dependent, but their citing her as an authority was largely out of respect, rather than subjugation. In the classroom it was their *independence* that was noticeable, as they were usually engrossed in their work, without the need for constant supervision. Although they covered the usual range of Reception class curricular activities, there was little or no wasted or 'waiting' time. By 9.05 a.m. all the groups were busily engaged in their first activity. Observation data show that Miss Dobson's on-task involvement level averaged at 81, high for a Reception class. The work appeared to be pitched appropriately, so no individual was inactive for long. Miss Dobson's assurance that they were a truly marvellous class seemed to have a positive effect on children's self-esteem.

We were not able to use the NFER Reading Test at the beginning and end of the year, since they were only 4–5 years old, but children's work was monitored on each visit and all six target pupils made good progress, though at different speeds and from different starting points. This may be explained by a powerful combination of positive expectations, skilful class management, well-organised and varied classroom activities, pupil independence, an intimate familiarity with each individual child's progress, harmonious personal relationships and considerable help from a classroom assistant who understood the language and cultural background of Asian children.

Miss Brown – Year 1

Miss Brown, a Year 1 teacher, was in her third year of teaching at Charldeen School when she took part in our research. As a newly qualified teacher joining the staff she had found the school's reading policy an invaluable tool, helping her to structure the children's reading and to plan for their development:

> It's been really useful.... I've used it to structure what the children are doing and I've been able to take the ones who are doing well a little bit further. It's very easy to know what you're doing in your own year group but you do get children who are sort of bright and are rushing ahead – so it's useful from a progression point of view, to know where to take them.

The reading policy was the result of extensive consultation by the language co-ordinator and the head teacher with staff at curriculum meetings. One of its central tenets was that every child should read to an adult every day. Miss Brown confessed that sometimes this target was not always realised, but she supported the objective without reserve and often used her lunch-time to catch up on readers:

> Hearing children every day is absolutely crucial and I do like to hear readers myself, not just delegate it all to mums and the classroom assistant, because reading's so important. It underpins everything else you do.

Children's reading within the classroom was structured through the use of a colour-coded collection of various reading schemes. Most children had free choice within a colour band. With the less able, Miss Brown herself chose the child's next book, usually working through one reading scheme's books before starting another. Miss Brown carefully assessed each child's stage of development, matching reading tasks to their ability. She explained how this worked:

> It depends on the child.... With James, these books are very simple and they've only got one or two words on each page and there's a lot to talk about in the pictures, so, for him, I would keep him on this particular set until he's been through all the very basic ones of those, and then I'll perhaps move him on to a different set. Once they're actually beginning to read, or beginning to recognise some of the words, then I let them have free choice within a colour band . . . . If I have a child who's on yellow books, say, and has been through the majority of what's in my box and isn't ready to move on, I can send them to another classroom, and there's different books in there, in the same colour band.

Phonics work was a strong feature of the classroom and was structured by the school's phonics policy which detailed the stages. Miss Brown's timetabled weekly phonics lesson was consistently reinforced by language games during 'on the carpet' sessions, and by discussing the sounds of letters with children while they were writing or reading. At the back of each child's reading record was written the alphabet, and whenever an adult read with a child, the adult was expected to check the child's competency at letter sounds. Miss Brown had also modified a published 'word list' scheme, which contained lists of words for the children to learn and which they took home at weekends. She explained that, with these, the emphasis was on 'sounding them out' with the intention of developing the child's word-building skills. She felt they were a particularly successful tool:

> I've found that as soon as the children start on the word lists, I can see an improvement in the way they start to approach their reading. It gives them confidence with their reading, that they know how to try and work out a word they don't know. And, of course, it links with their writing and spelling.

At the back of each child's reading record, in addition to the alphabet, there was also an initial list of twelve key words, which was gradually extended until 100 key words were known. Even with these, Miss Brown asked the children to learn them first by sounding them out, although she admitted that some parents seemed to test the children 'as if the words are sight vocabulary'. She regretted that a reduction in her classroom assistant's hours in the summer term had made it impossible to give as much attention to the pupils' learning of the key words:

> I don't practise those with them when they read to me. At the beginning of the year Lyn [the classroom assistant] used to do that. She'd have the less able children every day and she'd practise their words with them. Now I only have Lyn for 0.5 of a week so there's just not time to do the words every day. That's a real pity, because they came on so much better when they did that on a daily basis.

Accurate spelling and punctuation were valued highly. The researcher's observation notes contained many examples of the teacher highlighting these aspects of a child's writing, as she walked round the room discussing their work with them. Children in the class made extensive use of their own personal word books and commercial dictionaries. Spelling tests took place once a week. The same early morning routine applied every day: on entering the classroom children were to learn and check spellings, and then read further in their book before the register was taken.

Underpinning Miss Brown's very structured approach to the teaching of reading was a huge personal enthusiasm for books. This manifested itself in her classroom and in her teaching in a number of ways. Over the years she had built up a large personal collection of children's literature, which she used to supplement the school's own reading materials. These books were kept in a cupboard in the classroom but children were allowed to borrow them to read in school.

In interview, Miss Brown claimed 'I find every opportunity to talk about books'. Observation of her lessons showed that one of the main ways in which she did this was by having 'our author of the week'. She collected as many books as possible by one author and tried to read one each day to the class with time for discussion afterwards. During the week the books were attractively displayed in a specially designated 'Author's Corner' to encourage the children to read these books themselves at other times, some-thing children were frequently observed doing. Questions about the current books were included in the display, designed to set children thinking about the stories. Miss Brown was one of the few teachers observed in this study whose 'Author's Corner' books were changed on a regular basis. In some classrooms observed the same author's works were often displayed all term, or even all year, from September through to July.

Miss Brown used the organisation of her classroom to capture children's attention and maintain their interest in books and reading throughout the year. Her 'home corner' was a dynamic part of the classroom, changing each term from a home, to a shop, to a travel agent. Reading materials appro-priate to its current use were available to the children including newspapers, comics, magazines, brochures, catalogues and timetables. During the February half term she also moved her book and reading corner to another part of the classroom. Her reasons were twofold: she felt that, if the books were in the same place all year, the children were not constantly motivated to read them, and it allowed her to monitor more closely the children's reading during the period before registration, as it now contained her 'teacher's chair'.

A constantly reflective teacher, Miss Brown, critical of the way in which she had used the school's library in the previous year, changed her approach and felt she had improved the use of her library period to induct children into better understanding of libraries:

> Last year, I sort of just took them down and showed them how to find books and that was about it. This year, I've really focused in closely on how to use the library system – showing them the simple Dewey system and how to use books.

Miss Brown placed a great deal of emphasis on building children's confidence in their reading, as her comments about her least able pupil reveal, when asked what she would do if he could not read a particular word:

> With somebody like Paul, I would probably mouth the first sound of the word to see if he can get it right. Because that way he feels he's got it right – I haven't told him.

Her use of praise was noted regularly during classroom observation and seemed to be appreciated by the children. This was backed up by the systematic use of rewards, an approach highly developed throughout the school. Miss Brown believed that stickers and stars were good motivators, but she also demonstrated how she valued the children's writing through carefully assembled wall displays of all the pupils' work. A highly structured monitoring and assessment system was in place throughout the school. Each teacher kept a record card for each child which, for reading, incorporated details such as the child's phonological awareness, knowledge of key words, reading strategies and behaviour. This was then passed on to the next teacher so that a detailed account of progress was available throughout a child's time at the school.

A key feature of Miss Brown's approach to the teaching of reading was the way in which she differentiated tasks and reading materials to accommodate the wide range of reading ability within her Year 1 class, whether of high, medium or low ability. Oliver, a very able boy with a voracious appetite for reading, was allowed to take nine books home to read during the February half term. By this stage of the school year he had read 115 books from school since the previous September.

Oliver was a pupil of high ability who was making rapid progress. Miss Brown nonetheless provided him with individualised tasks to develop his reading skills even further. These included: giving him more detailed research tasks than were assigned to other pupils, where he had to write up what he had learned from a particular non-fiction book; talking about particular authors and why he liked them; and writing more book reviews, something more commonly observed with older children. He was given numerous opportunities to use the Dewey system in the school's library and was often observed using the contents and index sections of non-fiction books to find information quickly.

Miss Brown emphasised the importance of establishing a good relationship with parents, stating, when interviewed, that she saw them as 'partners in their children's education'. All teachers tend to say this, but our interviews with parents of pupils in her class confirmed the quality of the relationship. They described her as keen to listen to their concerns and ideas about their own children's reading, and willing to try to pay heed and act on what they said.

Miss Brown's class made considerable progress during the year. Her ability to match tasks and books to individuals, her undoubted industry and the careful structuring of her lessons and the children's programme may well have been instrumental in this, though they were not the only likely causes. Underpinning Miss Brown's effective teaching of reading were considerable class management skills. Her on-task involvement levels were consistently high, averaging 83. Lessons were carefully prepared and, if appropriate, materials were set out on tables before the children arrived in the morning, reducing the amount of time taken to settle children to tasks. Relevant development activities were in place so that children who finished their work early could extend it to a higher level. Children were well aware of the classroom routines and made efficient use of resources. Her relationship with the children was firm, but warm. Her overwhelmingly positive attitude towards reading and books was apparent to anyone entering her classroom and seemed infectious and hard to resist. As she herself put it:

> I love books, I really, really do. I'm so enthusiastic about reading and stories that my children just can't not be, really!

Miss Stinton – Year 2

Miss Stinton was in her first year at Hilton Primary School and had not been qualified as a teacher for very long. When she was initially asked to define the term literacy she was eager to penetrate beneath the surface of the concept:

[It's] enabling people to communicate through speech, writing and reading. Not just having the basics of that, but being questioned enough to understand what you're reading and what you're writing. It's not just getting by in the world of language, but having a bit more depth than that.

If Miss Stinton had only been interviewed and not observed, it would have been difficult to ascertain whether this statement was merely a pious ideology or reflected what actually happened in her classroom. As the school year progressed, however, observation of lessons and interviews with her pupils increasingly confirmed that Miss Stinton put a great deal of time and energy into ensuring that her philosophy became reality for the children in her class and was not mere rhetoric. Over the year all the children were regularly heard reading, irrespective of ability, and each kept a clear reading record.

When the researcher heard the six target pupils reading and interviewed them, it was notable that a premium had been put on understanding, and indeed on autonomy. All six, irrespective of ability, used a range of strategies to help them understand the text. They talked freely about the pictures in their books, self-corrected words when they realised they had made a mistake, tried sounding out words when they encountered difficult ones, or split the words up and looked to the pictures and the context of the story for clues. There was very high congruence between what Miss Stinton said she did and what was observed in the classroom. She had explained in interview what she would do if a child got stuck on a word:

> I'd encourage them to read the sentence again and see if that helped, so they're reading it for meaning. I might read the sentence to them and stop at the word, give it the sort of intonation, so it could help to give them a clue; encourage them to look at the picture ... it depends what stage they're at. If they were quite good readers already, I would encourage them to read on a little bit further. That sometimes gives them a hint as well. And look at the initial sound, maybe the initial two sounds, depending on the word. And if they really couldn't get it, I'd tell them because otherwise they're reading just for words rather than for whole meaning. If they're spending too much time on decoding one word then they've lost the thread of the story, which is what it should all be about really.

One of the two improvers identified by Miss Stinton was a girl called Marti. Her reading age improved from 6.9 at the beginning of the year to 9.3 at the end of the year, and she exemplified how this philosophy had been translated into practice. Marti told the researcher that she loved reading in Miss

Stinton's class, something she reiterated at the end of the school year. She was reading a play from a reading scheme and she had been encouraged to go through all the characters first, before starting on the text. She discussed the pictures and referred back to the character list to help her understanding of the story. As her confidence and understanding of text increased, Miss Stinton helped her gradually introduce more intonation into her reading and discussed what was happening with her. Marti was effusive about all aspects of reading and explained that it made you use your imagination more. She read a lot and liked silent reading and shared reading, time in the classroom which she used assiduously.

Silent reading and shared reading were not the only means by which Miss Stinton encouraged improvement in her pupils' reading. She tried to work explicitly on particular skills and combined this analytical approach with comprehension and enjoyment:

> I read individually with them and they do with other adults. I share lots of books and show them what I am reading, so I'm showing them the print as well. I teach them phonics too and blends, so they can decode the beginning of a word, but mainly encourage them to read for enjoyment and for meaning. Many of them are starting to use books for other purposes like information, finding out things.

This emphasis on understanding and using books for a purpose was neatly illustrated when the class was observed during a 'sharing time' period. One pupil, John, wished to show the rest of the class an encyclopaedia:

> *Teacher:* (*To the rest of the class*) Can you remember what it is called?
> *Pupil 1:* Is it like a dictionary?
> *Teacher:* That's a good idea, can you remember what it is called at the back?
> *Pupil 2:* Information
> *Pupil 3:* Introduction
> *Teacher:* Yes, it does start with 'In'.
> *Pupil 4:* Index.

> John turns to the back of the book, looks something up in the index and then flicks through the encyclopaedia to the relevant page. As the discussion continues, Miss Stinton used different opportunities both to expand the pupils' knowledge base and to learn more about how reference books can be used.

This was a good example of her making the acquisition of literacy something that penetrated beneath the surface.

Miss Stinton is another teacher in this study with good class management skills. Her on-task involvement levels were high and averaged out at 83, which meant that effective use of time was a significant element in her teaching. She also created a rich literacy environment. Her classroom had over 600 books in it and the pupils also had access to a new infant library that had just been restocked. Miss Stinton always had a display of books supporting the current topic and linked this to other features of whatever was the theme of the moment. When the topic was 'Communication', there was a 'hands-on' post office display in the classroom, which included envelopes, cards, forms and a post box. All areas were clearly labelled with information prompts such as: 'Use the index to research' and displays were regularly changed and updated.

Although Miss Stinton took great pains to structure activities and ensure that pupils were clear about what it was that they were expected to do, she also exhibited considerable patience when expanding the pupils' own attempts to comprehend the task in hand. She provided explanation, but also evoked interest by trying to fire the pupils' own imagination, often capitalising on curiosity. In one lesson she started to describe someone from a story, in an intriguing voice, while holding a little box in her hand:

> *Teacher:* This person walks very slowly into an enchanted forest. She's got a big black bag, and inside her big black bag there is ... what do *you* think?
> *Pupil 1:* A magic wand.
> *Pupil 2:* Toys.

The teacher continues to tell the story, asking for ideas as to which story she is telling; after a few guesses each time, she tells them a bit more of the story. When the children have guessed the story correctly she tells them that she is putting her box back into her cupboard now, because it is a magic box. The children all say 'Ahhh' in disappointment that it is over. The teacher then explains what she wants them to do and says when they have written their story it will go into a big self-made book.

She explained why she had done that type of lesson:

> It's just to inspire them really.... I introduced [a] magic shell earlier with them. It's really just to get their imagination going ... they put it in the middle and touch it if they need an idea. It's just getting ideas flowing, rather than just saying, 'Go and write a story'. And the other thing I might do ... I want to get hold of a cloak that's got pockets in it and pull objects out of that – as a story aid.

Miss Stinton's lessons were a combination of well-organised and stimulating activities and discussions, often involving plays, poems, games, sharing ideas. She translated her aspiration to help children understand what they were reading into action, reflecting a great deal on different ways of stimulating their imagination. She often explained something in detail to them when she thought it necessary, but at the same time encouraging them to be independent thinkers, so they became autonomous. During 'sharing books' time the pupils' discussions were very animated and observations of individual children showed that all appeared to be discussing their books and genuinely enjoying what they were doing.

Mrs Hutchings – Year 2/3

Mrs Hutchings, a very experienced teacher, had recently joined the staff of Suttwell School as a member of the senior management team and as language co-ordinator for Key Stage 1. Suttwell School gave language a high priority and had been placed highly in the local authority's league tables showing the results of national tests on pupils aged 11. She regarded the Schools Library Service as an excellent resource for topic packs and her own professional literature, so it was used extensively, as was the resources centre at the local university. The school was keen to bring in outsiders, such as story-tellers, poets and drama specialists, to provide the pupils with a rich variety of language experiences.

Although the approach to the teaching of reading within the school when Mrs Hutchings arrived had been closely structured around two core reading schemes, she explained that her own philosophy was firmly grounded in 'real books', and she had removed the existing scheme books from the shelves in her classroom by the end of the first term. She said she found the parents' expectations that their children would follow a reading scheme to be an unwelcome pressure, 'because I'm not used to teaching like that'. She particularly objected to the competitive element which she believed a scheme encouraged. Mrs Hutchings acknowledged, however, that some children needed a more structured approach to reading and was a keen advocate of the 'Longman Book Project', which the school subsequently acquired during the period of the research project for the Reception/Year 1 class and the less able Year 2 readers. She favoured this scheme because she felt 'it contains real books by real authors, offering the children the chance to experience a variety of styles, combined with a graded vocabulary'.

Mrs Hutchings considered most of the children in her class to be 'fluent readers', but she had some children who undertook extra literacy activities to raise their standard of reading:

> They're doing structured reading books with a lot of phonic input as well, plus whole word skills from when I work on the easel and

also we do spelling and reading of key words. I use a phonic work-
shop on the computer; usually they do that with the classroom
assistant.

The more able children were guided towards 'appropriate reading materials'.
Mrs Hutchings said she had 'roughly organised the class books according to
their difficulty', although they were not in any way colour coded. She
supplemented the school's resources with books from her own children's
library at home, finding that she needed to provide more early 'chapter
books', such as Young Puffins, for the developing readers.

Uniquely amongst the teachers interviewed in this LEA, Mrs Hutchings
indicated that if a child did not know a word when sharing a book with her,
she would stress the context cue first of all:

The first thing I usually do is read the rest of the sentence and get
the cue from that, then [I] suggest phonics, if it worked for that
word, or stress the picture.

This emphasis on meaning underpinned Mrs Hutchings' approach to the
teaching of reading, along with her conviction that books must always be for
pleasure. If children chose a book and then found they did not like it, she
insisted they change it:

I say to them 'If you don't like it, just go on to something else.
Don't continue with a book that you don't like. Don't read it!'

When asked what strategies were particularly important in improving children's reading, Mrs Hutchings highlighted both sharing books with
children and matching reading materials, not only to children's stage of
reading development, but also to their interests:

We do take time trying to fit books to children quite a bit – that
we think they would really like. If they seem to be getting a bit fed
up, we try and branch off a bit and do other things.

Classroom observation of her lessons revealed that a key feature of Mrs
Hutchings' approach to reading was that, when she was sharing a book with
a child, she allowed no interruptions from other children.

Many teachers in the study talked about the importance of engendering
in their pupils 'a love of books and reading'. In Mrs Hutchings' class children clearly seemed to enjoy their quiet reading time after lunch, when they
could share books with each other, or read individually. This was evidenced
by an extraordinarily high average on-task involvement score during these
sessions of 98, meaning that only one child was slightly off-task, and also by

the consistency with which the children brought their favourite books from home to share with the teacher and the class. Time was made available for this at the end of each quiet reading session.

Writing pupils' own books was a regular activity. It was also notable that there was a high degree of individual initiative in this class. Not only was writing a self-made book a task set by the teacher, it was also initiated by pupils themselves and undertaken in their own time or at home. They produced both fiction and non-fiction books themselves, including atlases, and these were displayed alongside the commercially published reading materials for other children to read. Time was regularly set aside for children to share their own writing with the rest of the class. The account below is typical of what took place in these sessions. Mrs Hutchings used them in a number of ways: to develop the children's speaking and listening skills, to explore with them their thoughts about their writing, to talk about words, to show they are valued as writers. She was also sensitive to the fact that some children might feel shy reading publicly in front of the whole class:

> As the children arrive in class, some tell the teacher that they have written stories at home. After the register has been taken the teacher invites these children to come to the front of the class with their stories.

> *Teacher:* This is a listening time. One person will be speaking, so the rest of you have to listen. (*Reading out the title of Claire's story*) 'The Party' by Claire, aged 6. Do you want to read it yourself to the class, Claire?
> *Claire:* (*Nods. She reads out her story, standing beside the teacher*)
> *Teacher:* That was lovely, Claire. Did anything give you the idea for that story?
> *Claire:* I asked my mum to give me a title so that I could then write a story.
> *Teacher:* What a good idea, Claire! Would anyone like to ask Claire anything about her story?

> Some children put their hands up. Claire answers the questions confidently. The teacher praises Claire again and then asks Charles to come to the front.

> *Teacher:* Charles has written a story, too. Are you reading it, Charles?
> *Charles:* No, you read it.

> The teacher reads it for him, using a great deal of voice expression. When she has finished she comments: 'I liked some of the words you used in your story, Charles, like "investigate".'

When the researcher interviewed the pupils in this class, nearly all of them responded to the question 'Who reads to you in class?' by saying 'the children at book time'. It was spoken with approval and was clearly a routine which the pupils valued and enjoyed.

Mrs Hutchings had generated in her class not only an enormous enthusiasm for books but also an awareness of style and words. The children often identified different authors' styles of writing and then tried them out for themselves in their stories. In one book read to the class by Mrs Hutchings, the story had appeared to come to an end, but then the next page had said, 'But that wasn't quite the end of the story ... ' and had continued. The children had been attracted to this strategy and in the ensuing two weeks many of them adopted variations of this piece of teasing intrigue in their own story writing. Mrs Hutchings regularly talked about particular words, exploring their meanings with pupils, whereupon these words would often appear in the children's writing. It was another feature of her teaching that was commented on with approval by pupils. When interviewed, one child explained how she had deliberately helped to build his vocabulary, saying that he liked reading 'because I can use good words like "exaggerate" when I'm writing'.

Lesson observations regularly identified incidents in Mrs Hutchings' classroom showing that each individual child was valued. Her interactions with the children were full of positive reinforcement: praise for good work, good effort and good behaviour. Every child's work was displayed on the walls. Humour was also a notable feature of her lessons and she frequently shared gales of laughter with the children. They responded by producing work of a high quality. Of the ten 7 year old children in the class who took national tests, nine scored above the national average in a not especially privileged area. Central to Mrs Hutchings' successful teaching of reading was the extremely high degree of involvement in the task, which ensured consistent concentration on their work by her pupils. The quality of these skills was brought into sharp focus when a student teacher took some of her lessons during a final teaching practice in the summer term of the observation period. In lessons observed given by the student, on-task involvement levels fell to 72. Mrs Hutchings' score over the year averaged 93.

Miss Lansbury – Year 3

Miss Lansbury had taught for twenty-five years, the first eighteen of them in secondary schools, and she was now the language co-ordinator at Broadlands Primary School, teaching a Year 3 class. She had attended a variety of LEA courses relating to literacy, which she described as 'very helpful and full of good concrete ideas as well as theory', and she seemed knowledgeable about teaching English, with a clear idea of what she was doing and why.

A noticeable feature of Mrs Lansbury's teaching was the use of information technology. She was very enthusiastic about using interactive technology for improving literacy, and Broadlands Primary was exceptionally well equipped with computers, so the pupils were very computer literate. They had individual floppy disks so that they could undertake extended writing and graphics projects, and they were used to demonstrating the various programs to the many visitors the school attracted. The computers were always in use, with children either writing their own work or using CD-ROMs to find out about Ancient Rome, or to work on their spelling, vocabulary and comprehension, as well as to record their own progress.

There was more evidence of the pupils' extensive use of computers in Miss Lansbury's classroom wall displays. These showed computer designs of bridges, word-processed factual information about how they had designed them, alongside poems about bridges. Books were also given a high profile, with table displays of books about the class's current topic and a book corner set in an alcove, attractively set out like a bower. The importance of reading was signalled in many ways to pupils. Both intrinsic and extrinsic rewards and recognition were common. The school had a 'Good Readers' board displaying names of pupils who had been doing well, and bookmarks were presented in assembly for progress.

Miss Lansbury was flexible and adapted her teaching to individuals. If a particular approach or book appeared not to be working very well for one child, she used her extensive knowledge of resources and individual children's interests to find something more suitable. The main reading scheme was *Story Chest*, which she liked because of its breadth and the inclusion of non-fiction poetry and plays as well as stories. She identified 'group reading' as her main approach to the teaching of reading, with the children arranged in ability groups. This, she said, was particularly appropriate for teaching a wide variety of reading skills, from inference and deduction to reading with expression:

> I think group reading is the single, most fundamental thing that has affected the teaching of reading in this school. I would always do it now because I think it works better than any other method. I think it's non-threatening because the children are in a group. They feel less threatened than in a 'one-to-one'. I think you can give them more attention than if it's one-to-one and, because you've got a group of four or five, you can actually teach them for 10 to 15 minutes, whereas if you're just hearing a child read, that's not really teaching reading at all.

Some children still needed phonics work and, for a few, she arranged paired reading sessions, with children of average ability helping poorer readers, which, she believed, helped them both. The children had a session with everyone reading each day, and there was what she called 'guided choice' of books from the class library. Miss Lansbury stressed the importance of reading in other curriculum areas as well, mentioning reading for meaning, following instructions in maths, and using research skills for topic work.

Miss Lansbury had a very pleasant, easy manner with her children, and personal relationships seemed extremely positive. Her response to noisy chatter was to signal disapproval not by reprimand but by using the word 'excited'. It was a code that the pupils understood, and the mention of it quelled any noise. She could modify their behaviour when necessary by making comments such as, 'Goodness, you are excited this morning!' When asked to find words to describe a castle in one lesson, the noise level from a particular group was getting higher, so she asked, 'Are you all right? I can hear you're getting excited!' They told her they were on their third page of words. She replied, 'Third page! My goodness. Three pages of ideas!' and the pupils continued with the work, pleased with themselves, but also modifying their voices in discussion.

In interview she stressed that her aim was to make the children independent, and this was reflected in her comments about their work, which she discussed with them in a noticeably egalitarian manner, talking to them as sensible people who just happened to be younger than she was. She gave explicit advice on the process of improving a piece of work, but left it to individuals to decide how to use it on any particular piece of work, which she said was theirs, so they must make the decision. 'Did you mean to leave us not quite sure about what he knew? Is that what you wanted?' she commented on one occasion, when children were redrafting a story. 'OK. That's fine. You're the author.'

This manner of talking to pupils did not appear to give *carte blanche* to the lazy or easily satisfied, as Miss Lansbury's praise for what they had already done was mixed with encouragement to do even better. She taught skills such as redrafting in a systematic and cumulative way, providing prompt sheets with questions for children to ask themselves. There were notices and charts on the walls giving guidelines about making notes, writing a draft, or finding more interesting words for a particular context, and these contributed to what seemed an unoppressive drive for improvement. On numerous occasions she would publicly urge the class to ask themselves the question: 'Is this the best, the very best, that I can do at eight years old?'

In one lesson observed, on the subject of 'punctuation and how to use question marks', she started by getting children to ask each other questions. After a number of expected ones, such as, 'Do you like cabbage?' and 'Have you got any brothers and sisters?', one girl asked Miss Lansbury, 'Is there some job you would have liked, if you weren't a teacher?' Miss Lansbury thought for a moment and then replied, 'Not really. Perhaps something to do with publishing books, but, no. On a good day, teaching is the best job in the world.' She said it with conviction.

Mrs Turner – Year 5

Mrs Turner, a Year 5 teacher, had taught at Hilton Primary School for many years and was one of their more established members of staff. She had seen many changes, including a new head in the previous year, but although maintaining what she regarded as her 'traditional' teaching style, she was always very interested in new initiatives and anything that might help her pedagogy. She was the school's language co-ordinator and therefore had a personal and formal interest in disseminating good practice in the teaching of literacy to the rest of the teaching staff.

For her work as language co-ordinator she was given a 'quite generous half day per week non-contact time', during which she had the opportunity to visit other year groups. Although she ran staff meetings for other teachers and disseminated information to teachers after attending courses herself, she recognised the professional knowledge of the other staff: 'I need to involve the expertise of those with experience of younger children', and she was prepared to 'bow to the superior knowledge of the Key Stage 1 co-ordinator'. Her approach to literacy was that of a team player, working to create a policy that involved the knowledge and input of all the school's staff.

Within her own classroom her approach to reading was enthusiastic and she adopted a varied approach that was designed to provide a high degree of structure in the first instance, but progression towards a more individual and independent approach for those who were able to cope with it:

> It depends on the ability of the child. The children who have specific problems with reading are still being given phonic work and we use the Oxford Reading Tree and ask the Special Needs Co-ordinator for appropriate worksheets and so on for them. We use ancillary work to do it. The more able readers are being weaned off the reading scheme and have a free choice of books at certain times of day, but other parts of the day they have guided choice and the same goes for the most able readers.

Her emphasis in teaching was on building confidence and matching the reading material to the individual ability of the child, to try to ensure that every pupil might experience success. She combined reading for pleasure with reading for a purpose, so that pupils could see why it was that they needed to be able to read. She offered them a wide range of materials, including reading schemes, plays, fiction and non-fiction, puzzle books, joke books and poetry. She also had a regular time in class where pupils were timetabled to listen to story tapes and, as mentioned earlier, in response to the lack of short commercially produced ones, she had taped most of the selection herself. Such sessions were carefully structured, with pupils asked to follow the text closely as they listened to the tapes. All her teaching materials were clearly labelled and well organised in a designated area of the classroom.

In Mrs Turner's class there was never any ambiguity about what pupils were expected to do. They had regular pre-programmed slots in the day for particular activities, which included story tapes, ERIC time when all pupils read, held at exactly the same time every morning and offering 'guided choice'. In the afternoon she also had a reading time which was 'free choice' and once a week there was a timetabled visit to the library. Mrs Turner always had a class reader, from which she read to the class at the end of every day and the pupils were expected to follow the text. She also made sure that she differentiated according to individual ability when helping children read their books, choose new books, or when she discussed the class reader with them. Differentiation was a particular issue in this class. When tested at the beginning of the year, the reading ability of these 9 and 10 year old pupils ranged from a reading age of below 6 to above 13:

> We have a class reader which for some stories, like the Victorian one I am doing at the moment.... We've all got a book and I read it for them to follow a text and hear it read with expression. I read it to them for 15 minutes at the end of the day, more or less every day. And then I also use it when we are talking about and discussing the story, to talk about characterisation, or plot, or language, so that they can then use the text to substantiate what they are saying. And in that way I have to differentiate by the sort of questions I will pose to the sort of people. I'll know that the least able are just staring at the book but they've got the feeling that they're doing the same as everyone else, so it's quite a useful, efficient way of quite a lot of people being able to discuss a piece of literature and presumably sharing in the enjoyment of sharing.

Mrs Turner's organisation, planning and class management skills were conspicuously well developed, and her class's on-task involvement averaged over 82 during the researcher's visits. Any instructions she gave were clearly expressed with attention to detail. She tried regularly to involve pupils in discussion to enhance their comprehension of the task. She talked with enthusiasm of the English language and took as many opportunities as she could to discuss different words and meanings with the class. On one occasion the children came back from an assembly and she immediately held an impromptu discussion with them about the story they had been reading:

> Mrs Turner starts by asking those who had been in assembly to talk to those who had not been there about the Greek myth they had heard, reminding them beforehand that there are 'lots of lovely long words to remember'.

Teacher: What was the story about?

One child starts the story off.

Teacher: Who did she marry?
Pupil: An old King.
Teacher: Can anyone remember his name?

A pupil answers correctly.

Teacher: Oh, well done. What nation did he come from?
Pupil: Troy.
Teacher: Yes, he was from Troy, he was a Trojan.

Mrs Turner continues the discussion, using questions and answers to recapitulate on the story, taking the answers one at a time and suggesting that pupils do not take the story forwards too quickly. The discussion ends with the teacher commenting on how many of the words and sayings from the Greek myth are now used in the English language.

This event, like many others, exemplified her style of teaching. It was structured, carefully pre-planned, but also flexible, related to individuals of widely varying ability, involved a high degree of social control, but stressed the pleasure and interest that children could find from the exploration of language.

Common features and differences

In this chapter we have described six teachers, selected from the thirty-five studied in this research. These six teachers ranged in experience from two years to over twenty years and were working in a range of schools, from a small village primary through to a large inner city school in Birmingham. Each teacher was unique, bringing her own individual personality and her own personal experience of what worked well to her teaching of reading. Some were highly organised in advance, others more opportunistic. Their approaches to teaching, the materials they used, the authors they favoured, the structure of their day, the context in which they taught, their views of pedagogy and of their pupils, were different. Some made skilful use of a classroom assistant, but others did not have one available.

Despite this uniqueness, a number of common characteristics can be identified from these six and the other highly competent teachers not described here. While the ten characteristics listed below may show a certain amount in common, however, the individual expression and manifestation of them was often different.

1 *Teachers had a high level of personal enthusiasm for literature and reading* which was translated into attractive well-stocked class libraries and book corners. In many classrooms the teachers supplemented the school's reading resources with their own personal collection of books, as in the cases of Miss Brown and Mrs Hutchings.

2 *Teachers had good professional knowledge*, not only of children's authors, but also of teaching strategies and pedagogy generally. In the case of teaching strategies, this was especially noteworthy with those who were language co-ordinators. All teachers knew of and used a variety of strategies, even though each had particular favourites, such as group reading, or vocabulary building.

3 *Literacy was made very important*. The classrooms themselves were rich literacy environments. Attractive and high-quality displays of all the children's writing, not just the best, dominated the walls in the upper Key Stage 1 and Key Stage 2 classrooms. Interactive displays which asked the children questions about items on show were common. Where lack of wall space limited the amount of displays, teachers produced class books of children's work. These covered all areas of the curriculum. In Miss Brown's class, the children's science work on 'Hot and Cold' was collated in an attractively made book and placed in the book corner for children to read. The importance of literacy was further emphasised by the recognition and celebration of it when it occurred, as described in the next point below.

4 *Teachers celebrated progress and increased children's confidence*. This was often done through drawing attention to someone who had made progress and using focused praise. In all classes there was emphasis on the satisfaction children could obtain from a job well done, while in some classes recognition was more formalised through the use of extrinsic rewards, such as stickers, stars, or certificates presented in school assemblies.

5 *Teachers were able to differentiate and match effectively teaching to pupil* because of their intimate knowledge of available reading materials and individual children themselves, taking account not only of varying levels of ability, but also of individual personal interests. This seemed particularly important with less able and more reluctant readers, where considerable expertise was required to engage and sustain the children's interest. Miss Dobson made skilful use of a bilingual classroom assistant, so that, by better understanding their language and culture, she could match the work closely to individual Asian children whose mother tongue was not English. By successfully differentiating tasks according to ability, these teachers ensured the children's confidence in their own reading.

6 *Systematic monitoring and assessment was notable*, though the form of it varied. Usually there was comprehensive written recording of children's reading strategies and behaviour, in addition to the books being read, but some teachers, like Miss Dobson, were also able to keep their records in their head and knew, without checking, what each child was achieving. The most comprehensive assessments included monitoring children's levels of phonic awareness and sight vocabulary. Some systems had been developed at school level but in most cases there had been some LEA input.

7 *Regular and varied reading activities were seen as crucial to improving the children's reading standards.* Some phonics work was undertaken in all the Key Stage 1 classes observed, although different teachers placed varying degrees of emphasis on this particular aspect. Language games were used to reinforce formal lessons. All teachers made strong links between reading and writing. Of particular note was the way in which these teachers made use of opportunities to highlight and discuss publicly many different aspects of literacy with their class, whether it concerned the meaning and use of words, what a writer of a book is called, or aspects of spelling and punctuation. The example described in the account of Miss Turner was typical of the way in which most of these teachers could capitalise on unplanned opportunities. The children in these classes were developing a rich vocabulary and confidence with which to discuss language and literature.

8 *Pupils were encouraged to develop independence and autonomy.* In different ways, even in classes where activities were highly structured, or where the teacher had a dominant personality, pupils were encouraged to develop ways of attacking unfamiliar words, taking their own reading forward, or backing their own judgement as authors when writing. Books written by pupils themselves were as highly valued as other books in the classroom and were displayed prominently for others to borrow and read, thereby giving the children's writing a genuine purpose and audience.

9 *Underpinning effective teachers' strategies for the teaching of reading were a high degree of classroom management skill and good-quality personal relationships with pupils.* These classrooms were orderly environments where the children understood the set tasks, knew where and how to access resources, and were able to concentrate on their work. The pupil on-task levels recorded during classroom observation were universally high, some being amongst the highest we have recorded in research projects in primary schools. This is not to say that teachers were dour and puritanical, lacking warmth or humour. Quite the reverse. Most of these teachers had a good rapport with their pupils, were able to joke with them when appropriate and could defuse the occasional potentially

disruptive incident with a light-hearted remark, rather than enter into a confrontation.

10 *Teachers had positive expectations.* All the teachers in this group emphasised that children should strive to reach a high standard, whatever their circumstances. Miss Lansbury publicly stressed the need for her class to do the very best they could for an 8 year old. All wanted children to redraft their writing to improve it. Miss Dobson regularly told the whole class how marvellous she thought they were. Even more importantly, perhaps, the teachers made the children feel that they were interesting young people and valued, so pupils knew their teacher had very high expectations of them all, not just a few.

10

THE PUPIL PERSPECTIVE

The pupil perspective has often been ignored in research. Although children are frequently tested or observed as a group, they are less likely to be interviewed or studied as individuals in class. Yet despite the argument that pupils' views, especially in the case of younger children, are not as reliable or 'mature' as those of adults, interviews with pupils can provide views of their world which sometimes corroborate and on other occasions contradict the perceptions of adults. Pupils often talk in a direct manner, do not have a professional reputation to protect, nor necessarily say what they think is expected of them. In this chapter the research into pupils from Study 4 of the Primary Improvement Project is reported, and in Chapter 11, several individual case studies will be described.

During Study 4 of this research, between six and eight pupils were studied in each of the thirty-five case study classrooms. Six of these consisted of two high, two medium and two low achievers, as identified by the class teacher. In addition teachers were asked to identify two pupils, midway through the year in January/February, who were thought to be improving at a greater rate than other pupils. The research team collected observation data on the pupils, recording what they did during lessons. Their 'on-task' and 'deviancy' was noted, as was that of the other members of their class as described in Chapter 1. They were interviewed regularly, with a semi-structured schedule asking what they read, who they read to and how they felt about reading, and they were often heard reading their current reading book. There were over 900 children in the thirty-five classes, and 258 of them were studied in detail, 130 boys and 128 girls. In Table 10.1 this is sample A.

In addition a further 355 children, sample B in Table 10.1, were given either an NFER or France reading test or, if they were under the age of 6, the LARR language test. Depending on the school's policy and existing practice in the school or LEA, we administered form A or B of the NFER Test or, in the one authority that preferred it, the Primary Reading Test developed by Norman France. The NFER-Nelson Group Reading Test 6–12 contains forty-eight graded items. Children are asked to complete a sentence

Table 10.1 Pupils in Study 4 of the Primary Improvement Project

A *Individual pupils' sample*

Number of high-ability pupils studied	70
Number of medium-ability pupils studied	70
Number of low-ability pupils studied	70
Number of 'improvers' studied	65
Total number of pupils in case studies	258[a]
Boys studied	130
Girls studied	128
Key Stage 1 pupils (aged 4–7)	133
Key Stage 2 pupils (aged 7–11)	125

B *Tested pupils' sample*

Boys tested	183
Girls tested	172
Number given NFER Group Reading Test	238
Number given France Primary Reading Test	88
Number given LARR Test	29
Total number of pupils tested (in 15 classes)	355

Note

a: Total does not add up to 275 as some of the 'improvers' were also in the original sample of six target pupils and three pupils (two medium, one low ability) left during the year.

by circling the correct word out of a possible five choices. The test provides both standardised age scores and reading ages. The Norman France Primary Reading Test (for children aged 5 years 9 months to 12 years 2 months) similarly is based on word recognition and sentence completion, also allowing for the calculation of standardised scores and reading ages. The LARR Test of Emergent Literacy is aimed at children in the age range 4 years to 5 years 3 months and can be administered with individuals or groups of up to four children. The assessment is intended to focus on children's early reading skills: recognition of reading material, identification of reading and writing activities, understanding of basic technical terms of reading.

No test gives a perfect measure of all the aspects of reading one might seek to elicit, but the two reading tests were selected because they gave valuable information on recognition and understanding, have relatively high validity and reliability, are widely used and accepted in schools, and could be administered without disrupting the work of the teachers concerned. The LARR test also has limitations, as does any language test of quite young children, but it did offer a useful indicator of early competence in fields related to literacy.

The tests were given in late September/early October and then again at the end of the school year in late June/early July. As was explained earlier, it was not possible to test all the children, nor even to test all the six 'target pupils' and two 'improvers'. The children tested came from fifteen classes, so test scores were available for 100 out of the 258 children identified for special scrutiny. Table 10.1 summarises the nature of the samples of children. Since forty-two children came from mixed-age classes (fifteen in Year 2/3 and twenty-seven in Year 5/6), these children were assigned randomly to either the higher or lower of Year 2/Year 3, or Year 5/Year 6, in Table 10.5 (see p. 225).

Did pupils 'improve'?

There are many different ways in which children can improve, one of which is on standardised test scores. Improvements in attitude might also be of interest, and 9 year old David, a Year 5 pupil who will be described in Chapter 11, is a good example of someone who started the year hating books and ended with a very positive attitude. Some children may also read more and better-quality literature as their school career progresses. These various types of improvement may be linked or separate. David, for example, improved enormously in terms of his attitude to reading and the nature and quality of books he consumed, but his standardised reading score only went up by 1 point.

In the majority of cases the six target children from each class for sample A were selected as requested, although two teachers chose six pupils irrespective of sex because they felt the general male/female distribution within their classroom was unequal. The researchers did not intervene in the choice of pupils and the decision was made on the teachers' knowledge of their class, not on any a priori guidelines. This meant that pupils who were categorised by one teacher as 'low ability' might have been categorised as of higher ability in another classroom. However, we did have reading test scores on 100 of the children in sample A, and as Table 10.2 shows, teachers' estimates of pupils' ability relate well to the test scores obtained at the beginning of the school year, even though, when they chose six target pupils, they did not know these scores. Analysis of variance showed that the test score means of the three ability groups differed significantly at beyond the 0.001 level; in other words, this would have happened by chance less than once in a thousand times.

Table 10.2 also reveals that the improvers they selected midway through the year tended to be children of below-average ability. However, teachers seem to have successfully identified children who were actually improving beyond the norm, as the improvers gained 6.5 points over the year, compared with the whole sample's gain of 4.1 points and the high, medium and low groups, who gained 4.4, 4.1 and 4.0 points respectively.

In terms of the test scores obtained, the whole sample did increase in

Table 10.2 Average beginning of year test scores and average points gain during the school year of the six target pupils and two improvers selected by teachers

Teachers' ability estimate	Average test score	Average points gain
High	109	4.4
Medium	99	4.1
Low	78	4.0
'Improver'	91	6.5

performance, though inevitably with standardised tests caution must be exercised, as they give but one snapshot of achievement and there are other reservations. The tests have a mean of 100 and a standard deviation of 15, so some two-thirds of children will score between 85 and 115 on it. The mean score of the sample B pupils tested went up by 4.1 points, from 95.4 to 99.5, but there was considerable variation between individual pupils and different classes. The extreme cases were three pupils who 'improved' between 26 and 32 points and two who 'declined' by 14 and 25 points respectively. Given some children's nervousness, possible lack of interest on the first or second occasion, or some other kind of artefact, such big changes often need explanation, and in Chapter 11 we report an example of a huge increase and a sizeable decline amongst two pupils within the very same class.

Some of the teachers in the sample of thirty-five who were selected by their head as being especially competent had rescued classes that had been badly taught the previous year. In these circumstances a class may be put 'back on track', in that it underperforms at the beginning of the year because of the legacy of the previous teacher, but achieves normality by the end of it. Also there is some evidence that children in any case slip back in test performance over the summer holidays. Most of the children were not tested until October, however, so this may or may not be a factor. These are just some of the cautions one needs to bear in mind.

In a fictitious class consisting entirely of 'average' pupils, each child would record a standardised score of 100 at both the beginning and end of the year. Among the 355 pupils on whom we had full 'before' and 'after' scores tested in fifteen classes, there were 62 per cent of children who improved their standardised score, 28 per cent whose score declined, and 10 per cent who achieved exactly the same level. These differences were significant on both a correlated *t* test and the Wilcoxon signed ranks test, as described in Chapter 6. Only one teacher's overall class scores actually declined, and that by less than 1 point, the others all increasing by between 2 and 11 points. In general, therefore, the whole sample does appear to be an improving group, though with considerable individual variation within it.

Pupils' reading

During interviews there was considerable focus on what children were reading, as well as on their progress or lack of it. Whenever pupils were asked if they had a current reading book they tended to say that they had, except for four children in Key Stage 1 and four in Key Stage 2. When asked who chose their book there were similar findings across all the stages, with the majority having chosen their own book, but in approximately a quarter of cases pupils had had their book chosen for them by their teacher. At all ages those who had their book chosen for them were more likely to be low-ability pupils. Occasionally the classroom assistant or special needs teacher was instrumental in selecting books for pupils, but the main responsibilities lay with the pupils themselves or their teachers.

The pupils gave a wide variety of reasons for what influenced their choice of books, which ranged from enjoying other books by the same author to previous knowledge of the book, but the most common specific reason given was the appearance of the book, this being more likely to be the case with older pupils than younger ones. Pupils were influenced by the front of the book or the pictures and one pupil summarised his choice by quoting the cliché: 'I really judge a book by its cover.' In some cases the pupils' personal preferences seemed paramount, and it was clear that they picked books they thought they would enjoy based on past experience:

> I like scary books or funny books and I like long books. I like getting into a book and reading it for ages and ages.
>
> (11 year old girl, medium ability)

On other occasions their choice of books had been influenced by what they had been learning about in school:

> I've been reading this non-fiction book recently. It's about dogs and cats. We had a pet assembly a few weeks ago, so I got this book out of the library.
>
> (7 year old boy, high ability)

Children were also asked what other things they read in school apart from their reading books. Although we are aware that pupils are exposed to a large range of printed matter aside from reading books, pupils were asked this open question to ascertain whether they were aware of text other than that in the form of a book. As expected, however, most pupils mentioned other story books they were reading, reading schemes, or specific fiction or non-fiction books.

Some did mention dictionaries, poetry or comics/magazines and occasionally pupils said that they read wall display work, classroom notices and worksheets. Children do have to read printed matter other than books in the classroom, but their responses suggest that 'reading' is still primarily perceived by the majority of pupils as something which involves a book. The child quoted below, however, read a range of books and used some of the other printed text displayed in his classroom to help him with his choice:

> [I've been reading] *Biker Mice From Mars, Joe's Cafe, There's a Hole in My Bucket, Puss in Boots*, signs and posters, so that I can find out about other books in the reading corner.
>
> (7 year old boy, high ability)

A 6 year old low-ability child was also clear about why words were displayed in the classroom and what she was expected to do. There was a clear routine that she followed and she knew this involved other printed matter apart from her reading book:

> Words off there [points to the display on wall]. Those books over there [points at the story books displayed] and flashcards [shows them to the researcher and then reads them].
>
> (6 year old girl, low ability)

When asked what they most liked to read most of the younger pupils aged 5 to 7 mentioned fiction books, some stating the ones they had particularly enjoyed, a few children liked reading comics or newspapers and some said they enjoyed the reading schemes they were on. Relatively few mentioned non-fiction books, and fiction was overwhelmingly more popular with this age group. At the junior stage, among 7 to 11 year olds, there was a slight shift in choice, but the majority of children still liked fiction best, comics, humorous text and reading schemes were also mentioned by a few, the number who favoured non-fiction had increased to about a fifth of the sample and there were also a few children who said that they enjoyed reading poetry. Fiction was popular across the sexes and the ability ranges, although the type of books favoured varied by age group and ability:

> Ordinary books like *Mrs Wobble the Waitress*.
>
> (7 year old girl, medium ability)

> All kinds of books except ones without pictures.
>
> (7 year old boy, low ability)

When they were asked what they read at home, there was a considerable range in children's background reading, which reflected the many social differences between them as well as the varying attitudes and aspirations of their parents and families. About a quarter of the older children had bought the books themselves, a similar number said they received them as presents. Nearly a quarter of children said they had obtained their books from the public library, while in just over a sixth of cases they came from the school or class library.

The younger children usually had books bought for them, either by parents or as presents. They also mentioned getting books from school, but did not seem to visit the public libraries in the same way as some of the older children. Two comments from high-ability infant school girls show how books were valued in their households and how this in turn encouraged them to read for pleasure and information:

> I read lots of animal books at home. We've got a great big tall bookcase full of non-fiction books. Mum sometimes buys me books. She'll say 'would you like this book?' and we always get lots of books to take away on holidays.

> Difficult books what I try to learn. And my bible because I want to learn about Jesus. And *My Body* book – I wanted to know how monkeys change into humans. I've got thousands of books at home.

Reading with adults

Nearly 90 per cent of 5 to 7 year olds said that they read to their class teacher, although this number was quite significantly smaller with 7 to 11 year olds, being slightly over half. Just over a fifth of the older pupils said that they read to other children, either in their own class or in another class, a slightly higher figure than that obtained with the younger pupils. One marked difference between the two age groups was that a fifth of the older pupils said that they did not read to anyone, whereas at Key Stage 1 virtually all the children read to someone and in a third of cases this included classroom assistants, which was only the case for a sixth of the older pupils. The frequency and variety of the people read to by some of the younger pupils is illustrated by the comment made by this 6 year old girl:

> [I read to] lots of people. Mrs Shaw [class teacher], Mrs Milne [classroom assistant], Mary [the dinner helper who comes in to hear the readers], and we read to the juniors, and the juniors sometimes help us do our work.

Older pupils are left more on their own, as it is assumed that the majority have mastered the basic skills relating to reading. In some cases it was difficult to know how the teacher assessed and monitored the reading progress of those pupils whom she never heard reading. In one Key Stage 2 class the teacher said he only ever heard the low-ability pupils read and consequently, when asked to name two pupils he thought had improved during the year, stated that he was unable to do so, precisely for this reason. However, the pupils in his class performed well on the reading tests we set, and read quietly during the daily silent reading sessions that we observed. This was a school in a middle-class area where many of the pupils had strong parental support, and the teacher appeared to concentrate his efforts on other areas of the curriculum.

Although the amount of time teachers spent hearing pupils read declined at Key Stage 2, the use of ERIC time was popular within both age groups. From the perspective of some pupils, however, it was not always the 'silent' reading period that teachers perceived it to be. In some classes pupils did not see it as a peaceful opportunity to read quietly, but rather as one where there were interruptions and distractions of different kinds:

> Sometimes [we have silent reading], when it's morning time, but everyone wants me to sit next to them to help them, but I know I can't help everybody.
>
> (7 year old girl, labelled by the teacher as 'medium ability',
> but more highly rated by fellow pupils)

> It's never quiet in this class.
>
> (6 year old boy, high ability)

Pupils were also asked whether they took their reading book home and irrespective of this whether they read to anyone there and who they read to. All the 5 to 7 year olds' classes took their books home, many doing so every day. The great majority of 7 to 11 year old pupils also took books home, although a sixth claimed they never did. In some cases this was because they had books at home that they preferred to read. Nearly two-thirds of the younger pupils said they took their books home every day, with this number dropping to about a third at Key Stage 2.

Approximately three-quarters of the 5 to 7 year old pupils read with their mother and about half read to their father; a number also read to one of their siblings. Half of the 7 to 11 year old pupils read to their mother and just over a quarter read to their father, with a similar number reading to a sibling. These differences between mothers and fathers reading with their children were hugely significant on a chi-squared test at beyond the 0.001 level (could have happened by chance on less than one occasion in a thousand). Boys were slightly more likely than girls to read with their brother, but girls were much more likely to read with their sister (this latter difference was significant at the 0.05 level, that is to say, would have occurred by chance on less than one occasion in twenty). A quarter claimed that they did not read out loud to anyone at home.

It is evident that, for many children in primary schools, there is a lack of a male role model, so far as reading is concerned, both at home and at school. Most primary teachers are female, as are classroom assistants, parent helpers and meal-time assistants. The pupils' responses show that children are more likely to read with their mother at home. This finding is in line with other studies of parental involvement (Minns 1990, Millard 1997). From a boy's perspective, therefore, the message seems to be, from an early age, that reading is something one does in the company of adult women, unlike sport, for example, which is often done in the company of adult males.

The stereotypes were not always in operation, however, as there were parents who still wished to hear older pupils read, even when they had mastered the decoding skills, and there were fathers who were as heavily involved in their children's reading as the mothers, if not more so in certain cases. One capable 11 year old girl stated:

> I sometimes read to my dad. If there is something interesting in a
> book or newspaper my dad sometimes reads it out, or gives it to me
> to read.

The trend to read to someone did decline both in school and at home as pupils got older. One child who was asked how reading in the juniors was different from when she was in the infants commented on the less directive role played by her teacher:

> In the infants the teacher calls you out one by one to read a book,
> but now you can read on your own without the teacher sitting
> beside you.
>
> (11 year old girl, medium ability)

Pupils were also asked if they ever talked to anyone about the books they read. Nearly two-thirds of 7 to 11 year olds said that they did, with discussions centring around the plot, the characters and which parts of the book they liked. They were most likely to talk to other children, either informally to friends, out of interest, or as part of a structured group reading session. One-sixth said they spoke to teachers and parents, so it did not appear to be perceived by the pupils to be something that they regularly did with their teachers, even though many teachers themselves saw it as an important element of their lessons. Some pupils mentioned that they effectively discussed a book by writing a book review first, which was then read by the teacher or other pupils. A high-ability 11 year old boy explained how book reviews worked in his class:

We have to write them [the books they have read] all down – what
we think about the book, whether we liked it, do we think anyone
else would like it.

The intended nature of book reviews was often elaborately explained by a
few of the teachers to their pupils during the classroom observations, but we
rarely observed them being read by the teacher or by other pupils in the
class. The younger pupils were also asked about whether anyone at home
had to write anything down to send back to school if they took their reading
book home. Just over three-fifths of the pupils said that someone did, with
slightly more of the lower-ability pupils saying that this was the case.

Pupil autonomy was also investigated. Pupils were asked whether they
had to ask a teacher, once they had finished a book, if they could change it.
About a third of 5 to 7 year olds said they simply went and changed it
themselves, while another third told the teacher first. A small number,
about 10 per cent, had to read the book to the teacher first, before being
allowed to move to another one. A similarly small number were given a
subsequent book by the teacher. The pattern with 7 to 11 year olds altered
slightly. Two-fifths of these pupils changed their own book without
informing the teacher, a quarter telling the teacher first. Only about 5 per
cent of pupils were expected to read from the book to the teacher first before
being allowed to make a change, and a similar percentage had a new book
provided by the teacher. While a quarter of the older pupils commented that
they would be expected to write a book review when they had finished a
book, fewer than 5 per cent mentioned that they would discuss the book
with the teacher or make a record of what they had read.

Four-fifths of the 7 to 11 year old pupils said that they were read to by
someone in class, and this was mainly in the form of a story reading by the
class teacher, often related to the topic they were doing, such as *Lady Daisy
and the Victorians*. Some older children also mentioned other pupils who read
to them, and occasionally classroom assistants or the head teacher did so.
Such mainly story-reading sessions usually took place at the end of the day,
or during an allotted reading time.

Reading strategies

Pupils in the study were asked about the strategies they use if they have
difficulty with, or 'get stuck' on, a word. When they read at school nearly
half of the 5 to 7 year old pupils said that they would ask the teacher, some
stating that the teacher would then tell them the word. A fifth of pupils
would attempt some sort of phonics-based strategy on their own, such as
sounding out the word, although in the case of this 6 year old girl she was
aware of the limitations of this method:

Sound it out, unless it's a 'silly' one. I start on the words in front
and then I read that word.

(6 year old girl, high ability)

In several cases, all in the same LEA, the pupils commented that they
thought the teacher would suggest a phonics-based strategy to them. Just
under half the 7 to 11 year olds said they would ask the teacher for help,
only six mentioning that they thought the teacher would suggest some type
of phonics-based solution. However, nearly half stated that they themselves
would use a phonics strategy. Others said they would look at the context in
which the word was set, some would persevere until they got it, while yet
others felt that they would ask their friends for help. Sometimes this
involved a 'leapfrog' strategy, bypassing the difficult word and hoping to
make sense of the passage later from the context:

I'd carry on and maybe pick up the story without that word and
maybe I might find out myself what that word means, because then
it would fit in with the sentence.

(8 year old girl, high ability)

An 11 year old girl of medium ability said that she also would adopt a
leapfrog strategy:

I leave it out and then go on to the rest, see what the sentence says
and usually the word will make sense.

In these two cases the pupils were not merely decoding the word but also
looking for its meaning. However, studying context was a far less common
occurrence than phonics-based strategies, and was only slightly more preva-
lent amongst the older pupils.

Pupils were asked what would happen if they 'got stuck' on a word when
they were reading at home. Two-fifths of pupils aged 5 to 7 said that an
adult in their household would tell them the word. One-fifth said that the
adult would help them by using a phonics-based strategy, and a slightly
smaller number said that the adult would suggest that they tried using
phonics themselves. One child did mention that she would look at the
pictures for help, but more common than picture cues was the use of initial
sounds or sounding out words. Some parents were both systematic and
determinedly persistent, as these two comments from high-ability 7 year old
girls reveal:

Mum says, 'What does it begin and end with?' and then I have to
get the word. Martin, my step dad, says, 'It begins with a 't'

[sounding it out]' and I have to try and get the word. Jason, my brother, just points to the word. If I can't get it, he tells me it.

They'd just say it out, sound it out. They'd make sure I know it. They make me say it lots of times.

The question was asked how children would behave if they found that a particular book was too hard for them in general. At Key Stage 1 the most popular response, in a third of cases, was that pupils would simply 'choose another book'. Less likely was that they would ask the teacher for help, or persevere with the book on their own. A few said they would simply give up and stop reading, so they could move on to something else. Half of the Key Stage 2 pupils would choose another book, about a sixth would ask the teacher, and another sixth would persevere.

I'd read a bit more, like a chapter. If it was really hard, I'd put it back. When I got better I'd read it again, because I'd understand it better and the words.

(11 year old girl, low ability)

Many of the 5 to 7 year old pupils found it hard to explain how they would know if a book was too difficult for them. Perhaps it seemed so self-evident to them, they could not find the words to express it to others, although some commented that they would know a book was too hard if the individual words were either too difficult or unreadable.

Older pupils tended to say that a particular book being too hard would be signalled by the difficulty of the individual words and whether they understood the meaning of the text. One high-ability 8 year old girl showed clearly that it would take more than a few difficult words to put her off:

If I tried reading it and I couldn't read any of the words, maybe if it was just a few words I couldn't understand, or words I couldn't pronounce, I'd carry on, because it would be a shame, if there were just a few [words I didn't know], that I would have to put it back.

What is interesting about this girl is that her strategy of being doggedly persistent appears to have paid off. Driven by a genuine love of reading and a strong desire to read new books, she was later found to be one of the most significant 'improvers' in the whole sample. During the year in which we studied her classroom behaviour and performance, her reading age increased from 8.2 to 13.2. This ostensible five-year improvement, as measured by a reading test, within a single year, seemed to owe a great deal to her determination and an exceptionally strong drive to acquire competence.

Only occasionally did pupils reveal more elaborate strategies for establishing whether a book was too hard for them. One high-ability 9 year old boy, having been taught a 'cloze'-type strategy by a previous teacher, continued to employ it even after she had left:

> [I would] put it back and read another one. How I would find out [that it is too difficult] is the five finger test. Every time you get stuck on a word, you put up one finger. If you get less than five, the book is just right for you. If you get more than five fingers up, it's too hard. If you get no fingers up, it's too easy. Miss X [the teacher who had now left] taught me.

Boys and girls

There was no particular focus on boys' and girls' reading performance specifically when we began the research, though the design allowed data to be analysed separately. As the research progressed several interesting aspects began to unfold, some familiar, some less so. Certainly there is considerable public interest in some of the data. When one of the researchers (Wragg 1997b) gave the Greenwich lecture, it was our data on the lower likelihood of fathers reading with their children that attracted most press coverage, even though numerous other findings were being reported at the same time.

Boys' and girls' ratings of their own characteristics

In the summer term, towards the end of the school year, all 258 target pupils in sample A were asked about their own personal characteristics during the interview. In this case a structured recording sheet was used, and the interviewer summarised the pupil's views on a 4 point scale, checking with the child first that the category chosen did match what the child had said. An even- rather than odd-numbered scale was used to avoid too many indecisive middle-point replies and four categories were thought to be manageable conceptually for the age spread from 5 to 11 year olds. The seven characteristics and the mean scores obtained by boys and girls are shown in Table 10.3. In each case the maximum possible mean score would be 4.0 if all children rated themselves at the top of the particular scale.

Boys see themselves as more determined than girls and rate their own progress more highly, but they estimate their own help at home to be lower, and this difference was statistically significant at the 0.05 level, that is there is only a one in twenty probability that the result could have been obtained by chance.

As a means of comparison we also asked teachers to rate their pupils on a 6 point scale on some of the same as well as on other characteristics, the bigger scale being used on the grounds that teachers ought to be able to make finer discriminations than young children, but again avoiding a middle point. The results of their scores can be seen in Table 10.4.

Table 10.3 Boys' and girls' ratings of themselves learning to read (258 pupils, 4 point scale; maximum possible score 4.00; the higher the score, the more favourable the self-rating)

Characteristic	Boys	Girls
How good are you at reading?	3.22	3.30
How hard do you try if you're stuck?	3.67	3.47
How much do you like reading?	3.43	3.57
How much help do you get at home?	2.49[a]	2.79[a]
How hard do you find reading?	3.14	3.17
How much will you try new words on your own (be independent)?	3.26	3.24
How well have you been getting on this year in reading?	3.68	3.53

Note

a: Difference significant at 0.05 level on an uncorrelated t test.

Table 10.4 Teachers' ratings of the target boys and girls in their classes (258 pupils, 6 point scale; maximum possible score 6.00; the higher the score, the more favourable the teacher rating)

Characteristic	Boys	Girls
How well do they read aloud?	3.51[a]	3.97[a]
How positive is their attitude towards reading?	4.40[b]	4.84[b]
How well do they concentrate?	3.78[b]	4.26[b]
How confident are they as readers?	3.98	4.23
How determined are they when they get stuck?	3.83[a]	4.20[a]
How much support do they get at home?	3.97	4.13
How much will they try new words on their own (be independent)?	3.83	4.12
How carefully do they listen?	3.95[a]	4.41[a]
How good is their oral vocabulary?	4.16	4.22
How much do they get done in a lesson?	3.78[b]	4.30[b]
How well have they been getting on this year in reading?	4.31	4.42
How high is their self-esteem?	3.87	4.14
How good are their social skills?	4.02[a]	4.38[a]
How wide a range of reading strategies have they got?	4.08	4.24

Notes

a: Difference significant at 0.05 level on an uncorrelated t test.
b: Difference significant at 0.01 level on an uncorrelated t test.

Table 10.4 shows that teachers see boys and girls to be much more dramatically different from each other than pupils themselves did in Table 10.3 and there are far more statistically significant differences. Not only do teachers judge the girls to be better at reading, which they indeed were on test scores, but they see them as more determined, better able to concentrate and apply themselves, with a more positive attitude to reading and greater social competence. While teachers do rate the help that boys get at home to be lower than that given to girls, the difference is not statistically significant. The same question did, however, produce a significant difference on the pupils' self-ratings.

There was a considerable halo rating in both sets of appraisals in Tables 10.3 and 10.4. There were very high correlations, of the order of 0.7 or 0.8 and above, between many of the characteristics *within* each data set, but none at all between the two sets. In other words, pupils tended to rate themselves similarly on various traits, teachers appeared to rate them similarly, but there was not one significant correlation between pupil ratings and teacher ratings. Even on items common to both lists, like 'determination' or 'progress', there were just very low statistically insignificant correlations. The two groups simply did not agree with each other on what they saw.

Boy–girl test score comparisons

Teachers' lower ratings of the boys' reading competence were supported by the test results obtained in this research. Table 10.5 shows the standardised test scores achieved by the 326 pupils in the sample who completed tests at the beginning and end of the year, rather than the LARR language test administered to younger pupils. It must be remembered that this is not a national stratified random sample, so conclusions must not be drawn about whole age groups *per se*. It is rather a sample of 6 to 11 year old pupils from the classes we observed during the research, so the boy–girl comparisons within each year group and the consistent patterns are of interest.

This sample of children was taught by teachers whose pupils, in every case but one, secured a gain in reading over the school year, so it is an improving group. Both boys and girls improved their standardised scores over the year. What is noticeable in Table 10.5, however, is that, compared with the girls, the boys start down and stay down. When tested at the beginning of the year the boys, as a group, were between 4 and 5 points behind the girls. At the end of the year there was still, on whole-group averages, a 4 to 5 point gap. This recurring pattern, of the boys starting a few points behind the girls and finishing the year still down, was recorded in three out of the four year groups tested, with the sole exception of Year 5, where the boys' and girls' profiles were similar.

A *t* test was used to check the statistical significance of any differences in mean scores. The difference between boys' and girls' scores was significant at

223

Table 10.5 Comparison of 326 boys' and girls' beginning and end of year mean standardised reading test scores (number of pupils in each sample given in brackets)

	Beginning of year	*End of year*
Year 2 boys (24)	90.50	99.04
Year 2 girls (21)	101.14	106.86
Year 3 boys (62)	93.47	97.06
Year 3 girls (64)	97.52	102.22
Year 5 boys (48)	94.85	97.17
Year 5 girls (40)	94.94	96.78
Year 6 boys (33)	91.18	96.36
Year 6 girls (34)	100.53	103.91
Total boys (167)	92.99	97.28
Total girls (159)	97.93	101.69

beyond the 0.01 level (in other words, could have occurred by chance on less than one occasion in a hundred). The improvement over the year for the whole group was also tested with a correlated *t* test and found to be significant at beyond the 0.001 level (could have happened by chance on less than one occasion in a thousand). Since it is easier for pupils who start with a lower score to get a higher mark on a second test than those who begin with a higher score (the phenomenon known as 'regression to the mean'), we ran several statistical tests on what are known as 'residuals', that is the test score gains statistically adjusted to take into account initial differences. It was important to do this because the initial test scores of the whole sample were a little below the national average score and boys in particular started from a lower base. When residuals were studied, there was no difference in the *pattern* of results reported here, except that the levels of significance were slightly lower. For example, the overall improvement rate was significant at beyond the 0.01 (one in a hundred) rather than the 0.001 (one in a thousand) level.

A comparison of the *rate* at which boys and girls improved showed no significant difference. Both boys' and girls' scores improved significantly over the year, but to roughly the same degree, that is the boys improved, but they failed to catch up because the girls improved as well. The boys started behind and, despite their improvement, they stayed behind. There are, therefore, two important points that emerge from this:

1   *Boys' reading can be improved.* Here was a group of above-average teachers, almost all of whom did manage to secure a significant improvement in their boy pupils' reading competence during the year. That they also

achieved a similar improvement rate for their girl pupils is immaterial. There should be no despair about the supposed inevitability of boys not learning to read well. If these teachers can improve boys' reading at a rate beyond the norm, others might do the same.

2   *Reception class and Year 1 teaching are vital*. If the boys start down in Year 2, but, when skilfully taught, do not lose further ground over the next few years, this underlines the importance of their getting a good start in Reception class and Year 1.

This second point, about the divergences between boys' and girls' performance from an early age, was illustrated by several of the critical events we recorded during observations. The following brief account of a boy and a girl, who started school on the same day and were observed throughout their Reception class year, illustrates very well how early differences can become a pattern.

Ben and Charlotte both started in Miss Williamson's Reception class on the same day in September. [Charlotte's story is told in more detail in Chapter 11.] In October the two children were given the LARR language test and both gained the same score, which was amongst the lowest in the class.

Classroom observation notes show that Charlotte, while capable of being high spirited and cheeky, was almost always on-task whenever books were being used. She paid attention to what Miss Williamson explained and pursued the start of reading with considerable enthusiasm. Ben, by comparison, though he never misbehaved, took on a glazed expression at the sight of books, and frequently stared round the room, rather than get on with his work. He was highly attentive when there was an activity like making a shaker out of two yoghurt pots and dried peas, and applied himself with great diligence.

As the year progressed, the cumulative effects of these two different patterns of behaviour began to build up. Reinforced by her relatively rapid progress, Charlotte took books home, persuaded her mother, who was a reluctant recruit, to help her, while Ben developed a set of strategies for avoiding book work. He would walk across the room, not distracting anyone, return to his seat, search his bag, look at what other pupils were doing, anything but look at a book or write some rudimentary scrawl. Only in group reading sessions was he active, showing that he was certainly not too dull to respond.

Not surprisingly, by the end of the year Charlotte had obtained the second-highest score in her class while Ben remained amongst the poorest performers. The sheer amount of time, let alone the degree of arousal, that Charlotte had brought to reading surpassed by far what Ben had spent. Charlotte was a competent reader for her age, but Ben had barely made a start.

The question remains, of course, *why* Ben made a poorer start on reading than Charlotte when, on the surface, they began with a similar language competence. It might be that the language test score of one of them was a less accurate estimate of language capability and reading potential than that of the other. The children were, after all, barely 5 when tested. It could also be the case, as is argued in countries where children begin school later, that boys tend to be slower developers in language than girls and so easily become demoralised in the early stages if they find learning to read too difficult. Equally it could be the case that Charlotte's relatively poor language background at home meant that she would in any case make more progress than others once school switched her on. The truth probably lies in a mixture of genetic and environmental factors that is not easy to uncover in a study like this, where gender is but one relatively small focus of attention.

Salient boy–girl comparisons

The differences we found between boys and girls are described in various chapters of this book, so we summarise ten of the more salient below:

1 Boys did less well on reading tests than girls at all ages tested from 6 to 11, except for Year 5.
2 Boys improved during the year at the same rate as girls.
3 Consequently, since boys started behind at the age of 6, they stayed behind the girls.
4 Boys said they were less likely to be heard reading at home than girls.
5 Teachers rated boys significantly lower than girls on: reading aloud, attitude to reading, determination, listening, concentration, work produced in class, social skills.
6 Boys were only slightly more likely to misbehave in class than girls, but some of their misbehaviour could be very distractive.
7 Boys often preferred books on adventure, sport and humour, while many girls preferred fiction to non-fiction.
8 Young infant-age boys had few male role models: almost no male teachers, classroom assistants, adult helpers were seen in infant school classrooms.
9 Only half of fathers read to 5 to 7 year olds compared with three-quarters of mothers, and only a quarter of fathers read to 7 to 11 year olds compared with half of mothers.

10 At home boys were slightly more likely than girls to read with their brother, while girls were much more likely to read with their sister (the latter was statistically significant).

How pupils see themselves – what they said in interviews

Only six pupils said in interview that they thought that they were not good readers, with the vast majority of the 5 to 7 year old pupils interviewed deeming themselves to be good at reading. When asked *why* they thought this was the case, the evidence and cues they cited were varied. Some status cues were derived from comparison with other pupils, information from parents or teachers, privileges, such as being allowed to select harder books, and other sources. This high-ability 7 year old girl combined several cues, including access to more demanding texts located outside the classroom:

> Yes [I am a good reader], because my mum said I'm the top at reading, because I choose from the corridor, like James and Eva.

Younger pupils tend in any case to say they are good readers. When asked for reasons, some do not give any, others reply 'because I am'. Even pupils judged to be of low ability by their teachers often said they were good, especially if the teacher gave them encouragement, as this low-ability 6 year old concluded:

> Yes [I am a good reader], because one day when I was very new in this class, I got a gold smiley face.

Most young pupils found it difficult to make objective judgements about their progress and proficiency. The difficulty was neatly illustrated by one medium-ability 6 year old boy, whose definition of his own competence at reading was referenced not against the performance of others of his age, but by the type of books in his environment.

> I think I'm a good reader at school. I'm not a good reader at home … I can't read my books at home.

The books available in his classroom were more suited to the competence of 6 year olds, which had given him confidence in his reading ability at school, but the range of books beyond his capabilities at home had served to undermine this confidence. As a result, reading competence for him was flexible and context related, rather than a norm-referenced or absolute concept, in many ways quite a mature view for someone so young.

Two-thirds of the 7 to 11 year old pupils thought that they were good readers, but a fifth thought that they were not, the majority of these having been categorised as 'low ability' by their teachers. These children said they thought they were not good at reading because they got stuck on words, or did not understand what they were reading. Most poorer readers seemed to realise by Key Stage 2 that they should be finding reading easier and have reached a certain threshold, and often the grading of books was their clue, as one low-ability 8 year old explained:

> No [I am not a good reader], because if I was better I wouldn't be on these books [pointing to the lower-level readers he was using].

Older lower-ability children were more aware that simply decoding words was not enough at this level and that comprehension was important:

> [My reading is] OK. I can read, but sometimes I don't understand what I am reading.
>
> (11 year old girl, low ability)

The 7 to 11 year olds were also asked what they thought they could do to improve their reading. Over half believed that more practice was the key. A few thought that they should try and read more difficult books and some felt that learning more words would help them. A few thought the answer lay in their own personal qualities, to 'try harder', while others identified particular techniques, like reading more slowly, or with expression.

Perceived purposes of reading

In one section of the interview there were questions about the purposes of reading, why pupils thought they needed to be able to read. Even 5 to 7 year olds were aware of the instrumental uses of reading within school and the most common response was that it enabled them to learn. Other reasons included 'for grown up life'; because a particular adult, often a parent or teacher, had said so; to read to others; for enjoyment; for employment; and 'to help read signs'. Some children who had already had difficulty with their reading were all too aware of the danger of being ridiculed as an illiterate in a largely literate society:

> It helps you to do your writing and when you're older, if you can't read, everyone will laugh at you.
>
> (8 year old boy, low ability)

Older pupils were no less utilitarian and functional in their responses. To enable them to read signs and instructions was the most frequently given answer, more so by those children who had been classified as of higher ability and some pointing out that it was particularly important from a safety angle. Employment was also a priority, with many stressing its place in helping them to get a job when they left school. Most knew that it formed part of their compulsory education and was in any case required of them, especially before they started secondary school. It was also seen as being helpful within primary school, helpful with writing, class work and if they wanted to pass tests.

> You remember some of the words and it helps you with your spellings and makes you more imaginative.
>
> (8 year old girl, medium ability)

> So I can read things on the page like maths and English.
>
> (11 year old girl, low ability)

All the pupils in the study were asked at the end of the interview whether they liked reading and the reasons for their answer. Only four of the younger pupils said that they did not like reading, because it was boring, or they would rather spend their time doing something else. The rest said that they liked it. Nearly half said that it was because they found it enjoyable in some way. Others liked it because of the pictures, because they felt it was an achievement or because they saw it as an aid to learning.

The overwhelming majority of pupils at Key Stage 2 also liked reading, but eleven pupils said that they did not. Nine of these were low-ability pupils who saw reading as a struggle rather than as a source of pleasure. Of those that did enjoy reading, over half said it was because they found it enjoyable, liking the stories that they read or occasionally the pictures. A few said it was because it stopped them getting bored, others found it relaxing or a means of escaping their troubles:

> Yes [I do like reading], because if something has happened it brings my mind off things.
>
> (8 year old girl, high ability)

One very able 9 year old boy found reading a useful way of firing his own imagination, especially if he could get inside the mind of authors and work out how they had conceived their stories:

> I enjoy it because you can find out what other people's imaginations are like. I can think how the man who wrote Tin Tin – how his imagination works.

The few who did not like reading said that this was because they found it boring or difficult, and two pupils said they only read because they had to.

The vast majority, however, claimed they liked reading, could see that it served a purpose and, so far as we could judge from observing them in class, most did in fact seem to take a positive attitude.

The 'improvers'

There were sixty-five children identified by their teachers part way through the year as improving beyond the norm. Some teachers had found it easy to identify improvers, naming pupils without hesitation, but for others it had been more difficult. The reasons for this varied, one teacher feeling he could not identify any improvers, because he rarely listened to them read, another believing that all the class had improved and it would be difficult to select just two. Some teachers chose pupils who were already part of the six target pupils we were already studying.

The risk in identifying improvers is twofold: first, they may not really be improving at all, and the researchers only had the teacher's assessment to go by; second, the very act of identifying two pupils thought by their teacher to be improving might become self-fulfilling, either because the teacher's expectation and labelling may boost the pupils' self-esteem and subsequent performance, or because teachers may, subconsciously perhaps, change their behaviour towards the children they have identified. In any case the well-known Hawthorne effect, whereby the effect of any kind of scrutiny appears to increase performance, may be at work. Nonetheless, we felt it was worth the risk, otherwise the problems simply combine to prevent investigators looking at the issue.

The sample of sixty-five improvers was studied in the same way as the 210 'target' pupils described above, but in addition we tried to elicit their own perceptions as to why they thought they had improved and how they felt they had got on with their reading since they had been in their present class. Most found it hard to articulate their progress in any depth, but the majority believed that they had improved, some suggesting that they had got on 'quite well' and others going so far as to enthuse that they were now 'brilliant'. Only two children said that they thought that they had got worse, although a few did not feel confident enough to say how they thought they had got on.

One 10 year old girl, Samantha, did have the confidence to believe in her ability. She had benefited particularly from a teacher who had matched the books she read to the appropriate level for her, after a teacher who had given her books that were too simple:

> I've got on really well. Before [in Miss X's class] they were all easy books so I didn't want to read them, so I just read them at home.

Samantha had clearly wanted more of a challenge and her new class had provided her with a greater range of books and with a choice that she liked. In her opinion it was this combination of matching both to a level suitable to the individual pupil and to her topics of interest that had led to an improvement in her reading.

Some pupils made their judgements about improvement on the basis of the speed of their progression through a graded or colour-coded scheme. Younger pupils especially seemed more able to talk about the indicators of improvement than about the reasons for it. The reinforcement of visible progress seemed in itself a sufficient motivator and justification. This group of children knew they had improved simply because they could see how they had moved speedily up the colours in the reading scheme or progressed to sitting at more highly rated tables. For some children watching the colours roll by was an incentive to read more, and little else was to be said, other than that they were driven on by them, as these two 6 year old boys in different schools explained:

> I started with yellow [colour-coded books], then I went to blue. After blue are pink.

> It's what table you are on. Red table have easy stuff. Blue is half and half, and green and yellow are really hard. I'm green.

It was not until the final interview at the end of the year that researchers specifically told the improvers that their teacher thought that they were doing 'really well' and asked why they thought this might be the case. Some children had difficulty explaining the reasoning behind this praise and said that they did not know, but over half offered explanations. About a quarter thought that they had redeemed previous failure, either in another class or in another school, some attributing their teacher's recognition of progress to a particular event:

> I've catched up, because in infant school I wasn't that good.
>
> (8 year old boy)

> Because I've just come to the school and I've caught up other people.
>
> (7 year old boy)

> Because once when I read to Mrs Benton, this word that some people don't know, I said it and I spelled it out first.
>
> (8 year old boy)

> She was shocked when I did my words. She was really happy!
>
> (8 year old girl)

Several pupils attributed their success to personal qualities of industry or determination, many believing that regular practice and application to the task had helped. Most then went on to identify specific elements of teaching, like whole class-reading sessions, the teacher linking reading and writing, or being able to read aloud to someone in the classroom that they felt had been beneficial:

> I try hard, the teacher likes what I am doing.
>
> (10 year old boy)

> I read every night, the more I read the better I get. You can find a hard book and are able to read it.
>
> (11 year old boy)

> I read all the things in the classroom, on the walls and in the book, there's lots of things that you have to read and I read them all.
>
> (7 year old girl)

> We read out the word and sometimes we look at the picture and Miss Roberts says 'work it out, don't look at the picture'.
>
> (6 year old boy)

> Writing [has helped me a lot], because if I was writing and I wanted a word and if I was reading and the word was in there, I'd just know how to spell it.
>
> (7 year old boy)

> I have help from Mrs Turner mostly, because I read to her a lot.
>
> (10 year old girl)

In order to try to elicit what it was that might have made the improvers actually improve, the pupils were asked: 'Do you think that what you do is the same as, or different from, other children?' The children primarily attributed the differences to ability, explaining that they were able to read harder books, or were simply better than the other children. Some, however, did manage to articulate what they did that was different, and their explanations covered a wide range of events. These included being more active and doing set tasks as directed, thinking about the sense of what they read, helping other children and reflecting on their own practice at the same time, and even, as the last quotation below illustrates clearly, being able to ride the gibes of their peers for being 'bookish':

I read everything everywhere. I *do* things, and they don't really look and see what they do.

> (7 year old girl)

I'm different [when reading out loud]. Some people don't read with much expression.

> (8 year old girl)

If they [other pupils] read my book and if it's too hard, they say, 'What's the word Mary?' and I say, 'Spell it out', and then they know the word.

> (6 year old girl)

Some people don't like it as much as I do. Some people think I'm daft reading, but I just like reading.

> (11 year old boy)

Parents helping their children has been a recurring theme in this research, and the influence of parents and others at home on children's progress, in terms of support, role models, resources such as time, money and attitude, was also studied through the eyes of the improvers who were asked if they could think of anything that they did at home that they thought helped them to get better at reading. Many said that they read to someone in their family, although this was more likely to be with their mother than their father and occasionally involved a sibling. A quarter also stated that they read to themselves in the evening, often before they went to bed. In addition to reading at home almost a quarter of the pupils also said that they did word games or spellings:

My mum makes up spelling words and I have to put them in the right order.

> (7 year old girl)

In the infants my sister asked my teacher to give me words in a box.
> (8 year old girl)

However, a quarter of children could not think of anything that they particularly did at home that had helped them.

Finally the improvers were asked whether being better at reading had helped them in any way. Overwhelmingly they thought that it had, with only two pupils believing that it had not benefited them. Although some children, particularly the younger ones, found it too difficult to explain the benefits, nearly two-thirds felt that they could identify the way their improvement had helped them. For some it meant that they now found some of the exercises set in class easier and their improved reading helped them with worksheets or tests, or just enabled them to get on with their work more easily:

> I get my work done quicker.
>
> > (7 year old boy)

> I can now read the worksheets.
>
> > (8 year old boy)

This in itself was a major achievement for some. For others it meant they could read harder texts, or access books they had previously found too difficult. For many it had boosted their general confidence to tackle school work:

> I can read stories to the class and it helps me write stories.
>
> > (8 year old boy)

> I didn't read most of the time in the lower juniors, but now I see other people reading it's getting more exciting.
>
> > (10 year old boy)

> Because at home I read real good stories out of the library and they're real good fun.
>
> > (5 year old girl)

11

PUPIL CASE STUDIES

The pupil perspective was an important focus of this research and in Chapter 10 there was a discussion of the general findings from interviews with and observations of the 258 pupils studied in detail. This chapter will focus on some of the individual children who were carefully monitored through the school year and consider what happened to them, whether they appeared to improve, either as indicated by test results when these were available, or according to other criteria. Different case studies are drawn from boys and girls in the four main categories studied, namely high, medium and low ability, and 'improver', in each case as selected by their class teacher. The case studies are actual illustrative examples from the four types, not overall stereotypes or fictitious composites. In each case the child's age is given as it was at the beginning of the school year.

Joseph, aged 6, Year 2

When Mrs Maple was asked to select her 'improvers' half way through the year she had no hesitation in choosing Joseph as one of them. We had in any case been studying Joseph since September, because she had nominated him as the low-ability boy in the original sample of six target children. By the end of the year he had become one of the most spectacular improvers in the whole sample. Mrs Maple explained how he had changed during the year: 'He had been almost unable to read at all when he came into the class. He's now really growing in confidence with his reading and has made a lot of progress.' Her initial appraisal of his low reading ability had been borne out by his result in a reading test administered at the beginning of the school year. His standardised score had been 78, well below the average score of 100, putting him in the lowest achieving 10 per cent of pupils in his age group.

Towards the start of the school year his speaking and listening skills made him a difficult child to interview and his concentration level was poor which meant he answered 'Don't know' to several of the questions, even those that were about his own feelings. When first interviewed he did manage to say that his mummy and daddy sometimes read his school reading book with him at home, and that, when he got stuck on a word, they would help him sound it out, or 'spell it out' as he put it. When asked what sorts of things he read at home, he simply replied 'my school book'. Joseph said he liked reading, but he could not explain why. He believed he was a good reader, but like many young pupils asked the question, his answer was based on his teacher having given him a sticker. He was not able to identify anything that he did in class which had helped him to get better at reading.

When the researcher first read with him he had to choose a book from the classroom, because he had left his current school reading book at home. He found the book difficult. He read slowly, without expression and no attempt at self-correction when he made one of his numerous errors. He was unable to recount the story, which may have been through lack of comprehension or interest, but later a lack of confidence in new situations became apparent, and this may have depressed his performance, though he had not done especially well in his previous class.

The transformation in his skills over the year was evident by the end of the summer term, when he managed to read an Oxford Reading Tree Stage 7 book, which was well beyond his earlier competence, fluently to the researcher with good expression, making excellent use of punctuation cues. At that stage, if he read something that did not make sense, he soon realised, re-read the story and corrected his own errors. He decoded the text faultlessly and was able to recount what had happened in detail. By this stage his whole reading persona had changed and he was no longer the shy, awkward child whose attempts at reading required huge effort and concentration. He now sat relaxed and confident, holding the book he was reading comfortably between his two hands.

Mrs Maple had recognised the potential for improvement early in the school year, but could not quite pinpoint what she believed had provided the impetus:

> He's the one that's improved the most out of all of them. I don't know what caused it, it just all clicked into place. He recognises nearly all the words now. But it's only in reading. He hasn't clicked with his writing or his maths, and his concentration is still very poor.

In Joseph's case increased personal and social maturity might well have led to improvements in these other important skills. Lesson observations indicated that the teacher's perception of his relatively low concentration levels was justified, as he did seem unable to focus for very long on any particular topic or activity, as this account shows:

This morning the teacher and pupils have been talking about 'opposites'. In pairs they have had to choose two 'opposite' characteristics. Joseph and his partner have come up with 'clever' and 'stupid'. Joseph is writing a story about someone who is 'clever'. The teacher is working with a small group of children undertaking a maths activity.

At the beginning of the observation period, some twenty minutes into the session, Joseph has only written one line and is making silly noises unrelated to what he is writing: 'Boom, boom, boom,' he says and giggles. No one pays any notice. Joseph then plays with his pencils, flicking one against the other. Classroom assistant realises he is off-task and moves to sit beside him. She points to his work.

Classroom assitant: Right, Joseph, what are you going to write now?
Joseph: (Screwing up his face) Don't know.
Classroom assistant: Come on, let's think.... If he's clever, what can he
                       do?

Joseph says nothing but starts writing.

Classroom assistant: Good boy.
Joseph stops after a few words and yawns.

Classroom assistant: What happens next?
Joseph: Don't know.

He looks away from the classroom assistant towards a neighbour, no longer responding to the classroom assistant. He picks up his pencils again and plays with them. He then rubs his eyes, yawns again …

Classroom assistant: Come on, Joseph. Get on with your work.

Joseph says 'I need a rubber' and gets up. He wanders around the classroom for some time before returning to his seat.

Despite Joseph's lack of application to other tasks, the improvement in his reading was substantial. By the time he was retested in the summer term he had moved considerably, from being in the bottom 10 per cent, with a score of 78, to one of 98, which placed him close to the average performance of 100. Joseph was not the only child whose reading appeared to have improved under the teaching of Mrs Maple, also the school's language co-ordinator, as the whole-class average standardised score had risen from 97.7

to 102.4 during the year, but his gain was the most spectacular. Her classroom was full of books of many kinds, as well as notices urging children to come and read or write in this corner or that, or intriguing questions. Her own personal enthusiasm for books was often public and seemed to give children a positive attitude to literacy.

When Joseph was interviewed for the last time at the end of the school year, he was asked why he thought he had become so good at reading. Unlike earlier in the year he now gave a considered response and spoke about how his attitude to reading had changed. The male members of his family appeared to have played a crucial role in this, both by supplying him with reading material and actually helping him. 'I started to practise at my books at home. My daddy told me the words and I got them in my head.' He went on to explain how the rest of the family had also started to support him and that his granddad now sent him 'loads of comics', especially the *Dandy* and *Beano*, as he liked reading those the best. His year-long pupil profile kept by the researcher revealed a stark contrast between his attitude to reading at the beginning of the year and at the end, when he said that he now liked reading very much, considered himself to be very good at it, and thought he got on very well with it in this class, though acknowledging that he still occasionally found it hard.

Joseph's case illustrates a number of factors that seem to have been important in bringing about such a marked improvement in his reading ability. His own change in attitude and the recognition that reading can be enjoyable was encouraged by his teacher's obvious enthusiasm for books and her careful matching of each child with appropriate reading material, which may have been particularly influential on the increase in Joseph's reading competence. Certainly he had grown enormously in confidence as a reader. An additional crucial factor may have been the considerable extra support provided at home, especially as both parents and grandparents were involved in providing reading material he enjoyed, albeit in the form of children's comics like the *Dandy* and *Beano*, and specific structured help. The close attention of two male members of the family was unusual, given that analysis of our sample had shown that fathers were less likely to read with their children than mothers, but it is not possible to say with any certainty how influential the presence of two male role models might have been. Certainly Joseph himself was very appreciative of what they had done to help him.

Miriam, aged 9, Year 5

The teacher of Miriam was a young practitioner with only a couple of years' experience. She displayed great enthusiasm for her work in general and the displays in her classroom were of an extremely high quality. However, hers was the one class in our sample of fifteen whose average standardised test result actually fell over the year, though only very slightly, and observations of her practice and evidence gathered during interviews suggest that one factor may have been a lack of monitoring of pupils' reading materials and progress. The target pupils, when interviewed at the end of the summer term, were unable to recall when they had last read to their teacher.

Miss Mumford had identified Miriam as a 'poor reader' who had little confidence in her ability, so she placed her on a 'book track', a trail of books along which she guided her reading. The books on the book track had been personally selected for the less able readers in her class by the teacher at the Schools Library Service as having the right degree of difficulty but with a more mature content. When interviewed in the first term of the year, Miriam told the researcher that she did not consider herself to be a good reader, 'because I get stuck on words all the time'. Reading had become a problem for her: 'I don't really like reading, because I get all the words wrong. I find it difficult to read.'

Miriam was not bereft when she encountered unfamiliar words, using a range of strategies, including breaking the unknown word into small parts, or sounding it out. While being observed in lessons her general approach to school work displayed a lack of concentration, and she was easily distracted by other events in the classroom. Both her teacher and her parents, when interviewed, described Miriam as a child who endeavoured to hide from her friends the difficulties she encountered with her reading and other school work, although she was a very sociable child who mixed well with her peers.

At the end of the year, she seemed to have made considerable progress. Her standardised score had increased by 10 points, from 79 to 89, and although Miriam herself believed she had made good progress during the year, when asked at the end of the school year whether she liked reading now, she replied 'Kind of I don't, kind of I do'. She explained this ambivalence as the result of becoming 'fed up' when she could not read certain words. The story was much more complex than that, however.

There is often an assumption that the involvement of parents in their children's learning, and a three-way partnership between them, their child and the teacher, will invariably be a good thing. Yet during interviews with both Miriam and her parents, it became apparent that parental involvement might sometimes be a negative factor and indeed in this particular case, had become a source of some friction between all three parties. At the beginning of the school year, her parents had met with the teacher to discuss what they perceived as Miriam's reading difficulties and had been reassured when the teacher explained the structured reading programme that would be available for their daughter through the book track scheme.

During interviews with Miriam herself, she indicated that she took her book home every day and read either to her mother or father. Miss Mumford's perception of the situation at home was that, although the parents were concerned, help was sporadic rather than regular, as they had another child with special educational needs: 'I think they have "blasts" with her and then she's left a bit.' The parents, when interviewed at the end of the year, expressed themselves as unhappy with the way in which they themselves had had to initiate discussions with Miss Mumford about Miriam.

Miriam's father was particularly critical of the lack of monitoring of her reading at school because Miriam was not keen to read at home, and he explained his own difficulties hearing her read by assigning blame to the other two participants in this somewhat strained partnership – Miriam and her teacher:

> They never seem to have the teacher listen to them anyway – it always seems to be parents or helpers. And the problem I've got is that Miriam will only read to me if she knows it well. I don't know why, I don't put pressure on her for it. It's something she puts herself under.

That reading had become something of a battleground at home also became evident from what Miriam's mother said in interview:

> When she comes home, she won't go and sit and read, she'd rather play.... When you try and sit there and go through it, she gets very cross, having to break things down, or maybe repeating things, she gets very frustrated and will tend to say, 'Go away. I'm not doing this any more!' ... She is so slow that you find it so frustrating to listen to, and she'll go, 'What do you think this word is?' and I go to say it and she'll say 'I wish you hadn't told me that. I'm supposed to break it up', and I'll say, 'I've given you the opportunity for you to break it up, you're struggling like mad, I'm trying to help you'. But she does get very, very frustrated.

The parents' lack of confidence in the teacher had led them into taking a more direct role in her reading at home. The materials they had selected for her to read included *Black Beauty*, *The Lion, the Witch and the Wardrobe* and *What Katy Did*. The vocabulary used in these books was way beyond Miriam's current reading development and so she struggled with the texts. This in turn demoralised her and her parents and made reading an uncomfortable and unpleasant experience rather than a pleasurable one. Miss Mumford seemed quite unaware that parental involvement was causing Miriam and her family stress and further undermining her self-confidence.

Both Joseph and Miriam described above, labelled 'low ability' by their teachers, showed considerable improvement during the year. This raises the whole question of labelling, as both these children may well have been more capable pupils whose achievement was held down and curtailed by personality or other factors. 'Improvement' in this context, therefore, may be more a matter of removing obstacles and barriers so as to unleash frustrated potential.

The involvement of parents was a common factor, but here the two stories diverge considerably. Joseph's improvement was more dramatic, being helped by encouragement and support from several sources: his parents, grandparents and his teacher. Miriam was also helped in her reading by her increased confidence. As she became able to decode words more efficiently she became less frustrated and this in turn helped her to comprehend what she was reading more easily. Her parents, however, with the best of intentions, so far as one could see, wanted to rectify the 'deficiencies', as they saw them, in the school by choosing books themselves. In the event they seem to have selected texts that were too difficult for her.

Whereas the harmony between home and school clearly helped Joseph, the dissonance between the parties concerned became a source of tension for Miriam and she became exasperated at home, though not at school, as the parents' programme of reading and strategies for helping cut across what the teacher did. Miriam's parents, correctly believing that her teacher might have done more to help her, tried to overcompensate and in the end exerted pressure which caused family stress. Miriam did improve beyond the norm and more than many others in her class, but her path was not as smooth as Joseph's and one speculates whether it might have been even more impressive had harmony reigned and had Miss Mumford monitored her pupils' progress more closely.

Marcus, aged 10, Year 6

Marcus was judged by Mrs Jenkins, at the beginning of the school year, to be of below-average ability. She chose him as a case study pupil because she said he was not very confident, due to his shyness, but was 'gradually coming out of himself'. She thought, therefore, that the 'low-ability' label she felt bound to apply at that stage masked his true capability. In September, when he took a reading test along with the other pupils in his class, the first part of his teacher's perception appeared to be confirmed. Although his chronological age was 10 years and 8 months, he scored a reading age of 9 years and 6 months, with a standardised score of 90, a 'medium to low' score.

In interview, early in the school year, Marcus discussed his strategies for reading, explaining that if he got stuck on a word he would split it up and see if he could work it out, but if he was reading with an adult he would ask them and if he felt a book was too hard for him he would simply put it back. He explained that he talked to his mother about reading, as she liked reading as well. He would tell her what happened at the beginning of a story, about the main adventure or story line, and what happened at the end. As the interview progressed his enthusiasm for reading began to show. He particularly liked books about animals and stories by Enid Blyton, but his lack of confidence was conspicuous. When asked if he thought he was a good reader he said: 'I love reading, but I don't know if I'm a good reader.' He explained that his love of reading was partially a form of escape, an antidote to boredom, saying:

> I love reading, if you get bored it gives you something to do. It takes away time – time goes by and you don't really know it.

In February, when Mrs Jenkins was asked to select two improvers in her classroom, she again chose Marcus, feeling that he had responded very well to the programme of work she had set him, especially as she had tried to match books to his interests:

> He's a unique little boy – a little gentleman. He talks to me quite a lot [saying he is] keen on animals. He talked a lot about it. I've suggested books he can read. He now feels more comfortable about who he is and his choice of books. He was new last year and his change of class has made him more comfortable.

Later in the year Marcus was asked how he thought he had got on with reading since coming into his present class. He said that he found reading a lot easier now and that he had more time to do it, because nearly every day he was told to get his reading book out and this was when he could sit and read. He also said that when they were given free time to do what they wanted, he chose to read. He commented that he read every single night and that the more he read the better he got, saying that now when he found a hard book he was able to read it.

The class teacher operated a system of quiet reading on most days, group reading where pupils read and discussed books together in groups, and she also read books to the class. Pupils had an individual reading record where they recorded the books they were reading. Marcus felt that being better at reading had helped him read harder books and had enabled him to find out more information for school.

At the beginning of the year, when Marcus was first heard reading, he read simple story books with large typeface, low print density and numerous pictures, the sort that 8 year olds might read. His reading was stilted and hesitant, although he was willing to attempt words he could barely manage. He ignored punctuation and often failed to distinguish sentences. Observations of his work in lessons during the year showed him listening with interest to the whole-class novel, almost always volunteering the first answer once a discussion started. By the middle of the year he had moved on to more fiction books that no longer had pictures, only text. Although his reading was still slightly staccato, it had become much more fluent and he read without mistakes, better aware of the punctuation in the text. He occasionally slowed down when reading, but this was usually to attempt unfamiliar words, which he was now able to decode correctly. He explained at this point that he just wanted to 'keep reading and moving on to fatter books'. He particularly enjoyed the books on animals that his teacher gave him.

By Easter Marcus was able to read chapter books, with small text, and was able to explain the story to date. He could read clearly and no longer pointed to the words. Even though he was reading a Mark Twain classic, *The Adventures of Tom Sawyer*, he found few difficulties with the text, with American expressions or the period language used. At the end of the school year, when the researcher interviewed him again and heard him read, Marcus was able to explain in correct detail the meanings of the text in the book he was reading. He attributed his success to perseverance, saying that he had been determined to keep reading harder and harder texts, even though some of the other children teased him for his bookishness. This marked determination and ability to resist the temptation to conform to the norms of his fellows was clearly a factor in his improvement, as was his teacher's carefully judged feeding of his voracious appetite.

His own perseverance and his teacher's skill appear to have paid off. By the end of the school year when he was tested again, his standardised reading score had increased by 9 points, from 90 to 99. Instead of being a year behind the average for his age, he was now operating at the norm, better equipped to tackle the more difficult reading assignments that would lie ahead of him.

Craig, aged 5, Year 1

Craig was originally selected by his teacher as a child of middle ability, or rather of middle *attainment*, since his teacher, Mrs Rothwell, described him as 'Bright but difficult, one who doesn't like to work'. In September, in his first interview, he said he didn't like reading 'because I have to do work' and that he didn't think he was good 'because I sometimes don't get it right'. His response to the questions about what he would do if he couldn't read a word, or found a book was too hard, was in complete contrast with Marcus above. He would walk away from difficulties: 'Leave it and find something else' was his preferred solution.

Craig showed poor concentration when observed in lessons, as well as several of the characteristics of children who are variously labelled 'attention seeking', 'hyperactive' or 'suffering from attention deficit'. Although he was friendly and communicative during interviews and informal conversations, he was not easy to interview, as he wriggled incessantly and kept asking if he could go. Similarly, when he read, his attention darted away from the book, occasionally coming to rest back on the text before taking off again.

When asked to read, Craig frequently commented that he had forgotten his book, as apparently he often did, and so had to choose another one, a process that took an inordinately long time. While reading he would stop at words he did not know and make no attempt whatsoever to decode, sound out, guess or work out from pictures what the unfamiliar word might be. Sometimes he would point at a word to ask what it was, and occasionally he stared intently at the pictures and commented on them. An event observed in the middle of the school year illustrates well how he frequently behaved in class:

> Craig was supposed to be working on an activity which appeared to be well within his capability. His group was cutting up photo-copied sentences from a story they had been read which they were then expected to arrange in correct order. Craig rushed ahead with the task, while protesting all the while that he was unable to do it, and stuck the sentences anywhere, making a complete mess and getting sticky with glue himself. Mrs Rothwell told him to slow down and do it carefully, so he pretended to tear up his paper in anger, seemingly trying to keep her in his vicinity. As he continued, he drew her attention to each thing he did, but when she moved to oversee another group, he immediately stopped work and watched some children building with Lego. By play time he had still not finished. When the other children went out to play the teacher provided a fresh sheet of paper. Together they worked through it methodically and Craig appeared to have no difficulty putting all the sentences in order.

When Craig was heard reading later in the year his behaviour had changed from that exhibited earlier. He showed interest in the book, and had become much more systematic about his reading. He pointed to the words and answered questions about the text, though he still expected to be told any words that he did not know. By the end of the year his reading behaviour had changed yet again and he was then able to read quite fluently. He read Pat Hutchins' *Goodnight Owl* and used phonic and contextual clues to work out words he did not know. His attitude had also changed, as he now admitted to enjoying reading and perceived himself to be 'very good' at it and trying hard to improve. At the beginning of the year, despite being one of the youngest in the class, he had achieved the sixth-highest raw score on the LARR Test, a score which seemed high considering the work he was observed doing in the classroom. By June, however, he had the highest mark in the class.

Craig's teacher, Mrs Rothwell, was in her first year of teaching. She had a pleasant, relaxed and calm manner with her class, and was well organised. She planned the children's work carefully with the teacher in the parallel class, and they worked together in many ways. When asked to try and explain Craig's improved behaviour and achievement in reading, she disclaimed responsibility for his progress, attributing it to a change in his home circumstances: 'He is with foster parents now, and has really settled down.'

Personal circumstances are major factors in the cases of Marcus and Craig, both boys appearing to be affected by their teacher and home life. In Marcus's case he had received parental support throughout his schooling, and his mother in particular had always shown an interest in what he did. The difference for Marcus was perhaps the change of school, moving into the class of a teacher who had a marked enthusiasm for books and the English language and was prepared to take the time to help match books to his interests. He also benefited from becoming confident enough to resist peer group pressure, so as reading became easier the range of books available to him became greater, reinforcing his growing interest in the written word.

In Craig's case the teacher did not appear to be such a major factor. She was a competent teacher, but lacked experience, being only recently qualified. Although it seems most probable that Mrs Rothwell's calm, friendly persistence had had its effect on Craig, other factors were undoubtedly influential too. A child like Craig, moving from one home to another, living with foster parents, can easily become confused and worried about what is going on in his life and so fail to concentrate on what is happening at school. The amount of time he actually spends on the task, therefore, is far less than it should be, as he competes for the affection and interest missing in his previous home life.

Not every problem can be solved by a teacher, and not every improvement is the result of a successful teaching strategy. Craig's achievement in reading seemed to be in an inverse relationship with the worries about his home life. As these worries decreased when he settled in with his new foster parents, his 'ability' seemed to increase, as did his confidence. A teacher may not have all the resources to compensate for problems at home, but Mrs Rothwell did not give up on a disruptive child, and the disruption that masked his true ability declined under her patient regime.

Andrew, aged 9, Year 5

Andrew was an immediately interesting child when observed in class. Mrs Turner, his teacher, picked him out without hesitation as a 'high-ability' boy, partly on the basis of a Cognitive Ability Test (CAT) he had been given which had yielded a particularly high score:

> He just stands out – in his responses, thinking and problem solving. This was confirmed on his CAT test.

In interview he was very articulate and was able to discuss his approach to reading in more depth than many pupils interviewed. When he met an unfamiliar word, he was quite at ease with reference books, including dictionary pronunciation conventions:

> If I don't know I sometimes go and look in the dictionary. I don't care what it sounds like very much. I just hope that some time I'll hear it said the right way. Usually if I've got to read something with hard words, I look in the dictionary and find out what they are and how to pronounce them.

He took opportunities to discuss books with the people about him, which included the people at his table and with his father at home. He read because he liked it and was aware that reading was important if he wanted to get a job and to get on in life. He thought it helped him learn things and got his mind working, but also for the humorous side of books, because some of the ones he enjoyed were funny.

At the beginning of the year he was already reading fluently, aware of the punctuation and the meaning of what he was reading, being able to explain clearly the story so far. When observed reading he would sit quietly immersed in his book, irrespective of what was going on around him. His written work was clear and imaginative, rarely showing any mistakes. At the beginning of the year his chronological age was 9 years 6 months, but his reading age was 13 years 3 months. When heard reading later in the year, he had started incorporating sound effects into his reading. By the end of the year he was not only fluent, but could talk accurately about grammar and punctuation in a text, explaining that an exclamation mark showed 'expression, as if you are surprised or in shock, or something amazing has happened', or that the apostrophe was used 'to show that some of the letters are missing from that ... it shows something belongs to somebody'. He attributed his extensive knowledge to his mother and father who talked to him a great deal at home.

When asked at the end of the year how he felt about reading he commented:

> I love reading because it's an easy way to get information and at the time you want, as long as you've got the book, unlike a video, where you have to go all through it, because in a book you've got contents and an index in books with facts.

He was not only able to decode fluently, but understood quite complex texts for someone of his years, with an insight that was far beyond his chronological age. He quickly grasped the meaning behind a text. He undoubtedly got a great deal of support from both his teacher and his parents, and in his view the impact of his father was considerable, a male role model not always present on this scale. Mrs Turner rated him as 'high' or 'very high' on all the attributes that you would expect a good reader to have.

Although Andrew seemed to possess considerable innate ability, this ability was also nurtured by many of the adults around him. He was given frequent opportunities in the classroom to be an independent reader and Mrs Turner provided numerous appropriate resources and written exercises which sustained his interest. She was often observed explaining to him, in answer to his many questions, and, from what he reported, his parents, especially his father, expanded his knowledge base at home, making reading a more meaningful experience. He was publicly encouraged in class, as were pupils of all abilities, reading out his written work and being praised by the teacher. The other pupils also recognised his ability and also informally enhanced his reputation by using him as a source of information and as a teaching assistant, which he accommodated in a good-natured fashion. Andrew is a good example of a high achiever in the field of literacy whose ability was strongly supported by both teacher and parents, so that his enthusiasm and love of books was not only sustained but enhanced.

Four 'improvers'

Teachers had different reasons for selecting children thought to be improving half way through the school year. In some cases they were pupils who did not have English as their mother tongue, so progress in speaking their new language often led to a spectacular leap in reading proficiency. Others were children whose true ability had been concealed through shyness, or other personal or home circumstances, and when these were mitigated their reading competence reached more closely the level that they might have attained in better circumstances. Sometimes the improver was a pupil whose interest in reading was thought to have been awakened by whatever the teacher had done. Occasionally there seemed to be no explanation, when a particular child, for reasons that might have been related to maturation, unknown external circumstances, or some unique interpersonal chemistry between teacher and taught, simply took off at a greater rate than the norm. The improvers described below cover various of these categories.

Amina, aged 5, Reception

Amina was a very lively, communicative, enthusiastic little girl who was not surprisingly chosen as an improver, as her growing competence would have seemed apparent to anyone who spoke to her over a period of time. She was perhaps chosen by Miss Dobson as an 'improver', rather than a 'high-ability' child, because her first language was not English, so she was rather quiet at the beginning of the school year. It was only when she became fluent and confident as an English speaker that she began to make rapid progress, and once she realised what was required by her teacher she was easily able to produce it.

Several explanations of Amina's success suggested themselves as she talked about her home life and family. She regularly went to the public library with her mother and explained that 'I read by my own in my bed'. She was proud of the desk she had at home and obviously enjoyed playing at 'being at school' with her younger sister as well as role playing with her toys. Her persistence was noticeable during classroom observation and this determination to learn to read spread over into her home life. One day she took a book from the book corner and showed it to the researcher, commenting proudly:

> When I had that book to take home and read, I made a writing of that ... all by myself. My mum was downstairs and my sister was downstairs and I was in my bedroom by my desk.

She had copied out the whole book and the pictures as well.

She knew that books could be taken home on Mondays and Thursdays and that 'it's very important we take it home', and 'If I like it, mum puts a happy face, and if I don't, she puts a sad face.' She had her own explanation for her success, however, which was that she applied herself diligently to her task in class: 'I concentrate and listen and do work and the others mess about.' Her class was not observed to be at all disorderly, but by her standards, other 5 year olds in the class did 'mess about', because they did not show her sustained concentration. She was aware that if she wanted to make progress, she needed to apply herself beyond the norm set by fellow pupils.

Amina was full of confidence and very happy to read. She had an inquisitive mind and when heard reading in January she clearly enjoyed reading and had a good memory which helped her to remember new words. She read *A Red Rose* from the *Story Chest* scheme and self-corrected. When faced with a new or difficult word, however, her strategy was to look and wait to be told what the word was, but when the word next appeared she remembered it and got it right. By June she tackled unknown words confidently using a good knowledge of letter–sound correspondence. When shown the word 'asked', which had caused her some difficulty, and asked to explain how she had worked it out, she replied: 'You'd have to spell it' and then elaborated '/a/ /s/ that's ass, then /k/ /e/ /d/, and then it makes together "asked".' She demonstrated similarly with the word 'felt' but said she did not know any other ways of working out unknown words.

It was clear that Amina understood what she was reading. She laughed at humorous references, self-corrected when what she said did not make sense, and was able to answer questions about the story. Most of the children in Amina's class had made a good start with their reading, but it was hard to identify any one element in particular that her teacher did with her which had resulted in her exponential spurt. With her innate ability and supportive home background she had absorbed the ethos of the classroom and flourished in a class in which reading was taught systematically and books given a high profile. Most noteworthy was a powerful personal drive to achieve, remarkable in someone so young, and this led to her high degree of dedication, both in the classroom and at home. Even though she was, at this stage, dependent rather than autonomous, she still learned quickly, so autonomy would probably come later. She seemed to spend much more time on learning to read than others of her age. While time alone is of relatively little import, when accompanied by intense concentration on a worthwhile task, it ought to be highly influential on learning.

Rachel, aged 7, Year 3

Mrs Lansbury chose Rachel as one of the improvers because of her all-round progress in decoding ability, comprehension, confidence and, perhaps most of all, in attitude. When Rachel came into the class in September, she had identified her as a poor reader with a negative attitude to reading, a time waster and a child who used her appealing 'little girl ways' to make it hard for teachers to push or challenge her with work she would claim to find difficult. Mrs Lansbury was very concerned that Rachel might make no progress during the year if her attitude and behaviour did not improve: 'Rachel has every work avoidance strategy in the book ... I've had to be firm'. She had spoken to Rachel's parents about her problems and although at first they were concerned about her being set extra work, they became helpful and pleased at the improvement she showed.

Rachel was a friendly girl, often observed talking to others in class. Later in the year it became clear that she was very pleased with her relative success and, quite possibly, with the attention it had brought her. Mrs Lansbury had been keen to ensure that Rachel's desire for attention would be satisfied through the reinforcement of positive, rather than negative behaviour, so she praised her whenever she did good work or was thought to have tried hard. When Rachel was interviewed and observed towards the end of the school year she had recently been given some words to learn, been tested on them and got every word right. Mrs Lansbury had shown exaggerated surprise and delight at this success. When Rachel was later asked why she thought her teacher had picked her out as someone who was doing really well with her reading, she laughed with pleasure and commented on this incident.

Rachel said she was aware of her improvement and was eager to reflect on possible reasons for it. She said that having a big spelling book had helped her, as had splitting the words up into bits, reading to herself at home and to her mother. She described the extra help she had received from another

adult in the classroom who had worked with her group, enjoying in particular being able to use her increasing reading competence to discover
knowledge for herself:

> Our helper gives us activities with our books, she'll say 'What does
> something look like?', and we have to look it up and find out.

Mrs Lansbury had also arranged for Rachel to do paired reading with
another child and, in helping each other, both were judged to have
improved. By the end of the year she had changed from being a poor reader
to being a reasonably fluent one, able to self-correct when what she said did
not make sense, saying: 'My mind told me [that wasn't right]. I knew it
wasn't right, so I looked again.'

Rachel is an interesting example of a child who appears to have improved
significantly because of her teacher's encouragement, high expectations and
flexibility. At the end of the year Mrs Lansbury felt that Rachel still gave up
too easily, but she was not prepared to let her waste time or quit without an
effort. She also made it clear to her that, although she had improved, she
thought she could do even better. She had tried to find methods and
resources that suited Rachel, and her regular routine of discussing children's
progress with them, and including them in decisions about their own
learning, seemed to help. Rachel was below average at the beginning of the
year with a reading score of 89, unable to manage many of the reading tasks
she was going to have to undertake. By the end of the year she could cope
with the work given in class, enjoyed reading, and knew she would get
praise and recognition for her success. This was clearly indicated in her
reading test result, which had increased to a near-average score of 97.

Charlotte, aged 4, Reception

Not all improvers received informed help at home, as the case of Charlotte
shows. When she started Reception class a month before her fifth birthday
she obtained one of the lowest scores in the sample on the LARR language
test. She had little preparation for school. Her mother had had a poor
academic record herself, frequently playing truant when she was a child: 'We
never read to her before she started school. I missed a lot of school myself,
like, when I was a girl.' Miss Williamson, a very experienced Reception class
teacher whose classroom had a rich language environment, had selected her
as an improver because she had taken to reading so quickly.

During the year Charlotte became excited at everything to do with
language. 'This word says "cow", c–o–w, cow', she would volunteer in a non-
stop torrent when observed. 'I can write my name' ... 'Do you know what
this book says?' Her teacher set her and the class several pre-reading exercises and drew their attention to the large amount of print in their classroom

and external environment. Charlotte created a number of simple self-made books and Miss Williamson steered her through a wide range of beginner fiction and non-fiction books.

By the end of the year she was the second-best reader in the class and obtained one of the highest scores on the LARR Test. Asked why she thought she had done so well, she herself attributed it to the help she had received from a fellow pupil: 'Because Daniel [the best reader in the class, who sat next to her] gives me all the words'. She smiled with pride at having signed up her own free private tutor.

Her mother, surprised at her progress, could not explain it. She had not particularly been helped at home. In interview she expressed astonishment that Charlotte had been interested in a crossword puzzle when she had seen her father doing one. She apologised all the time for not being able to help Charlotte, as she was not a particularly good reader herself. Indeed, Charlotte was often very persistent in her desire to learn to read and she had to be referred to her father when she met a word she did not recognise, as her mother often had no idea either.

By the end of the school year Charlotte was asking her mother to spell out words she did not know and actually showing her how to split difficult words into two. This was one of the few examples we encountered of a reverse of the norm – child shows parent how to attack a difficult word. Charlotte seemed to be a bright girl with a strong desire to learn to read, who only needed school and a skilful teacher to discover her talent in language and personal relationships. She will quite probably go far.

David, aged 9, Year 5

At the beginning of Year 5 David was adamant in our first interview: 'I absolutely hate reading. It's boring. I just don't like it.' Only his Liverpool Football Club comic was of any interest. This was an unusual response and his face distorted as he uttered the words. Interviewers will normally obtain a positive response to this question, as most children, when asked, will say that they like reading, almost as if this is expected. Some are indifferent and a few admit to disliking it, but David was one of the few to express strongly negative feelings, and almost the only pupil to use the word 'hate'.

Mrs Jackson selected him as an improver because his attitude to reading changed dramatically during the school year, as he went from being hostile to enthusiastic. As was the case with Charlotte, neither his mother nor his father ever read to him, even when he took books home. The school had a very positive attitude to parents and even before children commence school they are visited by one of the two Reception class teachers or by the head herself. During this home visit the teaching of reading is described specifically and each parent is handed a booklet written by the teachers which explains what the school does in the teaching of reading. Despite this preliminary visit and a programme of parents' evenings, David was still unaided by either parent.

When observed in class he was a seasoned procrastinator, able to turn finding a pencil into a five-minute task. Mrs Jackson ran an orderly classroom and the figures obtained from pupil on-task studies were amongst the highest we have ever recorded in classroom observation research. At the beginning of the year, less so at the end, David was often the one pupil not applying himself to his task. Mrs Jackson would often detach herself from a group momentarily to scan the class when pupils were working on their own or in groups. 'David, I'll be over in a minute', was a common public remark when she noticed him distracted from what he was supposed to be doing.

By the following June, however, he was transformed. 'Reading? I really like it', he said in his final interview. The interviewer reminded him of the beginning of the year when he had graphically described his intense dislike of everything other than his football comic. Asked why the change of heart, he was equally unambiguous:

> It's Mrs Jackson. She's given me some really good books, adventures and that sort of stuff, and books that made me laugh.

Patrick Burson's *The Funfair of Evil* had been particularly enjoyed. Mrs Jackson's personalised approach increased both the time and effort David spent on reading. She described in interview how she had sought out books on sport, adventure and humour, knowing that these would interest him. Although his reading test score had only improved slightly, by 1 point, from 95 to 96, his attitude and the number and range of books he read had soared. For a boy who was, by the end of the research in July, within a year of starting secondary school, where a hatred of reading would be a severe handicap, this represents a different, though nonetheless very important, kind of 'improvement'. It makes the interesting point that attitude, while not a substitute for competence, can be a useful accompaniment to it. In David's case, given the lack of support at home, improving his attitude to reading would have to be an important precursor to improving his competence at it, though whether he would go on to become a better reader in secondary school was outside the scope of this enquiry.

A big sinker and an improver within the same class

Mr Martin walked into his new Year 3 class of thirty-two children on the first day of the new term with his usual enthusiasm both for teaching generally and for the teaching of literacy in particular. He did not know, nor could he, that within the group were two pupils whose progress would diverge considerably during the year. The class was new to him and new to the school, so he explained to the pupils how their literacy activities would be conducted over the year. His exposition included content and process: the difference between fiction and non-fiction books, when they would visit the school library, that they would have a story time together. Then he seated everyone on the carpet and a long session took place during which he introduced the class to the different books on offer. He later explained why he did this:

> The idea was to choose books all in one place. If you do one table at a time, there's always one group who have to go last (thereby getting less choice).... There's the opportunity to introduce lots of books, authors, pictures and fliers. It provides an opportunity for the teacher to show his enthusiasm. It's a non-threatening, gentle way to get into choosing a book. The children then looked through them naturally.

However, despite Mr Martin's enthusiastic approach, marked sense of fairness and willingness to offer opportunities for all, at the end of the school year his class housed a pupil who had made one of the largest gains on a reading test in the entire sample and another who had regressed the most.

Like all the teachers in the sample Mr Martin had been asked to choose pupils who represented high, medium and low ability at reading. He chose Eva as a high-ability girl stating that she was unusual and very unworldly and Jack as a high-ability boy saying that he was very able, but was the youngest in the class, having 'loads of talent', but often working very slowly. It was Eva who made a staggering leap forward in her reading score and Jack who seemed to fall behind during the school year. Both were tested using the Norman France Primary Reading Test twice, with Eva scoring 102 at the beginning of the year and 134 at the end and Jack, by contrast, scoring 125 at the beginning and 100 at the end. Mr Martin's class average standardised score had improved by over 5 points during the year, but the pattern showed an interesting split, with fourteen high risers (gained 8 or more points), but five big sinkers (lost 4 or more points).

Eva's potential was celebrated by Mr Martin right from the start of the new year. On the first day of school Eva brought in a substantial book she had made over the school holidays, full of pages of written work all carefully presented. One child asked if he could see it. The teacher, who had everyone seated on the carpet, said he was going to share it with the whole class. Mr Martin told everyone that he thought it was amazing and he was therefore going to give her a Year 3 certificate which would be presented to her by the head teacher. He went through the different pages with the class drawing attention to the different things she had done and praising her on her work: 'I think it's amazing, I don't think I have ever seen anything like this from someone your age. It shows what an amazing young lady you are. I think it's brilliant.'

Mr Martin commented after the lesson why he had reacted to her work in the way he had:

> It was a celebration of what she'd done and an acknowledgement of her qualities [and also] to provide an inspiration to others. Her sister ... didn't get a certificate all the way through the school, so I wanted to celebrate. I hadn't planned it, it just happened. It was prompted by Sean who wanted to read it.

Lesson observation showed that Eva's and Jack's approach to work in class differed significantly. On each occasion when systematic observation of the six target pupils took place, Eva was always observed working assiduously. Jack, by contrast, only appeared to concentrate on his task sporadically. One day, when they were both working on the same written task, Eva wrote ten pages saying that it had not taken her very long because she had had all the ideas in her head. Her spelling was almost perfect, with one exception, and she used speech marks, question marks, apostrophes, abbreviations and exclamations without fault. She was able to read her own story with expression and explain why she had introduced irony into the text. She told the researcher that she always checked words she did not know. This piece of work was later marked by the teacher and given a star.

Jack was also observed working on the same task. He spent some of the time writing, but also sat and chatted with the boy next to him. When he had finished his conversation, instead of returning to work, he stared around the room whilst sucking his thumb. At the end of the lesson Jack has written one page and his story was selected by Mr Martin to read to the class. Although commenting that he had not finished, Mr Martin praised Jack for having made a good start.

On one observation visit, Eva again worked conscientiously throughout, whereas Jack was absent from school. In the last observation of the year, the pattern was similar to previous occasions. Eva worked assiduously on her task without losing concentration, whereas Jack was alternately on- and off-task, once again being observed sucking his thumb whilst staring around the room and fiddling with his pencil. He did, however, seem more on-task than off during this particular lesson and managed to complete about three-quarters of the task, using apostrophes and exclamation marks correctly.

The two pupils themselves seemed well aware of their own progress. In interview, Eva stated: 'I *love* reading. I *love* reading stories because it's exciting. Because I read lots of books and I'm older now, it's easier and you get on quicker.' Although Jack said that he *liked* reading because he too thought that books were exciting, he only thought that his progress had been 'all right'. Unlike Eva, who had no problems explaining any of the punctuation used in her book, Jack could not explain the difference between an apostrophe and a comma and had not mastered yet what speech marks were used for.

Mr Martin was a teacher whose on-task scores indicated that most of the time the pupils were highly involved in the tasks they were working on, with an average over the year of 82. His deviancy levels were, however, slightly higher than one would expect with this level of on-task involvement, averaging out at 5.3, above the average for this group of teachers of 3.5. This meant that three pupils might be misbehaving slightly, rather than this group's average of one or two. Midway through the year Mr Martin was asked to reflect on the pupils he had chosen and rate them on scales of 1–6 for their abilities as a reader and behaviour such as social skills, determination and independence. He rated Eva consistently higher, marking her high to very high (points 5–6) on most of the attributes whereas Jack was more consistently placed in the medium to high categories (points 4–5 on the scale).

Eva's home background was one of encouragement. Her mother, in particular, took every opportunity to introduce her to new experiences and encourage her to progress in her school work. Over the summer holidays she had taken her to numerous events and attractions and encouraged her to write accounts of these in the copious book she had brought into class at the beginning of the year. Jack, by contrast, was less fortunate and the teacher had succinctly explained at the beginning of the year that he was 'going through a difficult time', as his home and family life disintegrated.

The difference in the two children's home backgrounds was evident by the comments Mr Martin made about the two children at the end of the year. Of Eva he said:

> She is a voracious learner. She loves stories and words. She's read unbelievably, had loads and loads of book experience. If you look at her reading diary, it's phenomenal. I guess it may be due to less pressure [on her].

Jack had not had the same chances that year:

> He hasn't had an easy year, his parents have separated. He's probably stood still in terms of progress. He lacks confidence, has missed quite a bit of school, and is a bit of a loner.

These two cases illustrate the differences in the personal fortunes of two pupils in the same class receiving, on the surface, a similar education. Eva's mother was exceptionally interested in Eva's development and the pressure she may have inadvertently brought to bear on earlier occasions may have hindered her progress. Once Eva became more successful this pressure seemed to be relaxed and her increasing maturity and ability were able to thrive. The 'book of summer experiences' may have been an important turning point. Jack seemed a troubled boy who probably needed the extra support at home to give him confidence, but may not have received it whilst his parents were trying to resolve their own problems. As he missed class, day-dreamed, sucked his thumb, lost concentration, his reading appeared to regress. Even within the same class pupils' fortunes can diverge and produce quite different outcomes. 'Improvement' is certainly not a uniform process, nor are the conditions and opportunities for it universally bestowed on children.

Different patterns of improvement

In terms of test scores taken at the beginning and end of the school year, all except one of the classes showed a gain. The movement of scores was not uniform, however. The case of Jack and Eva's hugely divergent achievement in Mr Martin's class is the extreme case in the present study of differing progress under ostensibly the same regime, but there was no case of all the pupils in the class improving their standardised score at the same or even at a similar rate.

Indeed, although this was a generally improving, rather than regressing, set of classes, there was still an interesting diversity. In order to describe how some of these salient differences might look, in more readily comprehensible form, the sample of pupils was first split into three equally sized groups: the lowest third were labelled 'sinkers' (their scores had fallen by 4 points or more), the highest third were called 'risers' (their test scores had risen by 8 points or more) and the middle third were called 'similar' (they showed a movement of between -3 and $+7$ points, compared with first test score). Each class was then inspected to see what type of 'improvement' could be discerned and three different overall patterns of improvement emerged:

1   *Improvement pattern A – little change* Between a half and three-quarters of pupils stayed within a few points of their original standardised score, but a number of pupils improved by 8 points or more, while very few declined.
2   *Improvement pattern B – big riser* Over 40 per cent of pupils showed significantly increased scores of 8 points or more, with a similar number staying about the same and very few declining.
3   *Improvement pattern C – even spread* Over a third of scores rose by 8 points or more, roughly a quarter declined, and 40 per cent remained about the same.

'Improvement' is a portmanteau word which can in practice enclose many different forms inside itself, both in terms of the fluidity of movement within a whole class or group and the changes that occur in the accomplishments and fortunes of individual children. The analysis of whole-class patterns and the various pupil case studies in this chapter show some of the many kinds of improvement that can be witnessed in primary schools.

Accounting for the various causes and origins of changes for the better is no easy matter. Some seem to be explained by immense personal effort from the pupils themselves, often against the odds when children are unsupported at home, do not speak English, are teased for their bookishness, or acquire a reputation for poor behaviour. Others seem attributable to particular efforts by teachers or parents, reflecting some of the recurring themes in this research, such as matching books to interests, praise and encouragement, giving confidence, offering a path to autonomy as well as a degree of direction and structure. Most propitiously these conditions can act in powerful combination, though it is not uncommon for children's own personal qualities, like persistence and determination, sociability, concentration and independent-mindedness, to exert a forceful influence on their school achievement. In Chapter 12 we shall attempt to draw together the many strands in the development of children's literacy that have been identified as worthy of further scrutiny and comment.

12

IMPLICATIONS FOR POLICY AND PRACTICE

It is no easy matter, as we pointed out at the very beginning of this book, to study a phenomenon like 'improvement' in an environment as complex as that found in schools and classrooms. Trying to understand the inside working of individual children's minds, as learning takes place, poses an intractable set of problems. Inferences and conclusions drawn in the body of this book, or at the end of it, therefore, are inevitably tentative. We did not conduct experiments, as we wanted to investigate schools as they were and consider naturally occurring events and interactions. This involved analysing well over 1,000 written responses from schools throughout the country, observing numerous lessons where the principal focus was on literacy, and studying hundreds of children at different starting points in a variety of primary schools.

The difficulties of making inferences from natural occurrences have been acknowledged from the outset. Classroom life teems with thousands of micro-episodes, often hanging together in strings and clusters. These events are surrounded by thousands more outside the classroom, within families and other environments, when schooling may be reinforced, enhanced, or even undermined. In these circumstances, trying to ascribe any kind of learning to a particular source is hazardous. If children become better at reading, it may have come about because of the efforts of their teacher or parents, or despite them. They may in reality have been influenced by a certain person, author, style of teaching, or they may merely believe this to be the case. Improvement may have come about in the literacy-focused lessons we observed, or in the science, maths, art, and indeed other literacy lessons when we could not be present.

Even if a particular cause of improvement were to be found, it may have only a microscopic effect. As we described in Chapter 1, Gage (1985) reported how, in the field of medicine, despite the relatively small effect of beta blockers (2.5 per cent) and low-cholesterol diets (1.7 per cent) in helping heart attack patients survive a second coronary infarction, they were still adopted as part of an armoury of treatments for heart disease. Improving the teaching of reading may similarly need to seek numerous small contributions, rather than one single miraculously and universally successful strategy.

What does seem to be important is that, so far as we can see, improvement can be nurtured not only in different ways, but also in a variety of contexts. Our research suggests that several players can exert an effect on children's learning. It may well be the case that the real pay-off is in the classroom, what the research report written by Wang *et al.* (1993), described in Chapter 2, called 'proximal' factors, those elements nearest to teaching and learning, but we found some evidence of influence outside the classroom as well, from local authorities and parents. All the layers of education may have some positive effects, and when these work together, opportunities for children can be maximised.

Local authorities

It was because of this need to consider teaching and learning at several levels, and from different perspectives, that we tried to assess what role local authorities, schools, head teachers, language co-ordinators, class teachers, classroom assistants, parents and pupils themselves, might profitably play in children's acquisition of literacy in general and reading competence in particular. Local authorities underwent a period of considerable change after the 1988 Education Act. Some of them, like Birmingham, tried to be pro-active, and our research has shown that 94 per cent of heads in the city were aware of local authority initiatives, compared with an average of 46 per cent, less than half that number, in all the other 108 LEAs from which we obtained responses to the national questionnaire.

Local authorities, as we have reported in previous research projects (Wragg *et al.* 1996), are like a huge mixed ability class. Since 1988 several have become successful in a new, less proprietorial, role where support or inspiration, rather than direction or control, is stressed. Others have fulfilled their obligations with diligence, without adopting a high media profile, while yet others have made little impact on, or in a few cases even incurred the wrath of, their constituent schools. The local authorities studied in this research were equally varied.

Birmingham enjoyed considerable esteem among its primary head teachers. It differed in a number of respects from other LEAs in the way it handled literacy in its schools. For example, Birmingham offered its school-based language co-ordinators significantly greater support. They were more likely to be given non-contact time during which they could work with their colleagues (94 per cent of Birmingham schools, 46 per cent elsewhere), and extra payment (86 per cent of Birmingham schools, 49 per cent elsewhere). There were other differences, such as the higher profile accorded to reading activities, the public sponsoring of teachers' ideas, the staging of city-wide events, like the Year of Reading, the Chief Education

Officer's personal contribution through visits to schools, conferences and messages.

Birmingham was not the only LEA that undertook initiatives, however. Another authority we studied also had a Year of Reading, but fewer schools knew about it and it seemed to have less impact on the classroom practice we observed. The positive influence that Birmingham had on its schools was often driven by its Chief Officer initially, but the effect then rippled through schools, as first many head teachers became committed and subsequently class teachers themselves felt empowered to act. The combination of higher-level resourcing, with more money being spent on primary schools, personal inspiration from the centre, better communication and a sense of collegiality, seemed a powerful one, an unusually striking example of ideas and practices flowing along many channels, helped on by key people, like heads, advisers, language co-ordinators.

Effective communication between a local authority and its schools is one important starting point for any possible influence on classroom processes. Examples of effective leadership in action were given in Chapter 4, and the account of a meeting of the CEO of Birmingham with a group of the longest-serving head teachers illustrates well how this process worked in practice. The first important point is that there were seventeen such meetings of senior LEA officers and different groups of head teachers, so the encounter we reported in Chapter 4 was the last in a series. Second, the group size of twenty or so meant a great deal of work for the officers who attended them, but they made the judgement that, in winning the support of head teachers, it was a small price to pay. Third, the structure of the meetings was such that heads were asked (1) if reading standards could be raised and (2) who would do it. The almost universal replies of 'Yes' and 'We will' meant that the support and co-operation of key players was secured from the beginning.

The reaction of Birmingham heads to the challenge to raise standards was not unique. Our national survey showed that 97 per cent of schools thought that standards could be raised, though 29 per cent thought only 'with difficulty'. What happened in Birmingham, however, was a direct effort to harness these beliefs to action. These kinds of meetings, especially those with the most experienced and, in other circumstances, potentially most resistant heads, showed the effort that the LEA's senior officers were prepared to expend to address collegially, rather than peremptorily, the issue of improving literacy. It is open to argument whether the success and popularity that Birmingham enjoyed is unique, simply explained by the city having a Chief Officer who was regarded as charismatic, willing to send handwritten notes to individual teachers and put his personal stamp on schools, or whether the policies and actions can be generalised to other circumstances.

Certainly those LEAs which made a less impressive impact on practice could learn from the way that the distance between central administration and schools was reduced in Birmingham, and the type of efforts that were required to create a sense of community and support. In certain other cases the local authority was regarded as remote, not on the same side as heads and teachers, merely imposing an extra tier of bureaucracy, rather than helping schools in what some perceived to be adversity. In Birmingham the LEA was not only thought to be on the same side, but regarded as leading the charge. There was a qualitatively different climate, and the LEA offers a number of pointers to what a locally organised administration might achieve in circumstances where it is no longer the proprietor and has to influence by means other than direct power.

Schools

Alongside many differences, there were certain similarities in the way schools organised the teaching and learning of literacy. Almost all placed great faith in the role of the language co-ordinator, the fellow professional charged principally with advising colleagues and evaluating teaching; selecting, ordering and devising resources; running in-service courses; and often organising the school library and parents' evenings. Some 90 per cent of schools had such a post and in 10 per cent, often in smaller primary schools, the job was done by the head or deputy. A few heads professed that they themselves had little knowledge of the teaching of reading, but most of these believed that the role of language co-ordinator was, therefore, even more important. Yet few language co-ordinators had received much further training specifically on the teaching of reading since they had first qualified as teachers, and there does seem to be a strong case, if the role is as important as head teachers believe, for offering more training and support.

The tendency was for the official school policy to be empirically, rather than rationally, derived: in other words, a pragmatic approach, whereby existing practice was distilled into policy form. The belief was that intelligence lay embedded in actual practice. Policy was what teachers already did, or at least assumed they did. In the vast majority of schools books were sent home, as were spellings and other forms of follow-up work to be done at home. Much of what was done at school level, therefore, seemed to be based to a certain degree on deliberate and conscious structuring, though there were schools where less thought had been given to the overall management of literacy. This part-intuitive, part-sculptured, daily practice was then translated, usually by the head and language co-ordinator, into a written document.

Head teachers played different roles, some proactive, others less so. In one case study school the head teacher had researched and written her MEd dissertation on the teaching of reading. Fellow teachers were impressed not only by her professional knowledge, but also by the skilful way in which she and the language co-ordinator involved them in conceiving and implementing the school's policies on reading. The parents of all new pupils were visited at home by the head and Reception class teachers even before the children started school and the discussion of the teaching of reading was a central element of these preliminary talks. While certainly not identical, there was a high degree of accord between teachers about how they tackled the teaching of reading in their classrooms, and this seemed to be a direct result of their being so closely involved in policy making.

In certain other cases there was not too much congruence between policy intent and classroom action. We studied schools where what we observed in different classrooms did not always conform to what purported to be school policy, though it was more common to see a high degree of assent from teachers. Indeed, it was not always safe to assume that the leadership in literacy matters came from the head. There were individual teachers, whose practice seemed influential on the improvements noted, who worked not against their head teachers, but independently of them.

The national survey provided further evidence of the value that primary schools put on the creation of a positive and harmonious climate for literacy: 'Ethos and atmosphere' were regarded by respondents as the most important factor in improving reading attainment, and this aspect was put in first place, ahead of parental involvement, resources, monitoring/assessment and the allocation of time.

Despite the emphasis on what are sometimes regarded as more diffuse concepts, such as 'people' and 'climate', there were many examples of structured approaches to reading. Almost all schools (99 per cent) used one or more published reading schemes as a matter of policy, with just over half using several schemes and slightly less than half colour-coded books to show levels of difficulty. Over 80 per cent had written language policies, and most of those without seemed to be writing one. Systematic monitoring and assessment figured high on lists of what teachers and heads thought to be important. Phonic approaches to the teaching of reading were mentioned by teachers more frequently than others, though this may have been partly connected with the political climate of the day, when press criticisms may have put pressure on teachers to contradict accusations that phonics had been neglected. Targets for individual pupils were set by the majority of schools, though this was most frequently done with children who had special educational needs, often in the form of small steps that might be taken to increase competence a little at a time.

There was some discomfort with certain quantitative approaches to structure. 'Targets', for example, was sometimes a diffuse and elusive concept, differently conceived. Some heads were happy to think in terms of completing the building of the library as a 'whole-school target', but most schools (70 per cent) did not construe whole-school targets in terms of measured pupil achievement. Very few examples of pupils setting targets for themselves were reported. There was some scepticism, even in Birmingham, where target setting was widely used, about whether or not such moves would improve, or indeed even change existing practice. One overall conclusion, from the evidence derived from schools and local authorities, is that strategies to do with people and the quality of their life and work in school are valued more highly than structures, particularly when the latter have been externally imposed.

Teachers and classrooms

The thirty-five case study teachers we observed were in general highly esteemed by the heads of their schools, pupils in their classes were much more engaged in their work than many we have studied, and they also showed relatively large improvements in reading proficiency during the year, so these teachers did seem worth studying, both individually and as a group. However, as was pointed out in Chapter 11, there were several different patterns of improvement, both for individuals and for whole classes. We identified three salient patterns within the classes tested for reading:

1 *Improvement pattern A*, showing little change, between a half and three-quarters of pupils staying within a few points of their original standardised score, but a number of pupils improving by 8 points or more, and very few declining;
2 *Improvement pattern B*, the big risers, over 40 per cent of pupils gaining 8 points or more on their score, with a similar number staying about the same and very few declining;
3 *Improvement pattern C*, an even spread, with over a third of scores rising by 8 points or more, roughly a quarter declining, 40 per cent remaining about the same.

It was not unusual, therefore, to find, within the same class, pupils whose reading improved considerably, alongside others whose performance declined.

Teachers were observed using a wide range of strategies, and it was notable that the narrow functional definitions which some gave of the concept 'literacy' were not always filled out in their lessons, where they often demonstrated a much broader interpretation in their actual practice. Within this diversity a number of teachers expressed strong preferences for particular approaches. In Birmingham it was the use of 'Big Books' that was especially valued by some enthusiasts, while in other cases 'group reading' was seen as an effective strategy. It was noticeable to the researchers that even when people appeared to endorse ostensibly the same approach, the interpretation and implementation of something bearing the identical name could be quite different. 'Group reading', for example, was an elastic concept that embraced a variety of practices, and in Chapter 6 we described three contrasting interpretations of it. 'Paired reading' was another example of a flexible set of strategies that might involve an adult reading with a child, or two children in the same class or in different classes. In some cases paired reading was carried on assiduously from September to the following July, with few interruptions, while in other classrooms it fizzled out during the year.

Many extensions of reading were observed, often linked to writing. 'I can' and 'I do' books written by children themselves were popular in the early years. Sometimes these were accorded a proud place alongside real published books in the 'Author's corner'. Children's self-made books were popular generally, though what preceded the writing of them varied, and some teachers tried to mimic the whole process of publishing a book, from planning and drafting, right through to finalising and printing. In Birmingham the creating of one's own book was seen as a pupil entitlement, part of the Primary Guarantee the city offered its children.

The teacher's role in the act of reading itself was an interesting one. Although many stressed how important reading was to their pupils, few actually read silently on their own when their pupils did, as their role was usually to help and monitor. On the other hand, very few teachers mentioned in interview that they read a book to their class, yet this was a commonly observed activity, perhaps so taken for granted that teachers no longer thought about it consciously.

When it came to looking at teachers hearing individual children read there were many different views and practices. Some teachers and heads were hostile to the very idea, believing it to be a waste of the teachers' time. Others who did not state reservations quite so bluntly, nonetheless signalled their own lack of time for it by passing on the duty to classroom assistants, adult helpers, parents at home, or fellow pupils. In some cases teachers were especially keen to hear children read and there were head teachers who insisted that every child should be heard every day. In Chapter 7 we concluded, in the light of observations of what seemed to be successful practice, that there were six ingredients that were needed if teachers were to derive maximum benefit from hearing children read and conversing about the book. These were:

1 *Orderliness* – disruptive behaviour by other pupils can be a powerful distractor.
2 *Focus* – a strong focus on reading as the major activity of the moment, so that maths or other problems do not take the teacher away from the principal domain.
3 *Independence* – children reading alone need to be able to make their own decisions, so they are not too dependent on the teacher; equally, those

reading with the teacher need independence, so they can guess intelligently at unfamiliar words.

4 *Priority* – the child being heard needs to have top priority, except in emergencies.

5 *Importance* – reading must be made important, so that interruptions are frowned upon.

6 *Worthwhileness* – the book needs to be engaging and worth talking about.

It is tempting to try to find a number of universal truths from observations of these 'above-average' practitioners. As other investigators, some of whom were described in Chapters 1 and 2, have discovered, this is not as simple as it may sound. For example, several teachers observed gave prominence to the display of children's work and the celebration of it, as well as to the use of environmental print and the labelling of classroom features. Two teachers whose classes achieved amongst the highest gains in reading proficiency on standardised tests given early and late in the school year, however, showed little interest in display, and their classroom walls were relatively bare. It is not safe to assume that certain elements must be universally present in effective lessons.

We did, nonetheless, attempt to pick out some similarities amongst these arguably successful teachers, though it is noteworthy that these were often expressed in individual form. An illustration of this is that most teachers managed to secure a very high degree of pupil attentiveness to the task in hand, so that was common. What was different was the manifold means through which they achieved this goal, sometimes by fast-paced enthusiastic interactions prior to reading or written work, in other cases though a more quietly supportive, even private, approach to individuals. Some teachers made a show of publicly alerting the class to what was expected, or implemented clear rules of conduct, such as no talking or movement being permitted during sessions when reading was the highest priority.

The ten broad common factors we managed to isolate in Chapter 9, therefore, are offered with the proviso that they should not be regarded as universal prescriptions, nor should the absence of them in any particular classroom necessarily be regarded as an indicator of ineffectiveness. The ten features which several teachers manifested, in their different individual forms, were as follows:

1 A high level of personal enthusiasm for literature, some even supplementing the school's reading resources with their own personal collection of books.

2 Good professional knowledge of children's authors and teaching strategies.

3 Literacy being made very important, within a rich literacy environment.

4 Celebrating progress publicly and increasing children's confidence.

5 Being able to individualise and match teaching to pupils, particularly in terms of their reading interests.

6 Systematic monitoring and assessment, though the form of it varied.

7 Regular and varied reading activities.

8 Pupils being encouraged to develop independence and autonomy, attacking unfamiliar words, taking their own reading forward, or backing their own judgement as authors.

9 A notably high degree of classroom management skill and good-quality personal relationships with pupils, with some of the highest 'on-task' scores we have recorded.

10 High positive expectations, with children striving to reach a high standard, whatever their circumstances.

Pupils

Nearly two-thirds of the 355 children whose reading proficiency was tested during the school year showed an improvement on their standardised reading score, while over a quarter showed a decline. As was explained earlier in this book, since standardised test scores were used, the normal expectation is that children will remain on the same standardised score if they have improved over a period of time at the 'average' rate for their age group. The cohort of pupils studied in this research, therefore, improved well beyond the norm, and there seemed to be several possible explanations for this.

It is difficult, when trying to analyse teaching, to group or classify teachers without losing important idiosyncrasies, and it is not easy or desirable to squeeze children too readily into stereotypes. Certain pupils may share certain common features, in terms of the school they attend, their class teacher, or the books they read, but their individual life histories, families, attitudes, prior educational experiences, personalities and dispositions are nonetheless unique. Hundreds of different accounts could be given about the way they learn to read and what they do once they are proficient. To distil these discrete histories into generalisations is to oversimplify the complex, so it is a risk that researchers face with some degree of caution.

Reading support for pupils varied considerably. Some children read with a wide range of people: teachers, classroom assistants, meal-time assistants, parents, friends, siblings. A few claimed they read with no one, not even their teacher. In some cases particular adults seemed to have made a considerable impact on individual children's progress. It was usually a teacher who had selected books of particular interest, given encouragement, or equipped someone with specific strategies for reading alone successfully, but sometimes it was a parent or other member of the family. In the case of one of the most spectacular improvers, 6 year old Joseph, described in Chapter 11, his whole family became involved, parents as well as grandparents, and this seemed to boost both his self-confidence and his performance.

Most pupils in the study expressed a very positive attitude towards reading. Only four pupils in the 5 to 7 age group and only eleven in the 7 to 11 age group said they did not like reading, a mere 6 per cent of the sample. These were mainly children of lower ability or performance who were finding that learning to read was a struggle. By contrast, a large-scale study of 8 year old children by Brooks *et al.* (1998) found that a quarter of them said they had no interest in books. The high degree of pupil interest in reading secured in the classrooms we studied may well be a significant factor in the general success of children and their teachers. One of the most common reactions amongst the 'improvers', when interviewed at the end of the school year, was to say that they now enjoyed their school work more as a result of becoming more competent readers.

In addition to their enjoyment of books, however, many children also had a utilitarian/functional view of reading, appreciating that it would help them get a job, as well as read the many signs and instructions by which they were surrounded. They were also well able to make judgements about their own competence. Although young children often tend to say to interviewers, as a matter of routine, that they are 'good' readers, even if they appear to have little competence, they frequently reveal, on further questioning, that they have picked up numerous cues about the level of their own performance. Sometimes these are confirmed by comparison with other members of their class or subgroup, even when the teacher has made an effort to anonymise levels of performance by using colour-coded groups. In one classroom, being allowed to choose books 'in the corridor', which was where the more difficult texts were kept, marked someone out as performing beyond the norm. In other cases 'working on the computer' became an indicator of below-average achievement.

One feature that often came to the notice of researchers was the drive towards pupil autonomy. Ultimately children need to be able to read on their own, since this is what most older people do, and it was interesting to note the process by which autonomy was achieved. Many teachers encouraged independence from an early age. Depending on their age, between 30 per cent and 40 per cent of children studied could change their reading book whenever they decided. Many, though certainly not all, were well equipped with strategies to attack unfamiliar words and phrases. Most older pupils were well able to use phonics to sound out new words, or employ a 'leapfrog' strategy to skip over the unfamiliar word and seek a context which would help them return to it and make a better effort. In Chapter 10 there was a description of one 9 year old who was able to describe graphically the cloze-type strategy his teacher had taught him for deciding whether the books he was reading were too difficult, too easy, or about right.

By contrast with such autonomous pupils, the relatively large number of children in the 5 to 7 age group, about a half of them, who simply asked the teacher when they were stuck, can pose a problem. At this early stage some degree of dependence on the teacher is inescapable, but when too few children are able to seek help elsewhere, make an intelligent attack on an unknown word, use picture and context cues, or deploy some other independent strategy, then severe management problems can be caused. Those in quest of help may consume large amounts of the teacher's time, forming queues which prevent the teacher moving far from his or her desk. Since the teachers in this study were in general highly skilled managers of their classes, this was less of a problem than we have observed elsewhere. Nonetheless, even this very competent group had to cope with pupil dependency in the early years.

Autonomy may be a desirable outcome, but it is also double edged. Only 10 per cent of younger children and 5 per cent of older pupils said they were asked to read to their teacher before being allowed to change their book. Although a quarter of 7 to 11 year olds said they would write a book review after reading a book, only 5 per cent mentioned discussing the book with their teacher. They may, of course, have done so, but failed to recall it. However, an individual pupil discussing a book with a teacher was not something we recorded too frequently during classroom observation. Primary classrooms are rapidly changing environments and many demands compete with each other. Teachers have to tread a fine dividing line between autonomy and neglect: too much insistence on checking everything with the teacher before progressing and children will waste time in queues, become overly dependent, feel that they do not have a personal stake in their own reading; too little monitoring and there is no accountability, no means of knowing whether pupils have understood what they have read, or are making wise choices when they select their next book.

Individual pupil improvement was found in many different forms. There were examples of huge personal efforts by the pupils themselves, frequently against the odds, when children were unsupported at home, did not speak English, or were even teased for their interest in books and reading. One spectacular improver, an 8 year old girl described in Chapter 10, whose reading age went up from 8.2 to 13.2 in the year, showed exceptional determination and persistence for someone of her age. There were also striking instances of particular efforts by teachers or parents. These tended to reflect themes that have recurred more than once in this research, like matching books to pupils' individual interests, offering praise and encouragement, giving confidence, or helping children to become autonomous as well as offering them a degree of direction and structure. When these factors operated together they formed a powerful combination, especially if combined with children's personal qualities, like persistence and determination, sociability, concentration and independence of mind.

Parents and home

When schools were asked what new initiatives they were taking, or hoped to introduce in the future, the greater involvement of parents was the most frequently cited. This may be the result of the belief expressed by many teachers in interview that learning begins in the home. Sending home books, spellings, reading and writing assignments that were to be monitored by parents and entered in the home/school diary were regular occurrences in almost all the schools studied. No school expressed disregard for parents, and this was hardly surprising, given the pressure applied through school inspections and in the mass media to involve them in their children's learning. Most children in the 5 to 7 age group read to someone at home, and at least half of older primary pupils do so as well; home/school diaries are countersigned by many parents; spellings are checked; the general attitude of teachers towards parents is, in the main, extremely positive. On the surface, therefore, all appears to be well: schools do engage parents, and this is regarded *ipso facto* as a good thing.

In Chapter 8, however, we showed that, beneath the surface, the processes were not quite as unproblematic as might appear. The difficulties sometimes arose when parents tried to act in a manner regarded as professional, rather than amateur. In several schools the influence was largely in one direction, from school to home. When parents expressed reservations about what was happening, teachers saw it as their duty to explain what the school was trying to achieve, to persuade them about the rightness of existing practice, rather than change it: 'Some of these parents really don't understand what we're trying to do and how we go about it', as one teacher put it.

A common clash of ideologies occurred over hearing children read, for some parents the only method of teaching reading they remembered from their own school days. Another was about the different interpretations of what constituted 'reading', since some parents found it difficult to accept that looking at a picture book could constitute 'reading' as they understood the term. There were a number of exceptions to the 'one-way persuasion' solution to comment or dissent, like the school that received complaints from parents about children not being heard reading and so instituted a guaranteed weekly reading interview.

Many parents interviewed expressed ignorance about the methods used to teach reading, even in schools that had held parents' evenings. Their responses often began with 'I assume ... ', or 'I presume ... ', rather than with some degree of certainty. Yet successful evenings involving parents were very much appreciated, explaining, for example, how children might recognise, at quite an early stage, longer and more complex-looking words, such as 'elephant', a revelation which one parent described as an 'eye opener'.

Some parents seemed eager to play a more professional role, rather than the well-intentioned amateur role that teachers expected. Teachers tended to stress that reading at home was for 'fun' and 'enjoyment', avoiding any suggestion of drudgery, coercion, or indeed systematic teaching. Parents too were anxious to prevent reading at home becoming a chore, but several did want to be able to work more positively with their children, sounding out words, actually 'teaching' reading, rather than just hearing it. In a number of families there was tension and frustration when parents tried to push children on, expecting performance beyond what the child was achieving, or employed methods and approaches that were in contrast to what the child did at school. This frustration was summed up by the 6 year old boy described in Chapter 10, who said: 'I think I'm a good reader at school. I'm not a good reader at home. ... I can't read my books at home.' What he meant was that his parents were asking him to read books that were beyond his level of competence. Not surprisingly, at that early age, he gauged his ability relative to the texts he was reading, rather than to other sources of reference.

Parent helpers in the classroom also performed a modest role. Few were given any instruction on what to do, unlike classroom assistants. As a result, classroom assistants often heard reading in a systematic way, did group reading, or carried out some carefully planned and structured activities, whereas parents usually operated in an informal, unstructured and *ad hoc* manner. Even in Birmingham, where most schools made parents a central part of their agenda for improvement, there were schools where the head too readily assumed that certain parents might not even be literate in their mother tongue, compared with schools in similar areas that had higher expectations from them.

What was also noticeable was the prominent role played by mothers, compared with fathers. As will be described later in this chapter, it was more likely that mothers would hear their child read at home, complete the home/school diary, or help out in the classroom. It was extremely rare to see any kind of volunteer male presence in classrooms, especially in infant schools. Given the relatively poor performance of boys in reading in the early years and beyond, this raises the question of the need for more male role models, an issue which is discussed further in the section below.

The generally positive reaction of schools to the involvement of parents is a strong foundation stone on which to build, but there should be no doubt about the gaps, misunderstandings and lack of knowledge that exist, even in schools as effective generally as the ones studied in this research. Despite the efforts on their behalf, many parents still know little about how reading is taught, or about the specifics of what they can do to help at home, beyond exuding goodwill. Relatively few fathers become closely involved in their children's reading or are available to help in the classroom. Unwittingly perhaps, some schools may patronise their children's parents by glossing over their concerns, assuming that they are capable of very little beyond the most rudimentary, or, in the case of ethnic minorities, assuming too readily that they may not be equipped to help. In the many schools with a positive attitude, there are still steps that can be taken to strengthen the role of parents, even if this challenges some of the traditional assumptions about the limited role that parents can play in their children's education.

The performance of boys

The focus on the lower performance of boys in this research does not mean that other groups are not worthy of close scrutiny. There is a limit to what a research team can study and several aspects of boys' performance and attitude were regarded as worthy of attention during the course of this research. As we enter the next millennium the relatively low achievement of boys in literacy has become one of the biggest problems facing our society. For reasons given in Chapter 1, however, it is important for all children to achieve well in literacy and literacy-related activities in school.

Thousands of 'muscled' jobs, involving lifting, carrying, or other kinds of heavy manual work, have disappeared and are unlikely to return. The edge that boy school leavers used to have in the labour market, as employers favoured them for heavy manual jobs, barely exists any longer. Many of the jobs available to young school leavers involve work which is enhanced by the ability to communicate well. A poor start in literacy in the early years can become a handicap from which many pupils, boys or girls, will not recover in the secondary school. Improving the performance of boys, many of whom perform significantly less well than girls in reading in particular, needs to be given a high priority, but not at the expense of girls, whose achievements have improved significantly and should continue to do so.

A report from the Qualifications and Curriculum Authority (1998), entitled *Can Do Better,* attempted to summarise the position and suggest ways forward. It described how poorer language performance starts in the early years of pre-schooling, when nursery teachers watching under-5s at play soon discover that boys prefer action fantasy, careering around the room with few words but more sound effects. This is thought by some pre-school teachers to be dangerous, so it is often curtailed, though other teachers try to build more structured language into its raw energy.

In the present research, as reported in Chapter 10, we found what other investigators have often discovered, that boys in primary schools do less well on reading tests than girls. The boys in our sample scored on average 4 or 5 points below girls, at both the beginning and end of the year, in all the age groups tested from age 6 to 11, apart from Year 5. They were rated by teachers to be significantly below the girls not only in reading ability, but on social skills, and on personal characteristics such as concentration, determination, the ability to listen and, crucially, the amount of work they actually did in a lesson. They were also significantly less likely than girls to be read with at home, by anyone, not just by their fathers. The boys start down and they stay down in essential language competencies throughout the junior school phase, and the level of expectation from important adults like their teachers and parents is low.

The Qualifications and Curriculum Authority (1998) report confirmed this end of primary-phase deficit in its accompanying national test figures. In 1997 some 69 per cent of 11 year old girls obtained Level 4 in national tests in English, the expected 'average' for the age group, compared with 57 per cent of boys. There is, however, an important difference between 1980s and 1990s findings. There used to be an assumption, in the 1980s and earlier, that differences in primary school performance would not persist far into the secondary phase, that boys would eventually catch up and overtake girls. Evidence from public examination results at the age of 16 and 18 in the 1980s supported this assumption. In 1983–4, for example, 26.3 per cent of boys obtained five high-grade passes in the public examination at the age of 16, compared with 27.2 per cent of girls, a gap of less than 1 per cent. At the age of 18, in the same 1983–4 year, 11.1 per cent of boys passed three A level examinations compared with 9.5 per cent of girls.

By the late 1990s the belief that boys would surge ahead at the secondary stage was no longer tenable. A great deal of positive work had, quite rightly, been done during the 1980s to encourage girls to stay on at school and have stronger faith in their own ability. Year by year the gap between boys' and girls' performance in public examinations increased. By 1994–5 the figures for five high grades in the public examination taken at 16 no longer showed a tiny difference. The gap of less than 1 per cent had become almost 10 per cent in favour of girls (boys 39.8 per cent, girls 49.3 per cent). At age 18 the 1994–5 figures for three A level passes also revealed a growing deficit compared with the previous decade. Instead of boys outperforming girls, it was now the other way round (boys 20.5 per cent, girls 24.2 per cent). University entrance figures for the 1990s showed that, for the first time, more girls than boys were gaining entry to higher education. By 1995–6 there were 453,600 male compared with 470,500 female undergraduates.

The increase in girls' achievement was rapid and laudable, but boys' inability to match it increased the odds against them in later life. In the GCSE English examination, taken at the age of 16 and vital for employment purposes, the 1996–7 examination results showed that a high grade was achieved by 65 per cent of girls, compared with 43 per cent of boys. This last figure in particular highlights the importance of strengthening the performance of boys in the field of literacy in the primary school.

The Qualifications and Curriculum Authority (1998) report cited not only its own evidence but also some interesting case studies. Boys tended to read less than girls and cover a narrower field. Many preferred non-fiction and were reluctant to read poetry or certain kinds of fiction. They also wrote in a more restricted range of genres and tended to proofread and self-correct less thoroughly. Boys were less likely to be members of informal book circles, whereas girls often exchanged books with friends.

In the classroom observation studies in the present research we found boys to be only slightly less attentive than girls during lessons, and the small differences were not statistically significant, but there were a number of critical events noted where teachers were distracted from their work because of disruptive behaviour by certain boys in their class. However, we were studying a sample of teachers who manifested a particularly high degree of skilful classroom management, and even here some of the individual case studies showed examples of boys who were unable to concentrate for long on reading or language work, preferring activities and social interaction. National statistics showed that thirteen times as many boys (1,177) as girls (91) were excluded from primary schools for poor behaviour during the school year when the fieldwork for the research was carried out. Easier distraction and in some cases poorer behaviour generally means that, for various reasons, certain boys may simply spend less time on their task. The cumulative effect can be huge. Multiply inattentiveness by a thousand or more language lessons during the six years of primary schooling and this eventually adds up.

Trying to explain this sustained adversity is not easy. It may be a case of later maturation, as girls in primary schools have traditionally done better than boys in language. Research in which brain activity is scanned during language activities suggests that the female brain is active in both halves, the male brain predominantly in one. Many boys have seen the traditional male role as bread winner disappear in their own families, when male relatives, fathers, grandfathers, uncles, brothers, lost their jobs. It may be that this dramatic social change demoralises and demotivates, and that, in turn, lower motivation leads to less time being spent on the task in hand, so less learning takes place, or that loss of status leads to boys playing aggressive masculine, sometimes referred to as 'laddish', roles in order to restore it. Even if they can get a job, many of the boys now in school will have to retrain several times during their working lives, and most of them can look forward to many years of good health in their Third Age, the age of healthy retirement, so their appetite for learning needs to stretch way beyond the years of compulsory schooling. Language ability in general, and reading skill in particular, play an important part in their opportunity to benefit from lifelong learning.

It would be easy to develop prejudices, to despair when boisterous early years' rough-and-tumble play becomes adolescent 'laddishness', to assume that girls have a 'natural' edge over boys in English, both sides of their brain being active during language activity, but only one side of boys' brains, or that they are 'naturally' better at coursework. In the 1970s there was resignation at the plight of girls. Similar prejudices were rife: girls were said to be poor at maths and science, have no self-confidence, lack ambition to be anything other than a hairdresser or secretary, unable to cope with new technology, incapable of outperforming boys, who were believed to be more competitive. Yet a combined effort by teachers in many schools led to a dramatic improvement over the following twenty years. Many assumptions about the supposed 'natural' inferiority of girls were seen to be socially conditioned. Less was expected of them, so less was achieved. The same unwitting social conditioning may apply when assumptions are made about boys' poorer achievement in reading.

The Qualifications and Curriculum Authority (1998) report offered a number of suggestions, including the following:

- Steer boys away from playing entirely with construction toys in the early years towards language activities.
- Build more language into their fantasy activities.
- Capitalise on boys' enjoyment of discussion, drama, making videos, interactive technology, but making sure the boys do not dominate lessons.
- Investigate what boys are borrowing from the library; is it mainly non-fiction?
- Match fiction to their individual interests, such as sport, adventure, humour, if these are liked.
- Study the behaviour of boys in the classroom. Is it off-task? If so, why? Can their attentiveness be increased?
- See if mixed boy and girl groups work better than the single-sex groupings that often occur, explaining the purpose first.
- Encourage more boys to participate in the production of a class or school play or magazine.
- Ensure assessment covers a full range of achievement, not just narrative reading and writing, which may ignore strengths that boys may have.
- Try individual and group targets, for example encouraging boys to explore different writing genres or read a greater variety of text.
- Boys often see the purpose of literacy more if they can actually do something, so try extracurricular activities like arts festivals, book weeks, poetry readings, writers-in-residence.

If boys are to improve enough to be able to face the twenty-first century with confidence, a comprehensive and co-ordinated attack on their under-achievement will be needed. There are many areas in which action can be taken. In the 1997 Greenwich Lecture, one of the present researchers (Wragg 1997b) proposed a ten-point plan, covering the primary and secondary phases:

1 *Make an early start* Boys should be encouraged to attend nurseries, so they make an early start on language activities in particular and learn to behave well in class.

2 *Help at home* More fathers should help at home, especially with reading and writing, so language is not seen as a purely 'female' activity. Relatively few male role models were seen in classrooms during this research and fathers were much less likely to read at home with either boys or girls.

3 *Early intervention* There should be skilled individual specialist help for the many boys in infant schools who make a slow start to reading.

4 *Appeal to their interests* Humour, adventure, sport are among topics that appeal to young boys, so these should be incorporated into what they read wherever possible. Some of the most effective teachers observed during the research did precisely this.

5 *Improve behaviour* Some boys are easily distracted and then in turn distract others. Their behaviour in class needs to improve so they spend more time on their task.

6 *Alert teachers* When teachers became more aware of girls' underachievement their results improved. Awareness about boys' poor performance must be raised, not least amongst boys themselves and their parents, so that trying hard at school is not seen to be 'swottish', but normal.

7 *Use new technology* Many young boys like using new technology, such as CD-ROMs and virtual reality, and they often concentrate more when they use it.

8 *Involve them in their own learning* Today's pupils are tomorrow's citizens. They need to be directly involved in improving their own performance, so they can set themselves targets, maintain focus, ask questions of themselves, pick out important information, improve relationships, and know when to ask for help.

9 *Identify 'at risk' pupils* Early intervention in the primary school for those falling behind is essential, but there should be another safety net in secondary school, so that boys aged 13, likely to be 'at risk' when they leave, are identified and helped.

10 *Redesign the 14–18 curriculum* Provide a co-ordinated programme for 14 to 18 year olds for the twenty-first century, in which pupils can choose from sets of what are sometimes called 'academic' and 'vocational' modules, so that programmes can be tailored to individual needs and interests.

The education of all children to their full potential is often stated in official documents to be a top priority. The education of girls must not be neglected when addressing the problems identified, but unless the achievement of boys is improved, there could be immense problems in the twenty-first century.

Foundations for a literate society

The development of information and communication technology might, on the surface, appear to reduce the need for adults to be able to handle the reading, writing and understanding of text, but in practice it is not so simple a matter. Written text, and indeed the deciphering of icons, is still an important part of adult life, with or without technology, as we stressed at the beginning of this book. Many children attending school at the dawn of the millennium will live to the age of 80, 90 or beyond.

In the automated economy of the twenty-first century, no employer is going to get rid of two fork lift trucks and two drivers in order to employ twenty people with large biceps. If we want to improve significantly the overall national level of achievement for the twenty-first century, then it is the massive underachievement of boys that must be tackled vigorously. It is causing a major headache to those who educate them, and the evidence of their relatively low performance is now overwhelming at all stages of education.

There are many factors in this research which can help underpin a set of strategies to improve levels of literacy, thereby increasing opportunities for young people in the twenty-first century, both in work and in family and home life. Giving national and regional prominence to the importance of literacy is one valuable starting point. This would be lost, however, without intelligent action in schools, classrooms and in the home. Fortunate indeed are the many children for whom each of these locations provides a supportive environment. Sadly, some pupils suffer from lack of positive support in one or even all these settings. Many of the heads, language co-ordinators, teachers, classroom assistants and parents described in this book were above the norm in terms of what they achieved or the quality of help they offered children. What they did may not always be replicable, but they do offer models that can be studied and adapted as necessary.

The features that underpinned improvement were almost always closely related to the people who implemented them. Systems, techniques, policies, processes all offer an important framework within which success may be achieved, but in the end it is the interpretations and efforts of the individual people concerned that count. Children who became better readers had usually made great efforts themselves, but it was their teachers, parents and other helpers who had enthused about and celebrated their success, taught them strategies for attacking unfamiliar words, offered them interesting texts, recorded and monitored their progress and offered feedback on it, encouraged them to become independent as well as offered them advice when it was needed. Any effort applied to encouraging and supporting the key people involved is worthwhile, whether this is aimed at the pupils themselves, their teachers, their parents, or any others who are involved. Becoming literate is, after all, not only one of the greatest gifts that adults can bestow on the next generation, it is also one of their greatest entitlements.

BIBLIOGRAPHY

Adams, M. J. (1990) 'Why not phonics *and* whole language?', in W. Ellis (ed.) *All Language and the Creation of Literacy*, Baltimore, MD: Orton Dyslexia Society.

Adams, M. J. (1991) *Beginning to Read*, Cambridge, MA: MIT Press.

Aitken, M., Bennett, S. N. and Hesketh, J. (1981) 'Teaching styles and pupil progress: a re-analysis', *British Journal of Educational Psychology* 51(2): 170–86.

Alexander, R., Rose, J. and Woodhead, C. (1992) *Curriculum Organisation and Classroom Practice in Primary Schools: A Discussion Paper*, London: DES.

Alexander, R., Willcocks, J. and Kinder, K. (1989) *Changing Primary Practice*, London: Falmer Press.

Austin, G. R. and Garber, H. (eds) (1985) *Research on Exemplary Schools*, Orlando, FL: Academic Press.

Baddeley, A. D., Ellis, N. C., Miles, T. R. and Lewis, V. J. (1982) 'Developmental and acquired dyslexia: a comparison', *Cognition* 11: 185–99.

Barber, M. (1996) 'Creating a framework for success in urban areas', in M. Barber and R. Dann (eds) *Raising Standards in the Inner Cities*, London: Cassell.

Barber, M., Stoll, L., Mortimore, P. and Hillman, J. (1995) *Governing Bodies and Effective Schools*, London: DfEE.

Barr, A. S. (1961) 'Wisconsin studies of the measurement and prediction of teacher effectiveness', *Journal of Experimental Education* 30: 5–156.

Barr, R., Kamil, M. L., Mosenthal, P. B. and Pearson, P. D. (1991) *Handbook of Reading Research*, Vol. II, New York: Longman.

Barrs, M. and Thomas, A. (eds) (1991) *The Reading Book*, London: Centre for Language in Primary Education.

Barth, R. (1990) *Improving Schools from Within: Teachers, Parents and Principals Can Make a Difference*, San Francisco: Jossey-Bass.

Beard, R. (ed.) (1993) *Teaching Literacy Balancing Perspectives*, London: Hodder & Stoughton.

Bennett, N. (1976) *Teaching Styles and Pupil Progress*, London: Open Books.

Bennett, N. (1987) 'The search for the effective primary teacher', in S. Delamont (ed.) *The Primary School Teacher*, Lewes: Falmer Press.

Bennett, N., Desforges, C., Cockburn, A. and Wilkinson, B. (1984) *The Quality of Pupil Learning Experiences*, London: Lawrence Erlbaum.

Berglund, R. L. and Johns, J. L. (1983) 'A primer on uninterrupted sustained silent reading', *The Reading Teacher* 36(6): 534–9.

Blatchford, P., Burke, J., Farquhar, C., Plewis, I. and Tizard, B. (1987) 'A systematic observation study of children's behaviour at infant school', *Research Papers in Education* 2(1): 47–62.

Blatchford, P., Burke, J., Farquhar, C., Plewis, I. and Tizard, B. (1987) 'Associations between pre-school reading related skills and later reading achievement', *British Educational Research Journal* 13(1): 15–23.

Bloom, W., Martin, A. and Waters, M. (1988) *Managing to Read*, London: Mary Glasgow.

Boland, N. and Simmons, K. (1987) 'Attitudes to reading: a parental involvement project', *Education 3–13* 15(2): 28–32.

Bond, G. L. and Dykstra, R. (1967) 'The co-operative research program in first-grade reading instruction', *Reading Research Quarterly* 2: 5–142.

Bondi, E. (1991) 'Attainment at primary school', *British Educational Research Journal* 17(3): 203–17.

Brookover, W. B., Beady, C., Flood, P., Schweitzer, J. and Wisenbaker, J. (1979) *School Social Systems and Student Achievement: Schools Can Make a Difference*, New York: Bergin.

Brooks, G., Foxman, D. and Gorman, T. (1995) *Standards in Literacy and Numeracy: 1948–1994* (National Commission on Education Briefing. New Series, 7), London: National Commission on Education.

Brooks, G., Shagen, I. and Nastat, P. (1998) *Trends in Reading at 8*, Slough: NFER.

Brophy, J. (1986) *Socializing Student Motivation to Learn*, East Lansing, MI: Michigan State University, Institute for Research on Teaching.

Bryant, P. and Bradley, L. (1985) *Children's Reading Problems: Psychology and Education*, Oxford: Basil Blackwell.

Bryant, P. E., Bradley, L., McClean, M. and Crossland, J. (1989) 'Nursery rhymes, phonological skills and reading', *Journal of Children's Language* 16(2): 407–28.

Campbell, R. (1989) 'The teacher as a role model during sustained silent reading (SSR)', *Reading* 23(3): 179–83.

Campbell, R. and Scrivens, G. (1995) 'The teacher role during sustained silent reading (SSR)', *Reading* 29(2): 2–4.

Cane, B. and Smithers, J. (1971) *The Roots of Reading: A Study of 12 Infant Schools in Deprived Areas*, Slough: NFER.

Chall, J. S. (1967) *Learning to Read: The Great Debate*, New York: McGraw-Hill.

Chall, J. S. and Feldman, S. (1966) 'First-grade reading: an analysis of the interactions of professed methods, teacher implementation and child background', *Reading Teacher* 19: 569–75.

Chambers, M., Jackson, A. and Rose, M. (1993) *Children Developing as Readers: The Avon Collaborative Reading Project*, Bristol: County of Avon.

Clauset, K. H. and Gaynor, A. K. (1982) 'A systems perspective on effective schools', *Educational Leadership* 40(3): 54–9.

Clay, M. (1975) *What did I Write?*, Auckland: Heinemann.

Clay, M. (1987) *The Early Detection of Reading Difficulties*, 3rd edition, Hong Kong: Heinemann.

Delamont, S. (ed.) (1987) *The Primary School Teacher*, Lewes: Falmer Press.

Denzin, N. K. (1985) 'Triangulation', in T. Husen and T. N. Postlethwaite (eds) *International Encyclopaedia of Education* 9: 5293–5, Oxford: Pergamon.

DES (1991) *The Teaching and Learning of Reading in Primary Schools. Autumn 1990: A report by HMI*, London: DES.

DES (1992) *The Teaching and Learning of Reading in Primary Schools. 1991: A report by HMI*, London: DES.

DES (1993) *Curriculum Organisation and Classroom Practice in Primary Schools: A follow up report*, London: DES Information Branch.

DfEE (1998) *The National Literacy Strategy Framework for Teachers*, London: DfEE.

Doyle, W. (1978) 'Paradigms for research into teacher effectiveness', in L. S. Shulman (ed.) *Review of Research in Education* 5: 1977, Itasca, IL: Peacock.

Edmonds, R. (1979) 'Effective schools for the urban poor', *Educational Leadership* 37: 15–27.

Edwards, P. (1991) *The Changing Role, Structure and Style of LEAs: A Study of the Impact of the 1988 Education and Local Government Acts in Eight LEAs*, Slough: NFER.

Ekholm, M. (1988) 'Research on school improvement in Scandinavia', *Qualitative Studies in Education* 1(1): 69–78.

Fisher, R. (1992) *Early Literacy and the Teacher*, London: Hodder & Stoughton.

Fitz-Harris, B. (1993) 'The American way', *Managing Schools Today* 2(7): 24–8.

Fitzpatrick, K. A. (1981) 'A study of the effect of a secondary classroom management training program on teacher and student behavior', Doctoral dissertation, University of Illinois.

Flanagan, J. C. (1949) 'Critical requirements: a new approach to employee evaluation', *Personnel Psychology* 2: 419–25.

Freiberg, H. J. (1983) 'Consistency: the key to classroom management', *Journal of Education for Teaching* 9(1): 1–15.

Freiberg, H. J. and Driscoll, A. (1992) *Universal Teaching Strategies*, Boston: Allyn & Bacon.

Freiberg, H. J., Prokosch, N., Treister, E. S. and Stein, T. A. (1990) 'Turning around five at-risk elementary schools', *Journal of School Effectiveness and School Improvement* 1(1): 5–25.

Freiberg, H. J., Stein, T. A. and Parker, G. (1995) 'Discipline referrals in a middle school', *Education and Urban Society* 24(1): 421–40.

Freire, P. (1985) *The Politics of Education: Culture, Power and Liberation*, London: Macmillan.

Frith, U. and Snowling, M. (1983) 'Reading for meaning and reading for sound in autistic and dyslexic children', *British Journal of Developmental Psychology* 1: 329–42.

Funnell, E. and Stuart, M. (eds) (1995) *Learning to Read: Psychology in the Classroom*, Oxford: Blackwell.

Gage, N. L. (1978) *The Scientific Basis of the Art of Teaching*, New York: Teachers College Press.

Gage, N. L. (1985) *Hard Gains in the Soft Sciences*, Bloomington, IN: Phi Delta Kappa.

Gaines, K. (1989) 'The use of reading diaries as a short term intervention strategy', *Reading* 23(3): 160–7.

Galton, M. and Simon, B. (1980) *Progress and Performance in the Primary Classroom*, London: Routledge & Kegan Paul.

Galton, M., Simon, B. and Croll, P. (1980) *Inside the Primary Classroom*, London: Routledge & Kegan Paul.

Galton, M. and Williamson, J. (1992) *Group Work in the Primary Classroom*, London: Routledge.

Gambrell, L. B. (1978) 'Getting started with sustained silent reading and keeping it going', *The Reading Teacher* 32(3): 328–31.

Gardner, K. (1986) *Reading in Today's Schools*, Edinburgh: Oliver & Boyd.

Gath, D. (1977) *Child Guidance and Delinquency in a London Borough*, London: Oxford University Press.

Giaconia, R. M. and Hedges, L. V. (1985) 'Synthesis of teaching effectiveness research', in T. Husen and T. N. Postlethwaite (eds) *International Encyclopaedia of Education* 9: 5101–20, Oxford: Pergamon.

Goodacre, E. J. (1975) *METHODS: Including an Annotated Reading List and Glossary of Terms*, Reading: Centre for the Teaching of Reading, University of Reading.

Goodman, K. S. (1967) 'Reading: a psycholinguistic guessing game', *Journal of the Reading Specialist* 4: 126–35.

Goswami, U. and Bryant, P. E. (1990) *Phonological Skills and Learning to Read*, Hillsdale, NJ: Lawrence Erlbaum.

Gray, J. (1979) 'Reading progress in English infant schools: some problems emerging from a study of teacher effectiveness', *British Educational Research Journal* 5(2): 141–58.

Grogan, S. (1995) 'Which cognitive abilities at age four are the best predictors of reading ability at age seven?', *Journal of Research in Reading* 18(1): 25–31.

Hancock, R. (1991) 'Parental involvement in children's reading: a survey of schools in Tower Hamlets', *Reading* 25(1): 4–6.

Hannon, P. (1987) 'A study of the effects of parental involvement in the teaching of reading on children's reading test performance', *British Journal of Educational Psychology* 57(1): 56–72.

Hargreaves, D. H. (1997) 'In defence of research for evidence-based teaching: a rejoinder to Martyn Hammersley', *British Educational Research Journal* 23(4): 405–19.

Harrison, C. and Nicoll, A. (1984) 'The readability of healthcare literature', *Developmental Medicine and Child Neurology* 26: 588–95.

Hewison, J. and Tizard, J. (1980) 'Parental involvement and reading attainment', *British Journal of Educational Psychology* 50: 209–15.

Hodgson, J. and Pryke, D. (1983) *Reading Competence at 6 and 10: A survey of the styles of teaching reading in twenty Shropshire schools*, Shropshire: Shropshire County Council.

Hutchinson, D. (1993) 'School effectiveness studies using administrative data', *Educational Research* 35(1): 27–47.

Inner London Education Authority (1986) *The Junior School Project*, London: ILEA Information Section.

Institute of Education (1994) *Assessing School Effectiveness: Summary of a Research Study on Developing Measures to put School Performance in Context*, London: Ofsted and the Institute of Education, University of London.

Jones, M. and Rowley, G. (1990) 'What does research say about parental participation in children's reading development?', *Evaluation and Research in Education* 4(1): 21–36.

Juel, C. (1988) 'Learning to read and write: a longitudinal study of children in first and second grade', *Journal of Educational Psychology* 78: 243–55.

Juel, C. (1991) 'Beginning reading', in R. Barr, M. L. Kamil, P. B. Mosenthal and P. D. Pearson (eds) *Handbook of Reading Research*, Vol. II, New York: Longman.

Just, M. A. and Carpenter, P. A. (1987) *The Psychology of Reading and Language Comprehension*, Boston: Allyn & Bacon.

Kemp, M. (1986) 'Parents as teachers of literacy: what are we learning from them?', Paper presented at the Australian Reading Association, Brisbane.

Kulik, J. A., Kulik, C.-L. C. and Cohen, P. A. (1979) 'A meta-analysis of outcome studies of Keller's personalized system of instruction', *American Psychology* 34: 307–18.

Levine, D. K. and Lezotte, L. W. (1990) *Unusually Effective Schools: A Review and Analysis of Research and Practice*, Madison, WI: National Center for Effective Schools Research and Development.

Liberman, I. Y., Shankweiler, D., Fischer, F. W. and Carter, B. (1974) 'Explicit syllable and phoneme segmentation in the young child', *Journal of Experimental Child Psychology* 18: 201–12.

Marshall, H. and Weinstein, R. (1986) 'Classroom context of student-perceived differential teacher treatment', *Journal of Educational Psychology* 78: 441–53.

Mason, A. (1993) 'Reading research in the primary classroom', *Journal of Research in Reading* 16(2): 128–37.

McCracken, R. A. (1971) 'Initiating sustained silent reading', *Journal of Reading* 14(8): 521–4 and 582–3.

McNaughton, S. S. and Glynn, T. (1980) *Parents as Remedial Reading Tutors: Issues for Home and School*, Wellington: Council for Educational Research.

Meek, M. and Mills, C. (eds) (1988) *Language and Literacy in the Primary School*, London: Falmer Press.

Millard, E. (1997) *Differently Literate: Boys, Girls and the Schooling of Literacy*, London: Falmer Press.

Miller, L. and Lieberman, A. (1988) 'School improvement in the United States: nuance and numbers', *Qualitative Studies in Education* 1(1): 3–19.

Minns, H. (1990) *Read it to Me Now! Learning at Home and at School*, London: Virago.

Morais, J., Alegria, J. and Content, A. (1987) 'The relationship between segmental analysis and alphabetic literacy', *Cahiers de Psychologie Cognitive* 7: 415–38.

Mortimore, P. (1993) 'Searching for quality', *Managing Schools Today* 2(5): 10–13.

Mortimore, P. (1995) *Effective Schools: Current Impact and Future Potential*, London: Institute of Education.

Mortimore, P. and MacBeath, J. (1994) 'Quest for the secrets of success', *Times Educational Supplement* 25 March: 14.

Mortimore, P., Stoll, L., Lewis, D. and Ecob, R. (1988) *School Matters: The Junior Years*, Wells: Open Books.

Mudd, N. (1989) 'What Katie did', *Reading* 23(2): 80–4.

National Commission on Education (1993) *Learning to Succeed*, London: Heinemann.

National Curriculum Council (1993) *English in the National Curriculum: A Report to the Secretary of State for Education on the Statutory Consultation for Attainment Targets and Programmes of Study in English*, York: National Curriculum Council.

Nitsaisook, M. and Anderson, L. (1989) 'An experimental investigation of the effectiveness of inservice teacher education in Thailand', *Teaching and Teacher Education* 5(4): 287–302.

Oftsed (1994) *Primary Matters: A Discussion on Teaching and Learning in Primary Schools*, London: Ofsted Publications.

Oppenheim, A. N. (1992) *Questionnaire Design: Interviewing and Attitude Measurement*, London: Pinter.

Oxenham, J. (1970) *Writing, Reading and Social Organisation*, London: Routledge & Kegan Paul.

Phillips, L. and Norris, S. P. (1996) 'Longitudinal effects of early literacy concepts on reading achievement: a kindergarten intervention and five-year follow-up', *Journal of Literacy Research* 28(1): 173–95.

Plewis, I. (1991) 'Pupils' progress in reading and mathematics during primary school: associations with ethnic group and sex', *Educational Research* 33(2): 133–40.

Plowden Report (1967) *Children and their Primary Schools*, London: HMSO.

Preedy, M. (ed.) (1993) *Managing the Effective School*, London: Open University.

Pressley, M., Snyder, B. and Cariglia-Bull, T. (1987) 'How can good strategy use be taught to children? Evaluation of six alternative approaches', in S. Cornmier and J. Hagman (eds) *Transfer of Learning: Contemporary Research and Application*, Orlando, FL: Academic Press, pp. 81–120.

Qualifications and Curriculum Authority (1998) *Can Do Better: Raising Boys' Achievement in English*, Hayes: QCA Publications.

Raban, B. (1992) 'Reading research in 1989', *Reading* 26(1): 11–17.

Ranson, S. (1992) *The Role of Local Government in Education: Assuring quality and accountability*, London: Longman.

Reid, D. and Bentley, D. (eds) (1996) *Reading on! Developing Reading at Key Stage 2*, Leamington Spa: Scholastic.

Reid, K., Hopkins, D. and Holly, P. (1987) *Towards the Effective School*, London: Basil Blackwell.

Reynolds, D. (1976) 'The delinquent school', in P. Woods (ed.) *The Process of Schooling*, London: Routledge & Kegan Paul.

Reynolds, D., Creemers, B. and Peters, T. (eds) (1989) *School Effectiveness and Improvement*, Cardiff: University of Wales College of Cardiff.

Rich, R. W. (1933) *The Training of Teachers in England and Wales during the Nineteenth Century*, Cambridge: Cambridge University Press.

Riddell, S. and Brown, S. (eds) (1991) *School Effectiveness Research: Its message for school improvement*, Edinburgh: HMSO.

Riley, J. (1996) *The Teaching of Reading: The Development of Literacy in the Early Years*, London: Paul Chapman.

Roehler, L. R. and Duffy, G. (1991) 'Teachers' instructional actions', in R. Barr, M. L. Kamil, P. B. Mosenthal and P. D. Pearson, *Handbook of Reading Research*, Vol. II, New York: Longman.

Rutter, M., Maugham, B., Mortimore, P., Ouston, J. and Smith, A. (1979) *Fifteen Thousand Hours: Secondary Schools and their Effects on Children*, London: Open Books.

Sammons, P., Hillman, J. and Mortimore, P. (1995) *Key Characteristics of Effective Schools: A Review of School Effectiveness Research*, London: Institute of Education and Ofsted.

Samph, T. (1976) 'Observer effects on teacher verbal behaviour', *Journal of Educational Psychology*, 68(6): 736–41.

Sarason, S. B. (1971) *The Culture of the School and the Problem of Change*, Boston: Allyn & Bacon.

Scheerens, J. (1992) *Effective Schooling: Research Theory and Practice*, London: Cassell.

Share, D. L., Jorm, A. F., Matthews, R. and Maclean, R. (1987) 'Parental involvement in reading progress', *Australian Psychologist* 22(4): 43–51.

Shayer, M. (1996) 'Piaget and Vygotsky: a necessary marriage for educational intervention', in L. Smith (ed.) *Critical Readings on Piaget*, London: Routledge.

Simon, B. and Willcocks, J. (1981) *Research and Practice in the Primary Classroom*, London: Routledge & Kegan Paul.

Slavin, R. E. (1987) 'Cooperative learning: where behavioral and humanistic approaches to classroom motivation meet', *Elementary School Journal* 88: 29–37.

Smith, D. J. and Tomlinson, S. (1989) *The School Effect: A Study of Multi-Racial Comprehensives*, London: Policy Studies Institute.

Stanovitch, K. E. (1980) 'Toward an interactive-compensatory model of individual differences in the development of reading fluency', *Reading Research Quarterly* 16(1): 32–71.

Stanovitch, K. E., Cuningham, A. E. and Cramer, B. B. (1984) 'Assessing phonological awareness in kindergarten children: issues of task comparability', *Journal of Experimental Child Psychology* 38: 175–90.

Stoll, L. and Fink, D. (1992) 'Effecting school change – the Halton approach', *School Effectiveness and School Improvement* 3(1): 19–38.

Stoll, L. and Fink, D. (1993) 'Canadian pioneers', *Managing School Today* 2(6): 12–15.

Stuart, M. (1993) 'Learning to read: a longitudinal study', *Education 3–13* 21(1): 19–25.

Stubbs, M. (1980) *Language and Literacy: The Sociolinguistics of Reading and Writing*, London: Routledge & Kegan Paul.

Sulzby, E. and Teale, W. (1991) 'Emergent literacy', in R. Barr, M. L. Kamil, P. B. Mosenthal and P. D. Pearson (eds) *Handbook of Reading Research*, Vol. II, New York: Longman.

Taggart, B. (1993) 'Catalyst for change', *Managing Schools Today* 2(9): 12–15.

Tizard, B., Blatchford, P., Burke, J., Farquhar, C. and Plewis, I. (1988) *Young Children at School in the Inner City*, Hove: Lawrence Erlbaum.

Tizard, J., Schofield, W. N. and Hewison, J. (1982) 'Collaboration between teachers and parents in assisting children's reading', *British Journal of Educational Psychology* 52(1): 1–15.

Topping, K. (1995) *Paired Reading, Spelling and Writing – The Handbook for Teachers and Parents*, London: Cassell Education.

Van der Sijde, P. C. (1989) 'The effect of a brief teacher training on student achievement', *Teaching and Teacher Education* 5(4): 303–14.

Wang, M. C., Haertel, G. D. and Walberg, H. J. (1993) 'Towards a knowledge base for school learning', *Review of Educational Research* 63(3): 249–94.

Waterland, L. (1985) *Read With Me*, Stroud: Thimble Press.

Waxman, H. C. and Walberg, H. J. (1991) *Effective Teaching: Current Research*, Berkeley, CA: McCutchan.

Weber, G. (1971) *Inner City Children Can Be Taught to Read: Four Successful Schools*, Washington, DC: Council for Basic Education.

Weinstein, R. (1985) 'Student mediation of classroom expectancy effects', in J. Dusek (ed.) *Teacher Expectancies*, Hillsdale, NJ: Erlbaum.

Wheldall, K. (1989) 'Reading USSR Revolution', *Teachers' Weekly* 20 February: 16–17.

Wheldall, K. and Entwistle, J. (1988) 'Back in the USSR: the effect of teacher modelling of silent reading on pupils' reading behaviour in the primary school classroom', *Educational Psychology* 8: 51–66.

Wideen, M. F. (1988) 'School improvement in Canada', *Qualitative Studies in Education* 1(1): 21–38.

Wilson, B. L. and Concoran, T. B. (1988) *Successful Secondary Schools*, London: Falmer Press.

Wittgenstein, L. (1922) *Tractatus Logico-Philosophicus*.

Woods, P. (ed.) (1976) *The Process of Schooling*, London: Routledge & Kegan Paul.

Woods, P. (ed.) (1996) *Contemporary Issues in Teaching and Learning*, London: Routledge.

Wragg, E. C. (1993) *Primary Teaching Skills*, London: Routledge.

Wragg, E. C. (1994) *An Introduction to Classroom Observation*, London: Routledge.

Wragg, E. C. (1997a) *The Cubic Curriculum*, London: Routledge.

Wragg, E. C. (1997b) 'Oh Boy!', *Times Educational Supplement* 16 May.

Wragg, E. C., Wikeley, F. J., Wragg, C. M. and Haynes, G. S. (1996) *Teacher Appraisal Observed*, London: Routledge.

Wray, D. (1994) *Literacy and Awareness*, London: Hodder & Stoughton.

Wynne, E. A. (1993) *A Year in the Life of an Excellent Elementary School: Lessons Derived from Success*, Lancaster, PA: Technomic.

Young, M. and McGeeney, P. (1968) *Learning Begins at Home*, London: Routledge & Kegan Paul.

INDEX